Survival Artist

# Survival Artist

## A Memoir of the Holocaust

EUGENE BERGMAN

*Foreword by* LEON W. WELLS

McFarland & Company, Inc., Publishers
*Jefferson, North Carolina, and London*

LIBRARY OF CONGRESS CATALOGUING-IN-PUBLICATION DATA

Bergman, Eugene.
    Survival artist : a memoir of the Holocaust / Eugene Bergman ;
foreword by Leon W. Wells.
        p.      cm.
    Includes bibliographical references and index.

    ISBN 978-0-7864-4134-1
    softcover : 50# alkaline paper ∞

    1. Bergman, Eugene — Childhood and youth.   2. Holocaust
survivors — Biography.   3. Jews — Poland — Biography.   4. Jewish
ghettos — Poland — History — 20th century.   5. Holocaust, Jewish
(1939–1945) — Biography.   6. World War, 1939–1945 — Personal
narratives, Polish.   7. World War, 1939–1945 — Personal narratives,
Jewish.   8. World War, 1939–1945 — Prisoners and prisons.
9. Poznan (Poland) — Biography.   I. Title.
DS134.72.B47A3   2009
940.53'18092 — dc22                                        2009017858
[B]

British Library cataloguing data are available

On the cover: Eugene Bergman, 1935; background images ©2009
Shutterstock

Manufactured in the United States of America

*McFarland & Company, Inc., Publishers*
  *Box 611, Jefferson, North Carolina 28640*
    *www.mcfarlandpub.com*

For Claire, Sabrina, Bronek, David,
Evelyn, Juliette, Madan, and Kay

# Acknowledgments

To my daughter Sabrina Gail: you are my muse and my inspiration.

To my brother Bronek who has known me ever since my babyhood and without whom this book could not have been written.

To my friends and colleagues Madan M. Vasishta and Fat C. Lam with whom I am continually engaged in noble competition and to whom I owe valuable suggestions.

To the great Arturo Montoya, that other artist, one who has elevated living well into an art without becoming a hedonist.

To my computer and technology gurus Andy Lowe: and Steve and Dot Brenner, a hearty thank you.

Last but not least, kudos to the one and only my wife Claire for her good nature, loving-kindness, and forbearance.

# Table of Contents

*Acknowledgments*                                    vii

*Foreword by Leon W. Wells*                            1

*Introduction*                                         3

  I.  The End of an Idyll
      *A Foray into History*                        11
      *Growing Up in Poznan*                        15
      *The Germans Arrive*                          30
      *Escape to Lodz, Escape from Lodz*            38

 II.  Life in the Warsaw Ghetto
      *From One Ghetto to Another*                  42
      *The German Professor*                        53
      *My Father the Smuggler*                      56
      *The Real and Unreal Worlds*                  60
      *Vignettes*                                   64
      *The Siege and the Escape*                    72

III.  Dodging the Predators
      *Rescued by Dadek*                            82
      *Fobbing Off the Landlord*                   101
      *Mysteries of Mimicry*                       104
      *The Ghetto Revolts*                         113
      *Forays from the Kitchen into the Jungle*    117

IV. From the Uprising to Liberation

*Saved from Drowning and Shooting*          130
*Inside Insurgent Warsaw*          136
*I Become a Prisoner of War*          142
*My Life Among the Punks*          148
*The Liberation Comes*          162

*Afterword*          179

*Chapter Notes*          189

*Bibliography*          191

*Index*          193

# Foreword

## by Leon W. Wells

What I find most personally interesting about this fascinating memoir is the different experience of Eugene Bergman, a survivor from northeastern Poland. I thought that I knew the stories of other survivors in Poland, but it seems I did not. Galicia, where I come from, was the center of Chassidism, the region where the most religious Jews lived. In our house Yiddish was the only language spoken.

Bergman lived in the Western part of Poland, Poznan, near the German border. It seemed to have been completely different there. For example, as much as he claims that his father was religious, his mother spoke only Polish with the children. He also mentions that his whole family was blond-haired and blue-eyed. They did not look like the majority of Jews who had dark hair and dark eyes. These facts kept them from immediately being targeted as Jews and checked to see if the men were circumcised. In his memoir Eugene Bergman tells how his father passes as a Pole, a Christian. The author speaks of being hit with a rifle butt, an event which caused him to become permanently totally deaf.

The family moved from Poznan to Lodz, called Litzmanstadt in German; it is also in western Poland. Mr. Bergman writes that the ghetto there was placed under the reign of a Jewish "dictator," the elder of the Jews, Chaim Rumkowski, whom the Germans picked as their puppet after they had executed the city's most prominent Jewish leaders. If the Soviet summer offensive in 1944 had continued, the Jews of Lodz would have survived and Rumkowski would have become a hero. A similar situation was with Horthy, the head of the Hungarian government in 1944 who

1

tried to protect Hungarian Jews and as a consequence was deposed by Hitler.

He also mentions a German Jewish teacher who died of starvation, cold and abandonment. German and Austrian Jews more often committed suicide than Polish Jews. Also one should notice he says that, among the "Poles, like any other group, there were both swine and good people." I heartily agree with this philosophy. I was taken into hiding by a Pole who didn't even know my name. He risked his life and the life of his family had I been discovered.

I read this remarkable book with great interest. It opens new doors to the saga of Holocaust survival.

\* \* \*

Leon W. Wells is the author of five books on the Holocaust, some published in as many as twelve languages.

*Author's Note: For the last few years Leon Weliczker Wells and my brother Bronek have been meeting every Monday for lunch at a diner in Fort Lee, New Jersey, along with a few other Holocaust survivors.*

*There were eight of them originally. Three who were extermination camp graduates have moved on to another dimension, and a fourth one joined them recently. Of the four remaining ones, Bronek survived the war by impersonating a Pole, Leon by being hidden by a Pole, the third by living in the Soviet Union. The fourth man, who is 88 years old, was in Auschwitz during most of the war and had stopped coming to lunch. Once a month the friends traveled to Bayside, New York, by car to have lunch with him at a local diner near his house, until he became too incapacitated.*

*So it came about that, when so asked by Bronek, Mr. Wells agreed to read my manuscript and write a foreword for it.*

*I first met Mr. Wells at Bronek's eightieth birthday party. This tall elderly gentleman with a pleasant smile looked like a retired engineer (and in fact he was one) but when I learned his name I was awed. He is a former member of the Death Brigade, as recounted in his memoir,* The Janowska Road, *and he has experienced horrors unimaginable even to a Dante or a Goya.*

# Introduction

The photograph below shows young people smiling into the camera. They all look so handsome and idealistic, in the bloom of their youth for all eternity. It is a group picture of teenage boys and girls belonging to Hashomer Hatzair, a Zionist youth movement in my hometown, Poznan, in the 1930's. At this writing very few of them are still alive.[1]

I have another photograph. It shows a railway carriage with German soldiers leaning out its windows. Alongside the carriage is chalked the caption *Wir fahren nach Polen um Juden zu versohlen* (We're going to Poland to rough up Jews).

There were many trains like that going to Poland from Germany in September 1939. I had a photo, no longer extant, of another such train, showing a railway carriage with a banner on which is emblazoned the same slogan. It shows young German civilians laughing and waving from its windows. Perhaps no contrast is more eloquent than this one between the group photo of happy youths dreaming of a bright future and those of sightseeing soldiers and grin-

Teenage boys and girls belonging to Hashomer Hatzair, a Zionist youth movement in Poznan, at an outing in the late 1930's (courtesy Adam Redlich and Noah Lasman).

ning young thugs traveling with their government's officially sanctioned and avowed aim of beating Jews up.

Some years ago, Hagai Bergman, a relative from Israel, visited me in America. He asked me why it was that his father, David, my cousin, a concentration camp survivor, never spoke to him about his experiences in the concentration camp. I answered, "If you were to be beaten like a dog, humiliated day after day, would you want to talk about it to your children?" He did not answer, of course, but his face grew serious. He understood, all right. Yet here I am, talking about "it" to my children, and to whoever else happens to read this memoir. For one thing, David's wartime destiny, in its unrelieved steep descent, was much more straightforward than mine with its zigzags. From a life of hunger and deprivation in the Warsaw Ghetto he descended directly into the concentration camp inferno, where he stayed until the war's end, starved, beaten, worked like a horse, standing in roll calls for hours in rain, snow, and freezing cold.

The remarkable thing about David was his purity. He emerged from the concentration camp with his religious faith intact, and when I met him after the war in Tel Aviv he still observed all the Jewish ritual commandments, and continued to do so until the end of his life. Goodness simply radiated from him, and I never met a more saintly man. That kind of man simply could not do anything that he would feel ashamed of. By the same token, he was an absolutist and, like one, it was as if he expected Hagai and his other children to accept without going into what he thought to be sordid details the fact that his spirit was not broken by his martyrdom. However much I respect his motives, I regret the silence in which he veiled his past, because against the background of such sordid details his spirit would shine even brighter. Yet, he preferred to remain mute about them. As for the details, for example,

A railway carriage on its way to Poland with German soldiers. Chalked on it are anti-Semitic caricatures and the slogan: "We're going to Poland to beat up the Jews" (courtesy United States Holocaust Memorial Museum.

he was not the kind who, plagued by hunger, would steal a slice of bread from a starving fellow inmate, or who would curry favor with a kapo by ratting on another man for disobeying one or another fiendish Nazi rule. But this nature's nobleman did not feel it necessary to explain that to his family or anyone else.

But as for me, I cannot remain mute, at least not on paper since I am what people would call a deafmute. In this memoir I am paying homage to the devotion and self-sacrifice of my parents and brothers who saved my life countless times, and I can do that only by focusing on the details of our everyday life in the war. It was their example that made me determined to survive but not just at any cost. To survive in Hitler's Europe, in that wartime jungle world, I had to lie and cheat by living a double life, a life on the edge, but, like my family and David, though of course to a much smaller extent, I have not done anything that I could be seriously ashamed of.

Unlike David's one long agony, the path of my life has been winding through a series of hairbreadth escapes and daily attempts at pretending to be someone else to evade detection and death.

That has been the path of my brother Bronek's life as well. In some ways, his escapes have been even more hair-raising and his play-acting roles even more diverse. To boot, since he is my older brother and I was only nine when the war began, I have been able to enrich memories of my early childhood in the Poznan part of this memoir with his reminiscences. Owing to his wholehearted cooperation I have been able to flesh out some incidents from my prewar life which I only vaguely remembered.

This memoir is intended to illustrate the fate of not just myself but my family and more broadly the Polish Jewry and its surviving remnant.

Nothing like the Holocaust, this coordinated drive to exterminate a people scientifically, to grind the bones of the victims into fertilizer, render their fat into soap, process their hair into mattress stuffing, and extract gold teeth from corpses with pliers for smelting by the *Reichsbank*, has happened ever before. "The cruelties mock all norms and principles, they are beyond all limits of human understanding," as the so-called Ravensbruck Prayer, found on a scrap of wrapping paper in the camp after its liberation, puts it. This terrifyingly consistent policy of scientific carnage and industrialized processing of the corpses of human beings by other beings in death factories is the essence and the mystery of the Holocaust. I still do not understand why it happened. Nobody understands why, despite all the explanations offered, even though no other event in history has been as thoroughly and widely investigated. It lays bare the atavistic underside of European civilization. Even the photo of those German teenagers excitedly riding a train to bash Jews offers only a partial explanation.

It may be that to this day I still am leading a double life in the sense that my wartime persona now and then looks over the shoulder of my present persona. And when it does, it is usually to warn me about anything that is campy. Note that I am using the kitschy adjective "campy," instead of the more serious "inauthentic." After my wartime experiences most of what has happened to me is campy and a bonus.

My personal experiences are recorded here as a series of inchoate sense impressions of a young deaf boy. I have illuminated them in the broader context of the historic events happening around me. Does this mean that I have come to terms with my past after more than sixty years of trying to overcome it, attain closure, and live a so-called normal life? Yes and no.

Perhaps my experience in Martinique will offer a partial answer, with its anticlimactic closure when my bride Claire and I were stopped by a French gendarme.

Claire and I flew for our honeymoon to that French island and there I encountered a poignant reminder of my past. On arriving we checked in at a hotel and arranged to rent a car for the following day to tour the island, including the volcano on top of Mt. Pele. After we left the hotel next morning, we took the highway from Fort-de-France to Mt. Pele, about 20 miles north.

We drove up a serpentine road to the top of Mt. Pele, to stand at the lip of the crater of a volcano whose eruption in 1902 had destroyed the nearby town of Saint-Pierre according to a local brochure. The dark mouth of a dead volcano was not exactly an exciting sight, so, our curiosity slaked, we drove back down that steep series of hairpin turns until we saw a road sign announcing the town of Saint-Pierre, about six kilometers from the crater.

We toured the ruins of that town. According to the brochure, until the volcano's eruption the mountain was so peaceful that children played on its slopes and families from the environs picnicked on them. Then one day all of a sudden the huge tranquil green hill belched forth flames. The eruption was so quick and unexpected that the torrent of blazing hot gases and rock debris engulfed the town and killed its 30,000 or so inhabitants in a few blinks of an eye.

It was more than just another Pompeii, however, because it had been preceded by clouds of ash which had already buried nearby communities whose frightened inhabitants flocked en masse to take refuge in Saint-Pierre just before that town itself took a direct hit from the volcano. This last detail reminded me of the Jews from nearby communities who had flocked or been deported to the Warsaw Ghetto to escape death only to perish there.

We walked through the charred ruins of Saint-Pierre and in my mind I compared what had happened there to the Holocaust that engulfed Europe. It was as if nature were completely blind, as blind as justice is supposed to be but much more uncaring. It was as if the same impersonal force of nature caused the cataclysm that razed Saint-Pierre and the holocaust that engulfed millions in its flames.

As we were driving back to our hotel, Claire and I were stopped by a French gendarme who wanted to see my driver's license. At least that was what I figured, since I could not hear him. I handed him my license and, when he kept talking to me, that is, moving his mouth at me, I gestured at my ears. He raised his eyebrows, surprised to see that I, a deaf man, could be driving a car. Apparently that was a novelty in Martinique. It was funny to see how he raised his eyebrows and looked perplexed. I handed him a pad and a pen, after writing in French that I was deaf, and he wrote me back, asking if I could read lips, and looked even more surprised when I shook my head. Then I asked him why he had stopped us and found that it was because I was not wearing my seatbelt. He let me go since my international driver's license was valid and I guess he was too dumbfounded to ticket me.

It gave me a kick to engage in silent conversations with people like that. Back in Fort-de-France, we enjoyed a delicious dinner.

Did then my visit to Saint-Pierre put the Holocaust somewhat more in perspective, as another pointless cataclysm of nature? I mean, could it be possible to come to terms with the Holocaust by viewing it as a kind of natural disaster, like a volcanic eruption in Martinique or a catastrophic tsunami that kills thousands of victims in, say, Indonesia? Only in a way, because I, like other survivors, still find it extremely difficult to come to terms with it. Ultimately, I have to reject this natural-disaster analogy. In Saint-Pierre the thousands of victims died mercifully within minutes, if not seconds, while in Europe during World War II the Jews had to endure for years and years the torments of constant humiliation, affronts and chicaneries that sapped their dignity and self-confidence, and gradual deprivations ending in extinction. One after another, over the months and years, they lost their homes, their occupations and businesses, their material possessions, and kept being browbeaten until they ended up nervous wrecks, beggared, starving, and living in continual hope of salvation and in terror of the inevitable which finally came to pass.

I was no hero. I did not rescue anyone nor fight the Germans during the ghetto uprising or in the forests as a partisan. I exerted no influence on events. Even so, as I see it now, it was not entirely simplistic of me to tell Bronek once in my younger years, "Hitler is dead. I'm alive. I won." For I did win by dodging the constant perils and not just by merely and passively existing. Survival took being constantly on the alert and actively pre-empting possible snares. This memoir is also focused on describing the subterfuges by which my family and I evaded our ardent executioners.

My having emerged alive from the war was not just because the Germans, damnably thorough as they were, failed to find and kill absolutely every Jew in Europe. It was not just pure luck either, and I was not just a passive object of persecution. To survive in that menacing world of Jew hunters, in which the state was the oppressor and the laws and rules were designed to discriminate against, round up and destroy human beings of a particular "race," one needed to be on the alert every moment while remaining outwardly calm, to exert strenuous efforts at covering up and overcoming one's anxiety and pounding heart, to constantly face the terrors with a brave mien. More, even, to brazen them out by acting offended when challenged or questioned.

During the war I had dreamed of the West as a paradise, a world flowing with the milk and honey of human kindness and inhabited by superior human beings who were not tainted by experiences of misery and degradation and who felt empathy and understanding for those tainted by them. To me, in 1944, that paradisiacal world of the future became the West as personified by the carefree Frenchmen playing soccer in a fenced-off section of my prisoner-of-war camp or the elegantly uniformed English officers carrying tennis rackets whom I had seen at a railroad station in Germany, escorted by a German guard who looked and acted more like their batman.

My illusions were shattered, one by one, starting soon after the war in 1946 when American military policemen raided my family's home at the Zeilsheim displaced persons camp near Frankfurt in search of contraband U.S. foods and cigarettes. They came because my mother was operating an illegal grocery store inside the apartment, selling herring, vegetables, canned foods, and cigarettes to those camp residents who wanted to use them in bartering with the underfed postwar Germans outside. I saw then that one of these M.P.'s was practically a midget. He could not have been more than five feet tall, but he was wearing a full-sized helmet which made him look comical. Another time, I saw that some of the American servicewomen alighting from a khaki-colored army bus were fat and ugly. So, not all Americans were handsome and had lithe athletic figures.

About a year later, after my arrival in America in 1947, when I was having lunch at a crowded coffee shop in New York City, the questioning expression on the face of a middle-aged man showed me that he was asking my permission to sit down in a vacant chair at my table. I nodded and he sat down. His was a wooden face that seemed incapable of smiling. He had a stiffness of response like that of Buster Keaton, the face of a man who has experienced a personal tragedy. On learning that I was deaf he wrote me how miserable he was because his wife had not spoken to him for years even though they lived in the same house.

I was puzzled as to why he made these confidences to me, a teenager and total stranger. Perhaps because I was deaf and therefore not his equal as he saw it. (It is a response that I encounter and indulgently tolerate in some people.) Above all, these confidences were so foreign to me and my experience. I was puzzled as to how these two people who could not stand each other were able to tolerate living in the same house for so long. But that is another story and another question. So in this brave normal world people too can become emotional and mental wrecks even though they live in a peaceful country that was spared the emotional and mental ravages of war, not to mention the physical devastation. How was that possible? I found this encounter baffling. And to this day I wonder and still feel amazed when I meet with symptoms of lives that are ruined despite the absence of war — dysfunctional families, the birth of a child who is physically or mentally handicapped, people who are damaged even though they have not been exposed to the trauma of war.

I was not without my own mental scars, of course. When I emerged from the Holocaust I found that the lessons I had learned were of no value to me in the so-called peacetime world. To survive in Hitler's Europe, in that wartime jungle world, I had to learn how to lie, cheat, and be rude. In that world, the laws and rules were inverted, designed to oppress, exploit and ultimately destroy human beings, even and especially children like me.

Now I had to unlearn much of what I had learned if I wanted to survive in civilized society.

On my arrival in that society I might as well have been a forest savage transported to the shores of civilization. My wartime values now proved a handicap to me. I was stunned to realize that in the civilized normal world, kindness and courtesy were regarded as strengths, not weaknesses, and brute selfishness was not equated with having clout.

I could no longer elbow my way to be the first to board a bus, for example. In postwar Poland and Germany, I did that habitually and the docile crowd in front of the bus parted for me, reasoning that since a kid like me acted with such self-assurance I must be somebody in authority. When I tried this tactic the first time at a bus stop after arriving in America in 1947, the reaction of the people in the queue was different — they looked at me with angry faces and spelled me out. Another time, I needed a ride while walking on a two-lane highway in Westchester County, New York, so I stood in front of an oncoming car and waved at it to stop. In postwar Germany this tactic worked, but here in America, when the car stopped its angry driver cursed me and sped on. I had to learn to live all anew, to acquire good manners and be courteous, and it was difficult to me ... and it still is, sometimes. Some people still accuse me of being unfeeling or too ungracious in response to their confidences.

A word about the Germans: Some years ago I met a German writer, Horst Biesold, who authored *Crying Hands*, a book about the discovery that during the war the German deaf had been sterilized without their knowledge, in line with Nazi "eugenic" theories.[2] Under the grandiloquent "Law for the Protection of Offspring with Hereditary Diseases," serving to promote the "destruction of life unworthy of life," the deaf in Germany were subjected to compulsory sterilization and abortions. The book created a stir. Big deal, at least the most of the German deaf were left alive, if neutered. In my conversation with Biesold, when talking to him about my past, I spoke of "the Germans" and he objected, claiming that I should say "the Nazis." I told him I could not accept that but, all the same, I recognized that the Germans of the present era are no longer Nazis. Therefore, throughout this book, whenever I use the word "Germans" I mean the Germans of the Nazi era. And in that era they were indeed overwhelmingly fanatical Nazis even if, farcically, they could not tell a Jew from a Pole wearing an identical garb without the Pole telling them who was who.

# The End of an Idyll

## *A Foray into History*

What happened to me and my family can be better understood against the background of Jewish life in Poland, in the historical perspective, succinctly: starting in the 11th or 12th century with the pogroms accompanying the Crusades and after west Europe's Jews were accused of murdering babies, causing the plague, poisoning the wells, and so on and so forth. Many of these Jews found a refuge in Poland. Even after the deicide and blood libel accusations along with periodic expulsions in the West had largely ceased, this immigration continued, the principal reason now being the fear that the young would become tempted by the tastes and comforts of the West and become lax in religious passion and observance of rites.

The Jewish emigrants were driven at first by persecution and later by the same fear of assimilation and corruption of their offspring by the pleasures of life in the West that had motivated the Puritans to emigrate from Holland and begin life anew in America. It was not only the new ideas sprouting in the West but also the new fashions in dress and head coverings that clashed with Jewish customs. Multi-colored clothing, doublets, breeches, bodices, all clashed with the Talmudic prohibitions on emulating the fashions in dress of the dominant population. To distinguish themselves and emphasize their devotion to tradition and rituals, the Jews, like the Amish, wore more somber garb instead of following the innovations of fashion.

In those times Poland was much more tolerant toward Jews and unspoiled, a virgin land like America, offering Jews an opportunity for their own distinctive rich culture and religion to thrive in isolation from Western influences. As the Amish founded colonies in the wilds of America, the Jews founded shtetls in the wilds of Poland. Like the Amish, they lived in their own closed world, showing hardly any interest in their gentile surroundings. But unlike the Amish, the Jews in Poland, however insular they also were, did not confine themselves to agricultural pursuits, from which they were mostly barred anyhow. Since they were mostly literate, their culture being based on books, in Poland with its missing middle class they acted as middlemen between the landed gentry and the illiterate peasantry. In their roles as financial advisers, estate managers, millers, innkeepers, and money lenders, they were bound to interact with Poles and exercise an unavoidable impact on Polish life and culture. To cite just a few examples, initially their status was almost equal to that of the nobility and, according to a legend of origin, at one time a Jew, Abraham Prochownik, was king of Poland for a day. There is also a legend that another Jew, Saul Wahl, was likewise king of Poland for a day. Then too there are thirteenth-century Polish coins with an inscription in Hebrew: *Msk krill Polski* (Moshe the King of Poland), which reflect the impact Jews exerted on Poland's finances as operators of the first mints. The paramour of King Casimir the Great, Esterka, was Jewish.

The Jews in Poland enjoyed almost complete religious and cultural autonomy along with rights and privileges denied them elsewhere, and this prompted not just a material but a spiritual flowering of their unique civilization that had made Poland for centuries the center of a vibrant Jewish culture in the world.

Of course, this idyllic situation could not continue, and ultimately the Jews of Poland met an even worse fate from the Germans than did the Jews of Spain from the Inquisition. Nationalist ressentiments turned Poles into anti–Semites, smoothing the way for a more or less conscious acceptance of Hitler's campaign to exterminate Jews.

This was the paradox: throughout the ages the desire of the Jews to cling to their own religion and traditions preserved their ethnic existence for thousands of years but at the same time this very desire caused them to be regarded as strangers and aliens and subject to reprisals in whatever European country they settled in. Total assimilation would have meant total extinction of Jews as a people, and this they could not accept. As strangers, with their alien religion and customs, they were viewed with hostility by their hosts. By refusing to assimilate they survived as a people but not without suffering tortures and expulsions under the Spanish Inquisition and an almost crippling body blow in Hitler's Europe.

Yet, there is much more to this relationship between Jews and Europeans. After all, the only worthwhile personal relationships are those based on mutual toleration and respect for each other's identity. What applies to friendship between individuals applies equally to friendship between national groups. Jewish civilization in pre–Inquisition Spain was able to reach such an acme of flowering, and to contribute so much to the country's and Hebrew culture, because the Jews there used to coexist peaceably with the Muslims and Christians in a spirit of mutual toleration and respect. But that came to an abrupt end with the Inquisition. Centuries later, Jews in Germany, while coexisting peaceably with the Germans, nourished and enriched German culture even more, only to be crushed under the steamroller of Hitlerian anti–Semitism. As Martin Buber put it, "I testify: the symbiosis of German and Jewish existence, as I experienced it in the four decades I spent in Germany, was the first and only one since the Spanish Era to receive the highest confirmation that history can bestow, confirmation through creativity."[1]

In Poland, too, Jews creatively enriched the native culture. But here the pattern was different. It was a one-sided relationship. The history of Jewish contributions to Poland is a history of constant rejection. It is best exemplified in the one-sided response accorded to Adam Mickiewicz.

The list of acculturated Jews who enriched Polish culture is simply too long to enumerate here, but one name above all stands out: Adam Mickiewicz, Poland's greatest poet. His mother and wife were Frankists, that is, Jewish converts to Catholicism.[2] Perhaps because of his origin, which is for the most part unmentioned in Polish literature so as not to offend national pride, he propagated a kind of Polish messianism, claiming Poland to be the true martyred land playing a special role in the second coming of the Christian Savior. The martyrdom he meant was, of course, the loss of his country's independence to the partitioning powers — Prussia, Russia, and Austria.

Mickiewicz advocated Polish-Jewish reconciliation, seeing Jews as the elder brothers of Poles, with their destinies linked. That was a message the Poles ignored even though, ironically, they venerate Mickiewicz as their national bard.

Mickiewicz was only one of many. Whole shelves of books could be written about the seminal stamp left by Jews on Polish literature, science, and mathematics. There also were Polish Jews who gained fame in the greater world, such as Ludwik Zamenhof, the inventor of Esperanto; Bruno Schulz, the fantasist; the writer and Nobel Prize winner I. B. Singer; the founder of Hassidism, Baal Shem-Tov; and the pianist Artur Rubinstein, among many others.

It may be that, as an Israeli politician memorably put it, the Poles have indeed sucked in anti–Semitism with their mother's milk, yet it is a fact that all the great Polish writers and poets present a sympathetic and positive image of the Jew in their works. Only the second-raters spurt venom against Jews in their writings.

In the initially benign and tolerant climate of Poland, its Jewish population grew to three million, unprecedented for such a small country. German Reform Judaism, a deistic system more ethical than religious, with its belief that one could be a good Jew and a good citizen without strict observance of the traditional religious rituals, never sank roots in Poland. There, the Jew was either observant or an apikoros, an apostate. There was no middle ground. Such was the situation until World War II. Afterward, it did not matter since no Jews to speak of were left in Poland, at least until the 1990s and later.

In 1939 about 70 percent of Poland's three million Jews were religiously observant. The observant Jews were Yiddish speakers living in their own religious communities. They were easily distinguished by their beards, sidelocks, and garb. Their garb — black caftans, or long coats, and white shirts for men, and wigs and high-collared dresses for women — was as distinctive as that of the Amish and is said to be derived from the old Polish aristocratic costume which the conservative Jews retained after the Poles had adopted the Western form of dress. The caftans were black, long, and reaching below the knees, and the shirts white. In that somber combination of colors each observant Jewish male seems to be a priest by himself, like the Catholic and Protestant divines in their black-and-white vestments. The resemblance is not just limited to attire. The average observant Jew devotes his life to studying the Torah, also known as the Pentateuch, and the Talmud, that multivolume corpus of rabbinical writings. That would be like expecting the average Christian church attendee to be familiar with the writings of St. Thomas, St. Augustine, Origen, and other early Christian authors. In that sense, in addition to the similar black and white colors of his garb, the average observant Jew is just as learned, though in a different orientation, as a Catholic or Protestant minister. His very observance of the precepts of Judaism confers a kind of sacredness on his life.

Like the Amish, too, the Jews of Poland were totally immersed in their own rituals and traditions — and totally distinguishable. Even when they did not wear their exotic black caftans, they could be readily identified because of their different cultural characteristics: their faces were more expressive and they were more emotional and dramatic, like the Italians. Worst of all, in Polish eyes, they jabbered and gesticulated, in striking contrast to the subdued, stolid manners of the Poles, to whom Jewish manners seemed totally foreign, flashy, affected, and even grotesque. It was an ever-recurrent culture shock whenever the twain would meet. No wonder that the chances of observant Jews for survival following the German invasion by submerging themselves in the ambient Polish population were practically zero.

Poland was a country where everyone was expected to have a religious designation. Even the nonobservant Jews were willy-nilly also members of the *kehilla,* a communal organization based on religious association, since they figured in its records from birth through marriage to funeral and could opt out of it only by converting to another faith. That made it easier for the German catchers to identify them too by combing through the *kehilla* registries. For almost the first thing the Germans did on invading a city or a province was to sequester the *kehilla*'s records with their names and addresses of members. Even so, the nonobservant Jews or those with good Polish had better chances of survival than their observant brethren; they could blend in with the Polish population.

## *Growing Up in Poznan*

Poznan is my hometown. Located in northwestern Poland, in 1939 it was inhabited by a mixture of Poles and Prussians with a soupçon of Jews who in their turn were divided into German- and Polish-speaking Jews. In that year the city had a population of 275,000 but only about 2,000 were Jews. This was in striking contrast to Poland as a whole, where Jews accounted for a much greater part of the population, 10 percent, or three out of the country's then 30 million inhabitants, more than anywhere else in Europe, and even were in the majority in some towns and cities.

In Poznan itself though, before World War II there lived comparatively few Jews, the reason being that after World War I, when the formerly Prussian Poznan region reverted to the newly independent Poland, most of the Poznan Jews migrated to Germany. They thought German culture superior, and at the time they were right because in the second half of the nineteenth century the ideas of the French Revolution, with its emphasis on equal rights, finally percolated into Prussia. This prompted Otto von Bismarck to grant civil and citizenship rights to German Jews, with the tacit precondition that they would accept German language and culture and support the Germans against the nationalistic strivings of the local Poles.

In those times the unemancipated Jews living under czarist oppression on the other side of the border, in the Russian-occupied part of Poland, enjoyed no such protected legal status. To boot, they were disdained as boorish and loud rubes by their German fellow Jews because they would not accept the more secular, "enlightened" Reform Judaism.

The departure of most German Jews from Poznan after it was annexed to Poland following World War I created a void which had been filled only to a small extent by the Jews moving in from the interior of Poland. Twenty years afterward those among the émigrés who had Polish citizenship were to regret their decision when they were expelled from Germany back to Poland in 1938. A year or two later still, the remaining German Jews began to be deported en masse to the ghettos and extermination camps in Poland.

Those few and mainly elderly German-speaking Jews who had decided to remain in Poznan after World War I were nicknamed *Yekkes,* in reference to the formal suit coat or *Jake* in Hebrew-Yiddish that most of them wore, as a moniker of good-natured ribbing because they were thought to lack a sense of humor and were so stiff and formal that they were reputed to habitually wear suit and tie, unlike the "uncivilized" Jews from central and eastern Poland who arrived in Poznan wearing black caftans (but discarded them soon after they had been mobbed and beaten by the local rowdies). These remaining German-speaking Jews were considered both stuck up and gullible. Wags among the Polish-speaking Jews quipped that the *Yekkes,* those stuffed shirts, wore a tie or a cravat even in bed at night.

The distance separating these two groups was also due to the fact that the German speakers were for the most part secular Jews, members of the Reform movement, and therefore, in the view of their Polish-speaking Orthodox coreligionists, they were shallow and lacked deep spiritual qualities. That was not quite fair, since those German Jews stayed Jews after all and did not convert. All the same, these two groups lived in relative peace in Poznan and cooperated in running the Jewish community there.

In the first days of September 1939, before German troops entered Poznan, ironically enough some of these few remaining elderly German-speaking Jews were mistaken for Germans, since they had never bothered to learn much Polish. They were suspected of planting markers to guide German fliers to targets and hiding weapons. They were seized as German spies and escorted to prison while pelted with potatoes by Polish bystanders. That was a foretaste of their hard fate.

The Bergman family in 1935: Sara, me, Bronek, Dadek. Pesakh-Pawel is in the back.

My father came from Widawa, a hamlet in western Poland. As my brother Bronek remembers it, Father was born to a very pious and very poor family. *His* father, our grandfather David, wore a beard, side curls, and a black caftan and spent all days in the synagogue studying the Torah and other holy writings while leaving mundane worries to the care of our grandmother, an energetic woman who kept a little store with farm implements and attended to feeding and clothing their ten children. When they grew up, they scattered in all directions, three of them to America.

It seems that Grandfather David was an irascible and harsh man. In an extant photograph he is shown with an angry glare on his face. It was a miracle how his wife endured his hot temper and tyrannical outbursts without rebelling against him and against her fate. She must have been an extremely patient and tough woman. Besides, having a scholar for a husband is a matter of pride to a pious Jewish woman. As for my father himself, he was, perhaps in deliberate contrast to that curmudgeon my grandfather, an equably tempered man and a loving husband and father, endowed with a natural gravitas. Born in the Prussian-held part of Poland, he was a soldier in the kaiser's army during World War I and served in Berlin. Afterward he settled in Lodz, where he met, courted, and married my mother before moving to Poznan.

After the war of 1939–45 was over, when I found my mother again, she told me that when she was little she was driven to school in a horse-drawn carriage — her father was a textile manufacturer in Lodz and could afford it. In my mind I have a picture of a little pixie-faced girl lolling in that carriage with the coachman whipping the horse lightly as it stops in front of a schoolhouse. I was too young to remember her parents, but Bronek, who had once visited them after they had retired and moved to the country, where they cultivated an orchard, remembers them as a gentle and devoted couple, a kind of Jewish Philemon and Baucis.

Mother had attended a Polish school in Lodz and afterward worked for a while as a teacher until she met Father. She spoke Polish fluently, unlike Father, whose native language was Yiddish. At home she spoke to us in Polish and my father spoke to us in Yiddish. She read Polish novels, such as those of Zeromski and Sienkiewicz, while Father read only Yiddish books. He loved reading Sholem Aleichem, Icchak Perez, Mendele Mocher Seforim, and other writers with their delightful parables and half-tender, half-humorous stories of life in the shtetls.

I and my brothers grew up in a home where both these languages were spoken. Yet, despite their linguistic differences, my parents were a loving couple and Mother was a model Jewish housewife and parent, poised, pious and gentle, keeping a kosher home and kitchen, which mainly meant keeping dairy food and utensils separate from meat ones. It took the war for her real character to unfold fully when she became a rock for me and my brothers to lean on.

In Poznan we lived in a one-room apartment with kitchen on the first floor at 32 Jewish Street, a street that got its name from having been the center of the quarter inhabited by Jews. They had first found refuge there in the twelfth and thirteenth centuries, fleeing the Crusades and pogroms in the West. It was never walled in or fenced in and its inhabitants were free to come and go, so that it was not really a ghetto like those in west Europe in the Middle Ages. Yet it was there that Jewish life in Poznan had been concentrated for centuries, with a synagogue around the corner and

My fourth or fifth birthday party, 1934 or 1935, in the courtyard of 32 Zydowska Street. I am in the center of first row and wearing a white shirt. Bronek stands directly behind me. Dadek is in the third row to the right, with white headgear. My mother is second from left. Zosia is second from the top of the stairs.

a home for the Jewish aged nearby. There, the Jewish community grew, after it had been granted autonomy under the Polish kings, until it was sizable enough to be mentioned in fifteenth-century chronicles.

In the nineteenth century, following the partition of Poland among Prussia, Russia, and Austria, the Poznan Jews were accorded equal rights of citizenship by Bismarck's Prussia, so as to ally them politically against the local Poles.

These German-speaking Jews developed their own well-organized community with its imposing Grand Synagogue, smaller houses of prayer, cemetery, burial society (*Hevra Kadisha*), a library, a school, a ritual bath and a kosher butcher. There were also many charitable societies and foundations operating a home for the aged, the Rohr Jewish Hospital, an orphanage for boys, an orphanage for girls, a shelter for unmarried girls at least 14 years old, a shelter for indigent travelers, a school for poor schoolchildren, an association for aiding sick women and children, a society for distributing lumber and coal to the poor each winter, a home for the handicapped or what would be termed nowadays a halfway house, a society for clothing needy schoolchildren, a society for sponsoring the training of Jews in crafts and farming, a society for aiding indigent widows and orphans, a society for the vocational training of women and girls (sewing, nursing courses, etc.), a loan and savings association offering interest-free loans, and an association for sponsoring summer camps for indigent sick children — all for members of the community and Jewish visitors to the city.[3]

I cite them to show what a mind-boggling number of voluntary associations and foundations was operated by the small Jewish community of 2,000 in Poznan. The numbers of beneficiaries of all this charity were correspondingly small. The home for the handicapped had room for eighteen inmates. The orphanage for boys accommodated twenty-five. The orphanage for girls had room for seventeen, and so forth.[4] But then charity was one of the ethical commandments of Judaism and even in Prussian times the community consisted of not only bankers and factory owners but also of a big stratum of destitute Jews.

For all that, unlike their coreligionists in central and eastern Poland, the Jews in Poznan under Prussian reign were much more secular and mostly attended the synagogue only on the two biggest Jewish holidays, Yom Kippur and Passover. And since they usually supported the Germans against the Poles, after Poland had regained its independence in 1919 the local Poles were so antagonistic toward them that the numbers of German-speaking Jews shrank to an even smaller fraction of their former size and Poznan itself became notorious as the most anti–Semitic city in Poland. Those departing for Germany were for the most part the families of bankers, industrialists, property owners, lawyers, architects, and physicians, who hankered after so-called German culture only to regret it bitterly when Hitler came to power.

The void they left in the city proved too big to fill in numbers by the Jewish petty merchants, tradesmen, and craftsmen from the formerly Russian part of Poland who eventually replaced them. There were not many of these newcomers, owing to that special notoriety of local anti–Semitism. Consequently, in 1939 the Jews of Poznan accounted for merely about 2 percent of the city's population, compared to 10 percent for Poland as a whole, and inherited a ramified Jewish community structure that was too big for them.

In the 1930s more oil began to be poured on the fire by the rabidly anti–Semitic periodicals published in Poznan. They had names like *To the Pillory* (Pod Pregierz) and *The Spider* (Pajak). The covers of *To the Pillory* regularly showed lurid cartoons of Jews drawn to resemble bedbugs and rats with grotesquely long snouts charging en masse into the gates of Poznan. The motto below screamed "Don't let the kikes in!" As for the cover page of *The Spider,* it carried a logo of a grim horny-nosed spider trapping helpless victims in its web, their mouths open in agony while it sucks their blood. It urged Poles not to buy from Jews and not to rent housing or stores to Jews, and even published photographs of Christians who shopped in Jewish stores. Scurrilous papers like these accused the Jews of substituting rat meat for beef, adulterating milk with dishwater, adding worms to dough and kneading it with their feet. Aping the language of Hitler's Germany, these papers demonized the Jew as "the enemy of the world, the destroyer of cultures, the parasite among the peoples, the incarnation of evil, the ferment of decomposition, the devil scheming to poison and harm mankind." Hard to believe, but that was the language they used.

Apparently, the laws governing libel and privacy in Poland were rather loose. As a sidelight, after the war, in the 1950s, oddly enough, it turned out that the longtime Jew-baiting editor of *To the Pillory* was a Jew, a convert called Sekretarczyk. But then some of the most passionate anti–Semites are converts. Torquemada, he of the Inquisition, is said to have been a convert too.

These periodicals and, to a smaller but still considerable extent, the regular Polish press, also habitually published articles blaming the Jews for every ill there was, the Depression, joblessness, drunkenness, poor harvests, the plague of tuberculosis, and so on, and they urged Poles not to patronize Jewish businesses. They were popular reading among the Jews, too, a persecuted minority who felt outrage about being called nasty names and at the same time savored bitterly, even if disbelievingly, being viewed as masters of the universe, insidious and leering goat-bearded Elders of Zion plotting to subvert Christian civilization, at a time when they themselves were mostly so poor that a meat dish was a rare luxury for them. Among themselves, the Jewish readers of these reptile news-sheets circulated the old inside joke about Jews and bicyclists. (An anti–Semite claimed the Jews caused the war. The reply was, "Yes, the Jews and the bicyclists." "Why the bicyclists?" asks the one. "Why the Jews?" asks the other.)

The very existence of such periodicals pointed to the radical divide existing between Jews and Poles in an agrarian country where the rising native middle class had to compete for jobs in professions with the People of the Book and an economic war was waged against them by barring them from membership in professional associations, boycotting their businesses, and trying to legislate a ban on ritual slaughter.

Even the government and the judiciary were anti–Semitic: Jews were barred from government jobs and the courts routinely ruled against them, as for example, when Jews sued their tormentors. This is illustrated by one such suit, instituted against a so-called League for the Defense of the Fatherland and Faith in Poznan. Its members engaged in beating Jews. In that case, after his release from a hospital, a beaten Jew sued his tormentor, the league's chairman, a certain Noskowicz, a former organist who had been fired as a troublemaker. Noskowicz appeared in the courtroom together with his 12-year-old daughter. The judge asked her, "Well, little girl, were you with Daddy?" "Yes, I was." "Where was it?" "Near Freedom Square." "And what happened? First that Jew struck you, did not he?" "Yes, first that Jew struck me and then another Jew hit Daddy on the head from behind and then started to cry that we were beating him."[4]

Of course, the league's chairman was exonerated and the plaintiff had to pay court costs and compensation for the supposed libel. This courtroom farce was reenacted time after time until the abused Jews no longer bothered to sue. This incident was recounted by Wiktor Stachowiak, who, incidentally, had been the editor of the short-lived *Glos Poznanski*, The Voice of Poznan, a liberal newspaper that once reprinted by way of a satire a passage from a naturalist article in a German newspaper that said, "Doubtless, the rabbit is not a German animal, not even a Germanic one. That is because it is cowardly. There is no question, therefore, that it is an alien animal in Germany and merely abuses our hospitality. But as for the lion, it displays a number of traits that are indisputably purely Germanic."[5]

The antagonism toward the Jews was brought home directly to me in the late 1930s when anti–Semitism was raging even more fiercely in Poland owing to the example set by Hitler's Germany. As it happened, a man was paid by the local Association of Christian Businessmen to parade up and down the Jewish-owned stores in the alley around the corner from our Jewish Street, wearing a placard warning prospective customers, "Don't buy from Jews." His name was Jakubowski and I used to encounter him on my way to visit Father's store. He had a good-natured face with a huge and thick drooping mustache whose ends reached his chin. He had the drunkard's purple-veined nose and was very poor. The whole thing was farcical because he was actually a good acquaintance of my father and they used to chat amiably when they were sure of not being watched by one of Jakubowski's patrons, the Polish owner of a nearby big fabric store, who incidentally replenished some of his merchandise from my father at reduced prices. Besides, Jakubowski did not scare all the customers away, since some knew that Father asked decent prices for his merchandise. Those who feared to be identified on a snapshot published by *To the Pillory* would enter Father's store through its rear door after six o'clock.

By then, in 1939, I was old enough to read the message "Don't buy from Jews" on the placard held by Jakubowski, and once I happened to observe my father banter with him. At my age, eight or nine, I could not give a name to this whole thing but even then it struck me as a salient example of what Sartre later termed *mauvaise foi*, bad faith, while giving me a first intimation of the existence of anti–Semitism and its link to inauthenticity. It was not something natural but, kid that I was then, I accepted and thought no more of it. Now that I think of it I realize how false this situation was: my father bandying jokes with a man who was a walking advertisement warning customers not to patronize his store. I shall never understand why my father clowned like that, but I suppose it was an abnormal reaction to an abnormal situation. Or perhaps he was playing the good soldier Schweik.

Another surprising facet of my father emerged when he engaged in a verbal altercation with the Grosbergs, his competitors who owned a dry goods store diagonally opposite ours. One day, as Bronek stood outside Father's store, he heard Mrs. Grosberg begin for some reason to berate Father, who shouted back at her. A passing Pole chided Father for shouting at a woman and was about to hit him when Father ran off. Some Polish bystanders began to chase him but he ran inside another store that he knew had a rear exit, and he escaped.

Somehow he reached our home at 32 Jewish Street. His escape angered the Poles, and since the apartment house we lived in was known to be the only one in Poznan to be entirely inhabited by Jews, a crowd gathered in front of it and began to hurl stones and curses. It happened in broad daylight, at noon. We closed the shutters and sat in the dark until finally that crowd went away.

Bronek told me that story. It clashes with my exalted image of Father in wartime years. I am citing it for all it is worth.

The one-room apartment we lived in on Jewish Street served as a living room, a dining room, and a bedroom, all in one. I suppose in American parlance it could be called a studio apartment, though sans a toilet. It was joined to a dark and windowless kitchen annex through which one had to pass in order to enter the room, and the toilet was outside, in the hallway.

There were five of us: our parents and we three brothers. We brothers never called each other and our parents anything but affectionate Polish diminutives. Father was Tatus; mother, Mamusia; David, my oldest brother, was Dadek; Baruch, my middle brother, was Bronek; and I, the youngest, Eugene, was Genio.

All five of us lived in that one room. The windows opened into the courtyard, which also served as a playground where we kids would race around and play kickball and *srulki*, a game that demanded some dexterity: while throwing a pebble into the air a boy was supposed to pick up with the same hand five pebbles on the ground before catching it again.

That one room contained one large bed for my parents, a cot on which Bronek and I slept, and a sofa on which Dadek slept. As Bronek and I were growing boys, the cot was becoming too narrow for us, so that some evenings we not only engaged in horseplay but sometimes exchanged blows until our parents separated us. Dadek as the oldest was lucky: he had an entire sofa to himself. Perhaps that was why one morning when he was still sleeping, I gave in to temptation and playfully tickled his bare feet so that he woke up with a start. I still remember how my mother spanked me on the behind for that antic.

Dadek's sofa faced a dining table and chairs behind which a chest of drawers and an armoire hugged the opposite wall. There was hardly any space to walk around all that furniture. In that crowded one room I spent some of the most idyllic years of my life.

There was no hot water and we had to wash ourselves every day with cold water, summer and winter, except on Fridays when we walked to the Mikvah, the ritual bathhouse with a steam bath and an immersion pool in which I once almost drowned when I mistook its bottom for its surface and such terror struck me before I emerged to the real surface, gasping and spitting water.

We had no refrigerator and, instead of a pantry, we stored dairy products, fruits, and vegetables behind a partition in a place allotted to us in the cool building cellar. Each year in autumn, two horse-drawn carts, one full of potatoes, and the other with coal for the winter, would be unloaded for us and their contents shoveled into the cellar.

There was also the kitchen annex, dark and small, which was ruled over by Zosia, our maid and cook. At night it was also her bedroom. How she came to be with us is a story in itself. In prewar Poland maids were dirt cheap. Even a lower-middle-class family like ours could afford one. When

**David, or Dadek, my older brother, in 1938. This photograph, along with a few others, was saved by our Polish nanny who returned them to my mother after the war.**

Zosia was fifteen, she and her illegitimate one-year-old baby, Heniek, were thrown out by her parents and given shelter by our parents. She never identified the baby's father. She used to sleep in our kitchen, behind a curtain. The enterprising Tatus soon found out the address of Zosia's parents and talked them into forgiving Zosia. From then on her parents began to take care of Heniek while Zosia remained living in our kitchen and went home only on Sundays to be with Heniek.

That was where I grew up until the age of nine and the war, in that cluttered apartment. To this day I carry with me memories of a happy childhood there.

Zosia served also as my nanny. She would dress me and escort me to the elementary school, then do cooking and cleaning while Mamusia was helping out in the fabric store. When I was five or six, one day I got angry with Zosia because she would not let me wear a belt with my kneepants. To me, the belt was a symbol of being a big boy and no longer a baby. I was so furious that I walked out into the street wearing only my undershorts. I found myself in a crowded street and, because I was alone and wearing those undershorts, a policeman stopped me, his huge figure looming over me, giving me a big scare. He asked me, "Where's your mommy, kid?" and I was too tongue-tied to answer. Luckily, just then Zosia, who had been tailing me, showed up and got him to release me. She led me back home firmly holding my hand. Was I ever so relieved! Something like that one does not forget.

Zosia, who was Polish and Catholic, used sometimes to take me to her home where I met her family and, one time, was offered a ham roll, the first ham I ever tasted in my life, and asked to keep it secret from my parents. Heniek, her son, and I, Genio, were of the same age, became good friends and played together.

Tatus had first moved to Poznan from Lodz in the early 1920s at the request of his brother-in-law, Jakub Szachnerowicz, the husband of Regina, my mother's twin sister, who needed an assistant in his recently opened fabric store, but they fell out and Tatus rented a fabric store of his own located diagonally across the street. He and Jakub did not remain enemies long, however, since their wives were sisters and loved each other.

In that fabric store of his own, Tatus cut to order swaths from bolts of cloth that women bought for sewing into dresses. He also sold bed linen, window curtains, valances, that sort of things. Most of his customers were peasants who twice a week came to Poznan in horse-drawn carts to sell their fowl, vegetables, and other produce in Old Market Square, outside the Renaissance-style Town Hall, just a hop and skip from where we lived. After they sold their produce they would come to our store and buy fabrics for turning into eiderdown duvets, shirts, and underclothing, as well as garment accessories, thread, needles, and other sewing appurtenances. Some of them became my father's regular clients.

Dadek wanted to belong to Hashomer Hatzair, or Young Guard, a socialist Zionist scouting organization, but Father, an Orthodox Jew, would not let him because he thought it was too secular. Besides, among the fiercely anti-communist — because anti–Russian — Poles it was reputed to be communist and therefore doubly dangerous to a law-abiding citizen like my father. That youth movement, designed to encourage emigration to Israel, was so popular among Poznan boys and girls, however, that Bronek had, defying Father, joined it in secret. Surprisingly enough, when Father learned about Bronek's decision, he raised no further objections. I think that was because by then, in the late 1930s, not just the rightist but even the centrist Polish press began to praise the anti–Jewish laws passed in Nuremberg and appeal to the government to emulate our German neighbor. The socialist and communist parties were the only ones to reject anti–Semitism.

The young members of Hashomer Hatzair would listen to lectures about founding the Jewish National Home in Palestine, take lessons in Hebrew, and participate in literary and dramatic clubs on the premises of the former Reform synagogue that had fallen into disuse in the 1920s after the departure of most German Jews for Germany.

When the weather was warmer they would attend picnics and summer camps and go on group hikes. In the evenings they would light bonfires, bake potatoes in the embers, dance the hora, and sing folk songs — all innocently, because they were such idealists. These high-minded Zionist boy and girl scouts debated the merits of socialism versus communism and engaged in heated disputes about free love, but in theory only — in reality, they would blush if caught holding hands. They rebelled against their parents by not wanting to live any longer in a country where they were treated as second-class citizens because of their religion and dreamed of leaving for Eretz Israel, the Land of Israel, their own country. They did not smoke or drink and believed in the redemption of the Jewish nation through farm labor in Palestine, in reversing the anti–Semite's image of the Jew as a rootless parasite and restoring respect for their own people. Once back in their own land, in Palestine, they believed the Jews would again revert to becoming farmers and craftsmen, as they had been nearly two thousand years ago. To that end, every summer they would travel to farms where they practiced planting and cultivating crops, tending livestock, and operating farm equipment, in preparation for their dreamed-of move to Israel. The Germans were soon to give a macabre twist to this belief in the ennobling value of manual labor when, after invading Poland, they started savagely and methodically working their Jewish slaves to death.

But this practical experience gained was not all for the worse because, having learned how to work and play together and, above all, being nourished by their idealism and spiritual stamina, these Zionist youths survived in greater proportions than the Polish Jewry in general. They also were hardier owing to their scout training and more uncompromisingly disposed for armed struggle against the Germans, whether in the Warsaw and Bialystok ghettoes or in the forests of eastern Poland as partisans.

I wanted so much to join Hashomer Hatzair and wear its snazzy blue shorts, gray shirt, and blue neckerchief, but I was too little to qualify, and when I became old enough, it was too late owing to the war.

I think of these youths nostalgically. It was idealistic young people like they who had the guts to defy their elders and start the Warsaw Ghetto uprising and there, against all odds, keep battling the Germans in an unequal struggle for at least two months — longer than Poland and France. They did so because in their pioneering Zionist youth movements they had forged bonds of comradeship, learned how to work together, live communally, and organize themselves. They would not let their spirit be crushed. In the Warsaw Ghetto they fought in full knowledge that they were at least going to die with honor and not on their knees.

Our lives in Poznan were governed by the rhythm of religious rituals and holidays. Every Friday in the early evening, Bronek remembers, Tatus and we, his three sons, would walk in single file, like a duck and three goslings, to the ritual bath, which was presided over by Mr. Segal, a man with a wooden leg like Long John Silver of *Treasure Island*. After soaping and rinsing ourselves in a tub we would immerse our heads three times in a little pool, with us boys pretending that we were swimming, while uttering a prayer, that being the tradition and the ritual. After the bath we would don clean underclothing and holiday garments, and walk home with Tatus again proudly leading us. With the appearance of the first star in the heavens, signifying the onset of the Sabbath, we would walk to the shul, next to the home for the aged on Jewish Street in order to welcome there the holiday of the Sabbath Queen (Lecha Dodi). That little shul was nothing like a big synagogue. It also served as a place for regular weekday meetings with the object of studying the Talmud and the Torah under the rabbi's guidance.

Following the prayers we would return home where Mamusia and Zosia waited for us with a holiday supper. Before meals, emulating Tatus, we washed our hands from a pitcher and recited the prayer over the handwashing. A lace kerchief on her head, Mamusia would light the Sabbath candles, cover her eyes with her fingers and intone the benediction. The holiday supper almost always consisted of challah, a braided egg bread; gefilte carp; chicken soup with macaroni flakes; and chicken. Sometimes for a change it was beef stew with kasha. For dessert, there was crumb cake and tea. That was the Sabbath meal. Our weekdays were meatless and the fare was much plainer and mostly potatoes. Potatoes with herring, potatoes with borsht, potatoes with sour cream, potatoes with cabbage. In general, the Jews in Poland were so poor and ground down by economic boycotts and official anti–Semitism that the joke ran: if a Jew is seen bringing home a chicken on a weekday, someone in his family must be sick.

Before eating, Tatus recited in a singsong voice hymns of thanksgiving to the Lord and we all sang excerpts from Sabbath prayers.

Saturday morning we would walk to the Grand Synagogue, also called the Red Synagogue because it was built of red bricks, where we prayed until noon, with Tatus exchanging greetings with acquaintances before and after the prayers. We returned home for a lunch of chicken soup with square-cut flakes of macaroni or braised beef with potatoes and carrots. A bit heavy, that lunch, but then in Poland lunch was and is the main meal of the day.

After lunch we sang Hebrew songs and Dadek and Bronek discussed with Tatus last week's events and excerpts from the Pentateuch. Afterward, Tatus expected them to read aloud for an hour articles from Jewish newspapers published in Warsaw and Lodz or an entire chapter from a Yiddish novel. Bronek, in particular, bridled against it because he longed to join his peers playing soccer on a vacant lot blocks away but Tatus would not let him do so until the Sabbath ended at sundown, and by then it would be too dark and too late.

Dadek, on the other hand, just drank all this learning in. He was the scholar in the family, so brilliant that he was one of the very few Jews admitted to Poznan's College of Commerce. He was as frail as Bronek was robust. The doctors said he was anemic but the cod liver oil and iron pills they prescribed for him hardly seemed to work and he continued to be subject to fainting spells. It did not help that he had to endure anti–Semitic maltreatment at the high school. In the class, every time a teacher read his name at roll call, he had to hear comments like "Mangy kike. Christ killer!" When he was leaving the classroom he would get struck and pinched from behind, and when he turned around the perpetrators smilingly averted their faces. Not wanting to cause distress to his parents, he said nothing to them, but they could see the bruises on his face and arms and guessed what was happening. They knew better than to go to the college and complain, for they would only be met with a brush-off. They planned to relieve his lot by enrolling him in the fall in a Lodz gymnasium, a European cross between a high school and a junior college, where, for a change, most students were also Jewish. But that was to be in the fall of 1939 when their plans no longer mattered in face of the Nazi invasion.

On weekday evenings, once or twice a week, Tatus would go to the shul in order to study the Torah together with several other men, acquaintances with whom he also played cards weekly in a restaurant after dinner.

Sometimes Bronek and Dadek would attend the shul with him. Bronek still remembers the red armchair partitioned off by a braided yellow cord that stood prominently in a corner of the shul, next to the bookshelves. Tatus told him, "G-d forbid, never touch it." It was the armchair of Rabbi Akiva Eger, a charismatic nineteenth-century holy man and chief rabbi of Poznan whose name is venerated to this day in the pantheon of Hebrew sages.

We lived on Jewish Street in the heart of the small Jewish community. Though there were no ghetto walls, the community's members clustered together within a few blocks rather than spread out throughout Poznan. They found it comfortable to live together in a self-contained enclave with its own schools, temples, and other communal institutions — even if these had been bequeathed to them by their German coreligionists — and familiar religious customs and rituals. They formed friendships with Poles but always on an individual basis. Tatus was well-liked by his Polish customers and through Zosia I had my own Polish friend, her son Heniek.

Then the volcano of the war erupted.

## The Germans Arrive

On 1 September 1939 German troops invaded Poland, but they did not enter Poznan until the tenth of September even though the border was fairly near. The delay was due to focusing on first destroying most of the Polish army in the country's west by means of a massive double envelopment, with one pincer driving south from Prussia and the other north from Czechoslovakia. In that intervening period a panic erupted in my hometown and people bought up anything that could be bought for money in the stores. They emptied Father's dry-goods store in just one day. He spent all his money on buying new supplies from a warehouse and restocked his store, whereupon a new queue formed in front of it. But then everything stopped when German troops marched into the city.

Evening. Tatus took me to Old Market Square. Maybe he felt safer being seen holding the hand of a little boy, and besides he had been a German soldier in World War I and had nothing to fear, he thought. Standing in the crowd lining the sidewalks of the square, we saw green-uniformed German troops parading through it in serried ranks, with local

Germans welcoming them and handing flowers to the passing soldiers. Horses were towing wheeled cannon. Elegant officers watched the parade from the steps of the Town Hall, a smaller copy of the Palazzo della Signoria in Florence. It was a stirring martial sight but I was perturbed to see a couple of gendarmes frogmarching a somber civilian suspect, apparently a Pole.

Almost overnight, Poznan became Germanized, with names of streets and store signs changed. The city's Poles became henceforth treated as subhumans, reduced in status to flunkies and garbage collectors, but it was the Jews who were made to suffer most indignities. This ranking was exemplified by a sign hung on the door of a restaurant. Before the war it said "No Admission to Dogs and Jews." But now the sign was in German and "Poles" was inserted after "Dogs" and "Jews."

The caste ranked as the lowest was the Jews. The occupier ordered the sealing of Jewish schools and places of worship and seized the community's assets. The Jews were forbidden to use public transit and ordered to wear yellow brassards and later a yellow cloth star with the word *Jude*. The Grand Synagogue was stripped of its furnishings and Hebrew signage. The Holy Books were trampled and burned and the building itself converted into a swimming pool.

The humiliations inflicted on Jews were brought home to me in a most unforgettable manner. Schools were closed and we brothers had nothing to do. One morning in September I walked with Dadek, then seventeen, for a visit to Tatus's fabric store in the alley around the corner from our home on Jewish Street. As we walked, an unshaven man in striped garb stopped Dadek and talked to him using threatening gestures.

I had seen cartoons of convicts wearing such garb in the comics sections of Sunday newspapers, which by the way were largely reproductions of American comics, and was excited to behold a real, living convict. That man was, as I learned later, one of the criminals released en masse from Poznan prisons by their Polish wardens who fled before the advancing Germans and just left the cell doors open. But why did he stop my brother and what was he saying to him? Why did his face look so threatening? I could see that the convict had a brutish face with bloodshot eyes and what looked like a knife scar running at right angles to a corner of his mouth, which caused his face to have an even more frightening expression. From that vicious, scarred mouth he was spouting a torrent of words at Dadek, who stood there as if frozen while listening to him. The man was visibly losing patience and the scowl on his face deepened as he began to shout at my brother and finally shoved him in the chest so violently that Dadek retreated a few paces before his back hit a wall and he crumpled and fell. Even as he fell, there was a dazed look on his face.

The convict glanced around and as if by magic the alley emptied, with the few onlookers running inside the nearest storefront doors rather than face his gaze. He approached Dadek and searched through his pockets, finding only a few coins which he disgustedly pocketed. He spat, scowled evilly, muttered curses, and walked away, fortunately in the direction opposite to that of our home.

I cowered in the door of Tatus's store. Sensing that something was amiss, Tatus came outside and saw Dadek lying on the pavement. He ran to his son and helped him get up with such tenderness and delicacy and anguished expression on his face that it gave me a new perspective on him, Dadek, and on myself. That was not the godlike paterfamilias such as I had known him until now. And the affection he was showing Dadek, the first-born, opened my eyes, the eyes of the spoiled youngest child petted by Mamusia and Zosia, to the fact that the universe was not revolving around me and that other human beings had as much right as I to see and feel deeply and to love and be loved without involving me. Even I, the boy that I was, now saw and realized that Dadek, the brilliant, sensitive teenager who showed such promise as a thinker and scholar, was Tatus's favorite son in whom he had placed his greatest hope.

Until then I was the earth around which the Sun and other planets revolved. Now I became one of those planets, in my awakening consciousness. Or did I? This is a question of selfhood that every thinking being grapples with.

There was a stunned and sad expression on Dadek's face and his eyes were wide open. On helping him to rise, Tatus escorted him home, his arm around Dadek's shoulder while I stayed in the door of our store, with Fela's hand resting protectively on my shoulder. (Fela was the salesgirl.)

With the convict's disappearance, shoppers reappeared in the alley. The war was on and the buying panic continued.

When I returned home I found everything upside down. Mamusia was packing a suitcase with Dadek's clothing and, once she was finished, she embraced him, wiping her tears. Then Tatus and Dadek left for the train station. Tatus was sending Dadek to Lodz, feeling worried that my brother was now a marked man and the next time that convict met Dadek he would do something more drastic to him. To save Dadek from another such encounter he had instructed him to take the next train to Lodz, where he would stay with our relatives. Dadek left, not a day too late, because on the morrow the Germans banned Jews from taking trolleys and trains.

Next morning, I again visited Tatus's store, this time with Bronek. Once again the alley and the store were the venue of an event as vivid in my memory as if it took place today. A German soldier, a private, swaggered into the store. He asked Tatus straightforward if he was a Jew and, on receiving confirmation, demanded harshly that Tatus go with him to a nearby store selling cured meats. They went outside. Shocked and curious, I and Bronek followed them at a distance of several paces. My father was not going fast enough for the German, who walked behind him and kept shoving him in the back. On the way, Tatus stumbled, almost falling as his foot got wedged in a pavement crack, and this afforded an excuse for the soldier to kick him and curse him for a rotten Jew and "pig-dog." Father picked himself up wordlessly and they entered the butcher's store while Bronek and I waited outside. Through the plate glass window we could see Tatus pay for a large canned ham. They soon emerged, with the soldier clutching the can. He cursed my father again and departed.

What startled me was that the soldier was acting as if it were the most natural thing in the world to invade the store and maltreat and try to humiliate my father. After witnessing the convict's confrontation with Dadek the day before, the sight of my father being kicked by the German was the final blow demolishing the cozy world of my childhood.

My father, the heroic and admired figure in my life, kicked in the behind by another man! But the shock was cushioned by the differences between these two men that even I, the nine-year-old boy that I was then, could perceive. Tatus did not react to the kick other than stopping for a moment. He then straightened up and continued walking calmly as if he had merely tripped and fell. There was sadness in his face but otherwise it looked expressionless. The kicker, on the other hand, looked mean and petty. His triumphant grin was the smile of a loser, a nonentity who at last felt empowered, enjoying his power over another human being. I was to see that sadistic grin on many other Germans later.

Of course that pathetic soldier was not representative of the terrifying Germans I was to see later, the helmeted minions of death. Still, that incident was impressed deeply in my awareness, but not because it traumatized me. On the contrary, seeing — truly seeing — the fortitude and poise with which my father endured that shoving and kick and the brutality and insignificance of the assailant, I felt galvanized and derived from it inner strength. How could I think these supermen superior when I saw for myself how inferior, how base they were spiritually compared to my father?

Tatus walked back to the store with Bronek and me trailing behind. We did not dare walk abreast of him, feeling ashamed to show to him by our presence that we had been the silent witnesses of his humiliation. All that time, if he knew we were there he showed no sign of it. The expression on his face, what I could see of it, was bland and he walked on with measured strides as if nothing so monstrous had happened a moment ago. When we reached the store, he turned around to face us and held the door open for us. So he was aware of our presence!

But that was not the end of it. As if adding more drama to this shattering day, just then a pickup truck drew up in front of Grosberg's haberdashery store and two young men in the black uniforms of Hitler Youth jumped off from the cab. They strode inside that store and started to empty its contents, carrying boxes of hosiery, ties, shirts, and the like, and dumping them onto the pickup bed until it was full, too full for them to take things out of Tatus's store as well, so that instead they sealed it, ordering us out. It was on that day too that all Jewish stores in Poznan were sealed for subsequent confiscation of their goods, Tatus's too, with an armed German soldier guarding the stores in our alley. Luckily, there was a rear door opening into a courtyard and when darkness fell, Tatus together with Dadek and Bronek emptied the store of the most valuable fabrics through that door and carried it to our home. It was a wasted effort, because a couple of days later two Gestapo men in mufti searched our home and found and seized those carefully folded fabrics atop our mattresses and in our chest of drawers. Thankfully, they left us alone — thankfully, because as soon as a week or two later the penalty for such "sabotage" of our own property would be a labor camp or a death sentence.

Not long after, a radical turnabout in my life took place. In those early days of German occupation of Poznan, before the hail of official restrictions rained down on Jews, life was still fairly normal. I was still able to go out and play with other kids. We were playing on a sidewalk near a synagogue that was located just a few steps from my home. Our game was called *palant*. Its object was to hit with half of a broomstick a small piece of wood sharpened at both edges and see how far it would fly. The boy

who scored the farthest would be the winner. We were screaming and calling each other names in the heat of the game. One kid, Moshe, in particular used to scream at the top of his lungs every time he hit the block of
wood and claim he was going to break the world record, only to have it
fall a few feet from him. The other kids would laugh at him and he would
get mad. Then it happened: Moshe struck the block of wood so hard that
it sailed toward the sidewalk curb where it rebounded against the jackboots of a German soldier on patrol with his comrade. He shouted in German something like "Damned Yids!" apparently because most of us looked
Jewish and were playing near the synagogue, and he and his companion
started beating us children with rifle butts. I wanted to run but I froze in
fear. As I turned, I saw the shadow of one soldier growing larger and then
something hit me hard on the left side of my head. The world became
dark and I lost consciousness even before I hit the ground.

I awakened in a hospital, after lying in a coma for three days. When
I opened my eyes, I sensed that my head was bandaged and saw my parents, a white-coated doctor, and a nurse. They approached my bed and
faced me. For some strange reason the doctor and then my father moved
their lips but I could not hear them. How strange!

That was how I became deaf, though I was too young to realize it at
the time. From then on to this day I have been living like a man whose
ears are perpetually stuffed with cotton, with his eyes serving as his ears.
My life was turned into watching a continually unrolling reel of a silent
movie except that it lacks the jerky rhythm and the actors behave as in a
talkie: they make no exaggerated grimaces and do not flail their arms dramatically. On the contrary, their facial expressions and gestures are subdued, making it much more difficult for me to improvise in my mind
whatever subtitles suggest themselves to me according to these limited
visual cues. It is like watching a talkie without a soundtrack and zoom-
ing in on whatever moves.

As the saying goes, what a deaf man does not hear, he tries to figure
out for himself. From then on I have been constantly trying to figure out
the world for myself. Where the average person tries to figure out the
meaning of life, I have to figure out what directions is a passerby asking
me about, and fail, unless he writes it down for me. I became a constant
watcher, always bent on interpreting facial expressions of grimace, sadness, or laughter, gestures, posture, and movement. Did a person smile
and look happy? I smiled and looked happy in return. Did he look sad or

angry? I adopted a noncommittal expression on my face. Was his posture friendly, hostile, or indifferent? I adapted myself to whatever it signified. Was he asking me a question or offering me a present or chiding me or giving me an order? Were his movements slow or fast and what could it mean? Was he tired or lazy or was he in a hurry? It was and is a constant struggle to interpret meaning and attitude in a world that is not made for the deaf.

But that adaptation came with time. It was only gradually that I realized I was deaf when various members of my family began to tap me on the shoulder from behind to get my attention or, if in front of me, they moved their lips dramatically or gestured to make their wants known to me, as when my father pointed to a chair with his index finger for me to sit down.

There is much more to this strange and invisible handicap that has become my fate, of course: years later, on just one day in 1944, for example, my deafness saved my life and a quarter of an hour later caused my being fired at with real bullets, except that fortunately the bullets missed. My life was saved twice when I was rescued from drowning in the Vistula and then my rescuer demanded to see if my penis was circumcised but relented when I gestured to him that I was deaf. And some fifteen minutes later I evaded death a third time when a man shot at me more than once, after shouting in vain at me to raise my hands, without my hearing the shots, and then he too let me go after he realized I was deaf.

Incidentally, during the first three years of the war the only other deaf person I had met, or rather seen from a distance, was in the Warsaw Ghetto. He was a mentally retarded man who smiled idiotically while hurrying away from ghetto children who were throwing stones at him. I thus had a poor impression of other people who shared my handicap. It was only after I came to America in 1947 that I became aware of the existence of a large and thriving deaf culture which taught me the social graces I had missed in my Caliban-like existence during the war. Such are the consequences of a blow with a rifle butt.

Even before my head wound healed and I was able to walk again, my parents took me home, as it was dangerous for a Jewish child to stay in that hospital. For some time afterward I could hardly sleep because of the ringing in my ears, a condition known as tinnitus. I kept crying and complaining about that unending noise, which must have been heartrending to my parents. After a few weeks, though, that ringing stopped. I suppose

I was lucky because tinnitus plagues many deafened people for much longer periods of time if not for life. That constant hammering inside one's head is worse even than chronic migraine.

I can only imagine how my parents must have felt when I became deaf. The blow to them must have been all the harder in the context of the misfortune that befell them as Jews with the coming of the Germans. It did not help either that I, the youngest, was my mother's favorite child, petted and spoiled, and my becoming deaf only added to her worries. Upon my return from the hospital Mamusia stayed with me all the time, changing the bandage on my head and feeding me until I was well enough to walk on my own. My relationship with Bronek and Dadek also changed. In particular, I became closer to Bronek as he was nearer to me in age and I found it easier to read his lips in Polish than anyone else's. Much later, in the United States, psychologists developed the concept of the lifeline, meaning attachment between a deaf person and his hearing sibling or parent through whom he keeps abreast with the world. Already then, and for a few years afterward, Bronek served as a lifeline, a mediator, between me and the hearing world. My speech was then still good and my parents understood it, but they were not as easy to lip-read so that I relied on their use of pen and paper to understand them unless Bronek was there to interpret for me.

That was in the past. I have long since forgotten how to lip-read in Polish, and my daughter Sabrina has become my new lifeline in English, in emergencies.

My life was changed when I became deaf but I was too young to grasp the deeper meaning of that change. I came to accept my deafness as something natural, and besides I was distracted by the new atmosphere of terror in Poznan. I could no longer play with the other children outside. The brutal beating administered to me had so terrified the parents of other Jewish children that they kept them off the streets. With the schools closed and the streets dangerous, the children had at least the outlet of being able to play in the courtyards. In the courtyard of our building I played with other children all day long.

That was not enough to keep me busy. It was then also that I first conceived my passion for reading. I started to devour with my eyes all the children's books I could find, mine and those of my brothers who now were too old for them. In the evening, after lights were out, I would hide my head under a coverlet and continue reading by using a flashlight. Of course, this was no secret to my parents and brothers in that one room where we all lived and slept together. My mother would wait patiently a few minutes and then take away the book and flashlight to make me sleep.

The vise of more and more restrictions on Poznan Jews was tightening. The ownership of Jewish-owned businesses and stores was transferred to German "trustees." Jewish schools, libraries and synagogues were closed and, worst of all, the Germans seized from the offices of the Jewish community registries with the names and addresses of Jewish residents of Poznan, which they utilized later to round up them for forced labor, deportation, and slaughter — a technique which they later refined even more thoroughly in other cities.

## Escape to Lodz, Escape from Lodz

Sometime in October my father decided that we all would leave Poznan for Lodz, where we would join Dadek. That month the Germans began to deport Poznan Jews to labor camps where they starved them and worked them to death. Tatus felt we should quickly leave Poznan before we ourselves would be thus seized. We left for Lodz, the industrial heart and second largest city in Poland with a big population of some 200,000 Jews, where we might find safety in numbers and have a chance to live a more normal life, or so my father thought. Besides, most of our relatives lived there. He thought that we would stand out less there than in Poznan with its tiny Jewish minority. He was wrong about that, but when he realized his mistake, he reacted quickly again, as will be seen.

At any rate, what I remember most of my stay in Lodz was the kindness shown my family by my mother's relatives there, the heart-wrenching beauty of my female cousins, the well-appointed homes they had lived in before they all were evicted to the Baluty slum, and the endless card games they began to play at home after restrictions on Jewish life and a curfew were introduced. But these restrictions were only the first steps, leading to the expulsion of all Jews to the ghetto established in the Baluty slum suburb and their miserable existence and deaths in that vast sweatshop there.

Only one of my Lodz cousins survived the war in Europe. Her name is Lusia and at her liberation she was a slave laborer in a Czechoslovak factory to which she had been deported from Lodz.

My other surviving cousin, David, from Piotrkow Trybunalski, was liberated from a concentration camp. After the war he migrated to Israel where he was welcomed by his two brothers, Haskiel and Icchak, who had left Poland before the war and after many adventures ended up in Palestine. While still in Poland, Haskiel had won a national contest for the best Polish-language essay and was admitted to Poznan University. In the lecture halls he had to sit on a separate bench on the left side because he was Jewish. Outside the classroom the other students would taunt and assault him. The police did not interfere on the pretext of respecting university autonomy, that sacred cow in Europe. He endured his physical and psychological status as a pariah for a few months before finally giving up and leaving for Palestine with Isaac.

As for the card games, at the time I was a little kid and excluded from playing cards with my teenage Lodz cousins, whom I could only watch wistfully. That perhaps is why much later playing cards became a hobby of mine.

As in Poznan, soon after the German invasion Lodz became quickly Germanized. Polish street names and shop signs were replaced with German ones and the only newspapers to appear were in German. The occupier's policy was to annex western Poland, including Poznan and Lodz, into the Reich and deport all Jews either to forced labor camps or eastward, outside the new expanded boundaries of Germany into what was left of Poland, a rump province called General Government. In the case of Poznan this policy proved easy to pursue because of its small Jewish population, but not so in Lodz, the textile manufacturing center of Poland, with its more than 200,000 Jews. There were simply too many Jews to deport. The Germans solved this problem by decreeing the establishment of a ghetto in Lodz. It was to be in Baluty, the slum section of the city, consisting mostly of decrepit one-story wooden houses lacking water supply and sewage facilities, standing on crooked and mostly unpaved roads.

The ghetto in Lodz was placed under the reign of a Jewish "dictator," "the Elder of the Jews," a ruined businessman and educator called Chaim Rumkowski, whom the Germans picked as their stooge after they had executed the city's most prominent Jewish politicians. This "Jewish Residential District," as it was called by Germans who at first for propaganda purposes had avoided using the blunt term "ghetto," ostensibly became an autonomous Jewish area with its own police, municipal administration, and currency, the so-called Rumkies. These were signed by Rumkowski and decorated with six-pointed stars in various colors, a kind of Monopoly money that was good only within the ghetto. The ghetto was supposedly self-governing but in reality its "autonomy" was a sham and it was turned into a big sweatshop. Its inmates produced everything for the German war effort, mainly in the form of uniforms, shoes, boots, caps and other accessories for the German army, and were paid in food, actually in starvation rations. Making his wards "productive" for the Germans was in Rumkowski's proclaimed belief the only way of ensuring their survival. To that end, he had even succeeded in persuading the conquerors to transfer to Baluty some of the industrial machinery they had confiscated.

In Baluty, Tatus found for the five of us a single room in one such ramshackle house where we had to sleep on the floor. In the courtyard a well served as the source of water and an outhouse served as the bathroom. It was February 1940 and, even though we slept in our clothes, we shivered from the cold all night.

Sometime during that first night my father made a decision. He conferred with Mamusia and told us all to leave our suitcases and everything and just go out wearing the clothes on our back so as not to look suspicious.

That was in the early days of the Lodz Ghetto, before the barbed-wire fences and barricades isolating it had been erected, and before the German guards had been posted around it. We removed with scissors the yellow stars of David from our chests and backs and boarded a trolley that was traversing the ghetto. On that trolley we left the ghetto while it was still unguarded, not a day too soon. (A similar trolley was much later featured in Agnieszka Holland's film *Europa, Europa*.) There was no road back. Once we had left the ghetto Tatus decided to take us to Warsaw.

As it happened, even earlier, when the ghetto in Lodz was about to be established, Tatus had acquired a Polish identity card under the name of Feliks Krawczyk. He got it from a friendly Polish acquaintance whom he urged to report the loss so as to get a replacement. Money changed hands and Tatus's photo replaced the Pole's photo on the card with his own. At the same time he began to grow a thick but well-trimmed Sarmatian mustache that, given his aquiline profile, made him resemble Stalin, all the more so because he also wore his hair en brosse and was of stocky build, though he looked more dignified and his blue-eyed gaze was grave, unlike the dictator's narrow-eyed gaze.

In 1955, when I visited Israel for the first time I met my first cousins, Icchak and Haskiel, convinced Zionists who, embittered by their treatment as Jews in Poland, had migrated to Palestine before the war. They told me how impressed they had been by Tatus when he had visited them in their hometown of Piotrkow Trybunalski in Poland in the 1930s. As he was walking with them to the local cinema, people would stare at him because he looked like a Polish nobleman. His distinguished bearing, so unlike that of many Jews in Poland whom the endemic local anti–Semitism was almost turning into nervous wrecks and only intensified the scorn felt toward them by the Poles, probably contributed to his survival during the war.

What was my father thinking when he decided to become Feliks Krawczyk, a Christian Pole? Before the war, according to Bronek, Tatus used to enthuse about a then-famous movie, "Captain of Koepenick," based on a play by Carl Zuckmayer which was banned by the Nazis later. It was about a caper by a con man who exploited the German habit of blind obedience to one's superiors. He bought a Prussian captain's uniform, donned it and, on the strength of his uniform, ordered an army unit to accompany him to the town hall of Koepenick, a suburb of Berlin. There he arrested the burgomaster on suspicion of padding the books, sent him in custody to the Berlin military headquarters, and confiscated the municipality's chest of 4,000 marks, slipping out with his spoils and putting on civilian clothes. In its time that movie caused a big stir in Germany. It may also have influenced Tatus in his decision to start leading a double life himself. Then, too, Tatus may have had a premonition of a grim future for Jews. Whatever the reason, his decision to pose as somebody else saved him and his family for years to come.

But even if we all had Polish identity cards, that would not have been enough for going to Warsaw, because when the Germans decided to annex western Poland, including Poznan and Lodz, they set up a formal new frontier separating Lodz from Warsaw. Now Warsaw was inside the General Government. Movement between these two territories was closely controlled.

We thus were forced to take the low road. Instead of going by train we traveled eastward from village to village on hired horse-drawn peasant carts, trying to keep warm in the freezing weather by wrapping ourselves in blankets, with mufflers around our faces and necks. Once we crossed the frontier in an unguarded area, we took a local train to Warsaw.

This trip, only about 70 miles east, took us several weeks, and by the time we reached Warsaw spring had begun.

## II

# Life in the Warsaw Ghetto

## *From One Ghetto to Another*

We had escaped from one cage, the Lodz Ghetto, only to be trapped in another. In that other ghetto, in Warsaw, we remained confined for nearly three years, almost until the bitter end. I first learned about this new trap in a particularly stunning way, by seeing Aunt Dreizel rock back and forth while sitting on her bed with a grief-stricken expression on her face, as if a great disaster had happened. She was prophetically right.

When we arrived in Warsaw at first we stayed at the Orthodox home of my father's sister, Aunt Dreizel. It was there also that I first met her son my cousin David. He stayed with his parents in Poland rather than to follow his two brothers, who had left for Palestine before the war. He stayed because he was a more religious and more dutiful son. Fleeing the German bombardment of Piotrkow Trybunalski, he and his mother had moved to Warsaw, and that was where we met them.

It was a warm spring in 1940 and the trees were blossoming. That was also the first time I learned how tricky and conniving human nature can be. A tenant in our building organized a raffle with a turkey as the first prize. Most other tenants bought tickets to that raffle but the winner was found to be a cousin of the organizer. The others, their faces sour, grumbled that the raffle was rigged.

With the establishment of the ghetto we had to move there since we were living with Aunt Dreizel's family outside the proclaimed ghetto boundaries and they themselves were being evicted from their apartment. They had to scramble on their own to find a place to live in.

About 400,000 Jews, or one-third of the city's population, were living in Warsaw. Yet the ghetto established for them accounted for only 5 percent of the city's area. Within that area there were about 100 street blocks. The shape of the ghetto itself, once it became ringed by the wall, resembled a jagged oval one and one-half miles long and half a mile wide at its widest part.

Those Jews living outside the ghetto's boundaries were given a tight deadline to move into it. Tatus obtained a handcart somewhere. We piled on it our few belongings and joined a stream of people and carts that began to move toward the ghetto's boundaries. The carts were either horse-drawn and pulled or pushed by humans. They carried the most varied kinds of possessions: beds, divans, credenzas, armchairs, armoires, bedding. A much thinner stream of Poles moving out flowed in the opposite direction. As I walked and helped push the handcart I was overwhelmed by people of all ages rushing here and there, competing for the little housing available. It was baffling to see the normally self-confident and sure adults running around like scared chickens.

Luckily, Tatus found for the five of us in the ghetto a one-room apartment with kitchen at street level, on the premises of a former haberdashery store. We did not have to share it with other families. I do not know how he managed finding such a desirable apartment in that cramped ghetto.

In Poznan Tatus had been a small businessman, the kind of man who tended a store, prayed regularly at the synagogue, and played cards with cronies once a week. That was before the war. Now something changed in him. For the next five years he found in himself a new or awakened ability to keep his family alive by constantly living on the edge. God knows how much effort it required of him to remain always alert, never drop his mask, avoid uttering an incautious word in the presence of a stranger. The unmasking of a double life led by, say, a bigamous husband who spends part of the week with one wife and another part with the other, would at worst mean divorce and heartbreak but no loss of life, while the unmasking of the double life led by my father would have led to death, pure and simple, not just for himself but for his family.

The ghetto in Warsaw proved to be quite different from that in Lodz. For nearly three years, from its establishment in the fall of 1940 until the onset of its destruction in the summer of 1942, this walled-off and chaotic slum just north of the heart of the Polish metropolis was left largely to its own devices, unlike the ghetto in Lodz, an enclave on the city's outskirts whose dwellers were turned into a drab mass of proles subject to much closer supervision by the Germans.

The Warsaw Ghetto was a place of glaring social contrasts with opulent restaurants, cabarets, and deli stores offering a variety of luxury foods to smugglers and their like who got rich quickly while the more numerous starving wretches, or "useless eaters" in German terminology, loitered outside.

On my wanderings through the ghetto I would now and then pass such places. The smells wafting from them whetted my hunger but I hurried past them quickly because of the fearsome bouncers guarding their doors. These bouncers kept at bay the wretches loitering outside and hoping for a lagniappe. Many of these paupers were slowly and miserably expiring of starvation, cold, and disease, because the Germans had imposed strict and ever stricter limits on food rationing and stopped the importation of any medicines or articles of personal hygiene. Everything was in very short supply, even clothing, which meant that the ghetto dwellers wore tattered garments that literally fell apart with wear and tear. As an unintended consequence, almost the only thriving businesses in the ghetto were, next to the stores and restaurants for the rich, funeral homes serving to accommodate the steeply rising death rate, and sewing establishments to which the not-so-destitute brought their garments to be patched up.

Yet, the new elite of smugglers and the well-off wore natty clothes and stuffed themselves with rich food in the restaurants and coffee houses. In another society or culture the starving, shivering wretches would revolt and assault those bastions of plentiful food and affluence, but not in the Warsaw Ghetto, perhaps because rioting was not in the Jewish tradition and perhaps also because these beggars and paupers were too undernourished and weak to revolt. These opposites of wealth and misery were in such glaring contrast with the ghetto in Lodz where, under the one-man rule of Chaim Rumkowski, "the Elder of the Jews," everybody, aside from his cronies in the bureaucracy, was in the same boat of working hard and barely subsisting on totally inadequate food rations.

The ghetto functioned as a semi-autonomous city until July 1942. It contained thousands of people who were saved from starvation. Owing to its central location in Poland's capital, it was easily infiltrated by smugglers, without whom the ghetto would have been depopulated by famine within a month. The Lodz Ghetto in contrast contained a much higher proportion of starving paupers because of its hermetic isolation from the city. Located in Baluty, an outlying northern slum suburb of Lodz around which most houses were razed, it was surrounded by a hostile German population. This isolation was reinforced by the ban on sending and receiving mail. No food parcels could be sent to the ghetto either. The cordon around the ghetto was made even more impenetrable by the eviction of the local Poles to boroughs farther away from Baluty. That ghetto was encircled only by barbed wire, a far cry from the Warsaw Ghetto's three-meters-tall brick walls topped with broken glass, but its isolation was much more complete than in Warsaw.

Owing to that practically absolute isolation in hostile territory, escape from the Lodz ghetto was impossible, whether on the surface or underground — since Baluty lacked a sewer system, escape through sewage canals was not possible either. Also owing to that isolation, smuggling was impossible and, since there was no food to buy on the black market, money was no good there. Anyway, it was Monopoly money, owing to the forced exchange of German and Polish currency for the Rumkies, the ghetto's own currency which bore Rumkowski's signature and was worthless outside the ghetto. The only thing the Rumkies were good for was to pay for the meager food rations allotted to the owners of food coupons. After the war I saw samples of that currency bearing Rumkowski's signature and six-pointed stars in various colors, and its very existence made me realize how sizable the Lodz Ghetto was, like some quasi-independent city-state, with a population nearing 200,000 at its peak.

It is pertinent to ask here how it happened that the Lodz Ghetto, the most populous ghetto after the Warsaw one, remained unresponsive to the Warsaw Ghetto uprising in 1943 which spurred revolts in smaller ghettoes, to which emissaries had been sent from Warsaw. But no emissary, no news of the revolt in Warsaw, could reach the cordoned-off Lodz Ghetto on the other side of the border, in Germany. To be sure, there was a resistant youth movement in the Lodz Ghetto too. But no echo of the revolt in Warsaw had reached it owing to the very isolation of the Lodz Ghetto, its lack of contact with the outside world. Anyway, even if they had known what happened in Warsaw, sealed off within this hermetic cordon as they were, the Lodz youths were unable to obtain arms and were in no condition for an armed struggle.

Rumkowski, the "chairman" of the Lodz Ghetto, acted like a little dictator, aping the authoritarian style of the Germans. This elderly white-haired man enjoyed the fruits of his privileged position by bossing everyone else in the ghetto and marrying a woman much younger than himself. The historian Ringelblum cites an anecdote about Rumkowski: "'We have gold currency in the ghetto,' he declares. 'How's that?' someone cries with amazement. He raises his fists and says, 'The labor of our hands is our gold.'" In other words, he damned himself by confusing human lives with a metal.[1]

Rumkowski was not alone in his obstinate belief in redemption through "productive" labor. The heads of some other ghettoes also placed great emphasis on such "rescue through labor," and they too turned their bailiwicks into sweatshops. The average Jew living in those ghettos believed in this slogan as well — until he was disabused of it. This was part of the age-old Jewish policy of either bribing hostile powers-that-be or becoming economically indispensable to them. Ultimately, but not completely, Rumkowski's belief proved mistaken.

There was, however, also another reason for this mass psychosis. Long before the war, as the tidal wave of anti–Semitism surged, Jews were continually being reproached for being parasites and strangers without a country of their own. They were made to feel guilty even though there was no reason for their feeling so. After all, whichever country they lived in, their assimilated coreligionists contributed to its economy and enriched its culture. Still, they could not help feeling estranged by these accusations, which were a blow to their self-esteem and caused them to be defensive. That also accounted for the rise of Zionism, with its appeal of return to a land of their own. That also accounted for the popularity of Zionist youth movements. That, finally, also was the reason why people like Rumkowski took these reproaches to heart and wanted to prove otherwise to their maniacal tormentors. But a ravening wolf cannot be appeased.

Rumkowski slavishly tolerated successive deportations of children and old people to the killing camps, with the illusory object of saving the core of the Jewish people, those strongest and most "productive"— until they too were deported to the killing camps along with himself. Typically, he once appealed to an assembled crowd of parents to surrender their children to the Germans. The enormity of his self-delusion was revealed in that appeal. He declared, "Brothers and sisters.... I must cut off limbs in order to save the body. I must take children because, if not, others will be taken as well."[2]

Adam Czerniakow, the head of the Warsaw Jewish Council (*Judenrat*), the ghetto community council, would never have said that. He was too sober to entertain Rumkowski's illusions. Besides, the situation in the Warsaw Ghetto was quite different. Czerniakow never advocated the idea of turning the ghetto inhabitants into "productive" workers slaving in factories for the benefit of the German war effort in the misguided attempt to ensure their survival. The Germans may have viewed him as a mere tool for transmitting their orders, but that was not how he viewed himself. If he did cooperate with them by providing them with laborers whom the Judenrat paid a fixed if very low wage, that was done only with the view of doing it on an organized way rather than letting the Germans brutally seize people off the street for unpaid forced labor, even though then, too, nothing could be done to minimize their savage abuse of the laborers. They were kicked, beaten, made to work without gloves and warm clothing in the brutal cold, and subjected to many other forms of maltreatment. Czerniakow did not abuse his powers, and he killed himself rather than to sign his name to the first-ever deportation order for the Jews of Warsaw, which included children at that, in July 1942.

The ghetto in Warsaw, unlike the one in Lodz, was situated almost smack in the center of the capital. It was surrounded by a Polish population that was more neutral than hostile, and this made possible a lively covert exchange of goods and services.

The ghettos in Warsaw and Lodz stood out because of their great size and were similar in some other ways as well. Even though it was basically a big labor camp, however unique, the Lodz Ghetto with its 200,000 inhabitants was, like its Warsaw counterpart, the scene of a lively cultural life, with concerts and theaters that were free to stage plays as long as these were inoffensive to the Germans. It was a prole city rather than a labor camp, for at least the inmates lived in their own homes, slum hovels rather, however cramped and unsanitary, and not in barracks under the direct supervision of the SS, and did not have to report for roll call at dawn. The Lodz Jewish Council even administered its own prison, police, hospitals, and other municipal departments. For all that, its autonomy was a sham since it was a chicken coop to the German fox, who could enter any time it liked and wring at leisure the neck of any "chicken" it caught.

It may be that Rumkowski with his "productive" approach was more successful than Czerniakow. The fact remains that the Warsaw Ghetto was decimated in 1942 and razed in 1943 while the Lodz Ghetto survived

technically longer, until August 1944, and actually was the only functioning ghetto (not a regular labor camp) to have survived that long. Still, when
it was liberated by the Red Army it contained only about 900 Jews, all but
some 10,000 of the others having been killed in the concentration camps.
Those 10,000 had survived the camps and were liberated by the Allies.
Contrast this with the more than 28,000 who were able to escape from
the much more porous Warsaw Ghetto and hide out on the Aryan side.
These are authoritative estimates.[3]

The Lodz Ghetto also owed its prolonged survival to the presence of
a large number of Jewish textile craftsmen who were forced to resurrect
the garment and haberdashery industry that had made Lodz famous in
Poland, this time for the needs of the German army. Ultimately, however,
it too was doomed, like the ghettos in Vilna and Bialystok whose chair-
men had followed Rumkowski's approach in vain. Its doom was preor-
dained because its continued existence in a territory already otherwise
denuded of Jews and incorporated in the Reich attracted, like a nail that
still stood out, the manic attention of the Nazi planners of the Final Solution, that plot to annihilate all Jews. Besides, it was feared that the ghetto's
productive capacity was about to be rendered useless by the impending
onslaught of the Red Army, though five more months elapsed before that
would happen.

Even if Czerniakow in Warsaw had wanted to follow Rumkowski's
path and turn the Warsaw Ghetto into another huge sweatshop, the choice
was not up to him. The Jewish community in Warsaw was the largest in
Europe and correspondingly the ghetto there was twice as large as in Lodz,
with a population that at one time during the war exceeded 450,000 and
consisted mainly of professionals and petty merchants and artisans rather
than skilled industrial workers. Because the ghetto was located next to
downtown Warsaw and not in a suburb, it could not be as tightly sealed
off as it was in Lodz. The Germans, expecting it to wither on the vine,
constricted the supply of food until it was not enough even to subsist on,
and they cut off the supply of medicines and articles of personal hygiene
like soap. However, it was too porous to isolate and too anarchic, making it much more difficult than Lodz to subdue the inhabitants and har-
ness their labor. As a consequence, this prompted the Germans with their
martinet mentality to ultimately deport the Warsaw Jews to the killing
camps sooner.

In Warsaw our home was located in a tenement on Rymarska Street.

Later we lived on Ogrodowa Street, a few paces from the brick wall that separated us from the Aryan side, meaning the non–Jewish side in the pseudo-racial Nazi jargon. That wall was ten feet high and topped with sharp shards of glass intended to lacerate the bodies of would-be trespassers. It was erected by conscripted Jewish laborers around the ghetto along street sides and at intersections. Attempts to surmount it or otherwise to exit from the ghetto to the Aryan side were at first punished with jail and later with death.

Because we lived so close to the wall, ours was a dead-end street, fairly quiet and deserted. Yet, it was just two or three blocks from the main thoroughfares such as Leszno Street, which always teemed from dawn till curfew hours with masses of people hurrying aimlessly, just so they could escape overcrowding in their homes, without a place to go. They could not be just strolling as they seemed driven by some nervous inner tension. The passersby were so packed together that for more elbow room some walked on the roadway instead of on the sidewalks. The congestion only grew worse as more and more people were dumped into the ghetto or flocked into it on their own from the countryside around Warsaw along with German, Austrian, and Czech Jews.

Not that the packed roadways mattered much since there was no traffic other than occasional three-wheeled cycle rickshaws, carts horse-drawn or pulled or pushed by humans, and the trolleys bearing Polish and German gawkers that traversed the ghetto without stopping. After some time these trolleys were rerouted outside so as to tighten the cordon around the ghetto. There was also a separate trolley line for the ghetto dwellers only, with horse-drawn trolleys painted yellow, bearing the blue-on-white circular shield with the star of David in front, but after a while it too ceased operating.

In the fall of 1940, in the early days of the ghetto, when I was ten, I happened to meet Julek, a classmate of mine from the elementary school in Poznan. He and his family also gravitated to Warsaw like us. In Poznan, he used to be my best friend. He was in the same first-grade class, and I would often walk with him after school to his home. His parents had been a well-to-do young couple and lived in a villa with a cook of their own. Whenever I came to his house they would invite me to what passed in Poland for lunch but was actually dinner and serve me such fancy dishes as veal cutlets with what I now know to be called potatoes Dauphinoise and the like.

I had lost track of him after the Germans entered Poznan and I became deafened. Now in Warsaw I was of course delighted to encounter him on the street. We shook hands and by force of habit I accompanied him to his new home, thinking innocently maybe that I would be offered such dainties again. But I knew better once we entered a dilapidated tenement and climbed dark, evil-smelling stairs. Julek knocked and, when we entered, it was a strange sensation to see that he and his parents were now living in a partitioned-off and ill-furnished half of a room smelling of unwashed laundry. In Poznan they had lived in a big multi-roomed house. And now here in Warsaw, instead of being served exquisite entrées and Viennese pastry, I shared with Julek and his parents their meal of boiled potatoes and salt.

Their former air of welcome was gone. They cast uneasy glances at me. I had a feeling that, unlike in the past, they were begrudging me even those potatoes, and they probably did. It was a depressing occasion.

Afterward Julek and I drifted apart. I never saw him again but I just hope he survived.

That first winter in the Warsaw Ghetto, 1940–41, was even colder than it had been in Lodz. There was no heat, of course. Only the very rich could afford coal. In the evenings, at bedtime, my hands were so frozen that they felt as if they were burning. Mamusia would warm up some water in a pot on a stove and dipped my hands in to give me temporary relief. I had no gloves then. It took some time before my parents were able to obtain them for me.

I used to go to a playground of sorts because it was just about the only open space inside the ghetto. It was Tlomackie Square, which faced the neoclassical Grand Synagogue. The largest synagogue in Poland, with a capacity of 3,000, in a grandeur and renown it was the equivalent of Manhattan's Temple Emanu-El in Polish terms, except that its columned portico had been erected in Neoclassical rather than Romanesque style, and it was crowned with a cupola. I would come to that square every day to gambol with other children, kick a ball with them, and run around in what was just about the only park area left in the ghetto. Still, by then it was not a park anymore and there was no grass left. It was just raw black earth, littered with rubbish and crisscrossed by a series of anti-aircraft trenches left over from the siege of Warsaw more than a year previously.

One day I enlisted with Toporol, an organization devoted to promoting agriculture among Jews, which launched a drive for planting vegetables in the ghetto and recruited children for that purpose. I helped to clear the square of rubbish, rocks, and weeds and plant vegetable seedlings in its black soil. As a reward I received a Toporol identity card with my photo on it, of which I was inordinately proud. This was the first time in my life I had received my own identity card, with my photo on it, and I fancied myself an official, a person in authority, in an era when being official meant being somebody.

Some time later I mislaid that card and looked for it in vain. It was not in my pockets, nor under my bed. I went back to Tlomackie Square in the morning but found it changed almost unrecognizably: somebody who was either starving or malicious had torn up and extracted the onion, potato, and other seedlings that we kids had planted only yesterday.

The loss of that card was a big blow to me. I was no longer a person in authority, a big shot. Seeing how upset I was, my brothers decided to return to the square with me on the following days. We kept turning over clods of the soil until finally, by a fluke, we found my Toporol card. But it was not whole anymore. Some ill-wisher had torn it into several pieces, as if to make fun of my aspirations. This as well as the sight of the van-dalism perpetrated on those vegetable plots was too much for me. That was the end of it and I did not bother to apply for a new card as, besides, Toporol abandoned the idea of growing anything on the square: it would only invite the scavengers again.

The square also holds other memories for me: my wife's grandfather had been a major donor to building a library annex, the Judaic Library, next to the Grand Temple, as I learned years later in the United States. That annex, the only surviving part of the temple, is now the site of the Jewish Historical Institute. The temple itself was blown up by the noto-rious Jurgen Stroop as a finale to his suppression of the Warsaw Ghetto Uprising on May 16, 1943.

He boasted, "The festive official finale of the Grosse Aktion was the dynamiting of the Grand Temple. The preparations took 10 days. The temple was solidly built. Blowing it up all at once had to be preceded by planting and wiring explosives. What a lovely spectacle it was! From a pic-torial and theatrical viewpoint it was a fantastic image. When it was ready to be blown up, an engineer officer handed me the plunger. I waited with my hand on the plunger. Finally, I cried *Heil Hitler* and pressed the plunger. The flames of the thunderous explosion rose skyward. A beauti-ful palette of colors. An unforgettable allegory of the triumph over the

**The Grand Synagogue in Warsaw was demolished by the Nazis, but the Judaic Library on the left survived.**

Jewry. The Warsaw Ghetto ceased to live. Because Adolf Hitler and Heinrich Himmler wanted it."[4]

The square fronting this temple was also where I broke my arm. While playing tag with other kids I fell into one of those six- or eight-foot-deep anti-aircraft trenches. I do not remember if I was pushed by the other kids or stumbled and lost my balance on my own, but fall I did and broke my right arm when I automatically extended it to cushion my fall.

I clambered out of the trench with someone's help and came home exhausted, thinking nothing of it. After awhile, however, the pain in my arm became so unbearable that I lay down and began to moan. Mamusia then decided that I should go to a hospital and Dadek picked me up and carried me piggyback to the nearby Czyste hospital. It must have been in the early days of the ghetto because the hospital still had X-ray equipment, and it revealed that my arm was broken. They put it in a splint and bandaged my arm, stiffening it with gypsum, a practice discredited by modern medicine — and to this day my right arm is shorter than my left.

# The German Professor

One memorable day in the summer of 1941 comes to my mind. On that day, as usual since the last few weeks, I was to be tutored in speech and lip-reading. The tutor, one of those German Jews recently deported into the ghetto, had a blotchy red face and bulging lips and wore a handsome red-and-blue checkered coat that was a noteworthy rarity as already then most people wore shabby clothing. He boasted another rarity — gleaming leather shoes, in a place where most people had already worn their shoes out until they were full of holes. In the ghetto he still kept buffing his shoes until they shone, as a matter of pride and Germanic discipline. He had been a professor at some German school for the deaf. My parents had engaged him to teach me lip-reading and speech. Lip-reading was out of the question, however, because he knew little if any Polish and I knew no German.

He was thus reduced to teaching me how to pronounce discrete vowels and consonants, which he mouthed in a very graphic and off-putting way. These lessons were a chore. I dreaded having to touch his pink wattled throat in order to feel vibrations when he pronounced gutturals and place my hand in front of his lips to feel the expulsions of air when he hissed sibilants and other such consonants. Not a very pleasant sight. I suppose it did not amuse his former pupils at the school for the deaf either. At least I did not have to touch his nose, which had a wart on it.

By then I suppose I had developed that flat unaccented speech of the deaf which makes people eye me with astonishment or bafflement when I address them, but because of the physical revulsion I felt toward that teacher and his methods, I hardly profited from his speech lessons. As for lip-reading in general, I never could learn it properly in Polish, though for some reason I was always able to lip-read my brother Bronek. After I arrived in America, lip-reading in English was an even greater problem to me, except for the simplest and most elementary words like "coffee" and "milk."

This inability to lip-read has often in my life caused me problems with people who were simply dogmatic in their belief the deaf could join the normal world, as they phrased it, if only they would learn to speak and lip-read. They also believed that lip-reading is a skill that can be learned, not the talent that it actually is and one needs to be born with, which I was not.

Anyway, one day rather than face another such ordeal with the tutor, beset by a strange inertia, I decided not to come home from Tlomackie Square, my favorite playground, at the appointed hour.

About a quarter of an hour later, at an intersection fronting the square I saw Dadek, who was plainly looking for me, reasoning that he would find me there. He passed me just a few paces away but failed to notice me among the dense crowd of pedestrians crossing the intersection. A messenger from my parents, he was given the task of bringing the truant home where the tutor was waiting for me. I felt uncomfortable about deceiving him, but the prospect of facing the German tutor and his physically crude methods overcame my scruples and I walked away in the opposite direction where my brother could not find me. Dadek's figure still stands before my eyes as he was slowly walking, looking to the left and right, and shortsightedly peering in the faces of the passersby in search of me, wearing his habitual look, a look of pondering some absorbing mystery. It was a look that I cannot forget to this day.

I could imagine how uncomfortable the tutor was, sitting there and waiting for me in vain while my parents were guiltily offering him excuses for my absence and he kept politely denying the discomfort he felt. Yet, I could not stomach that situation and grew more rebellious. I could not tarry near Tlomackie as Dadek might be still there looking for me, so I wandered through the ghetto, paying a visit to the sidewalk hardware stall managed by my cousin David, who was watching over a jumble of old pots, pans, and kettles for sale. Benignly smiling, he was as always pleased to see me, and the feeling was mutual even if we could not communicate well. That was the last time I saw him until after the war when I met him again at the Zeilsheim displaced persons camp in Germany in 1946, before he left for Tel Aviv to join his brothers.

When I finally arrived home after my wanderings through the ghetto, it was late in the afternoon and the tutor had left. My parents gave me a look of reproach, which made me feel much more guilty than a hiding would.

My truancy worked. My parents figuratively threw up their hands and discontinued the speech lessons. That was in the summer of 1941. A few months later, in the winter, I happened to see my tutor again while I was walking down a street. I almost did not recognize him because the lower half of his face looked caved-in, but I identified him by the wart on his nose. He was sitting on the sidewalk. I felt uneasy seeing the once dignified professor in this humiliating posture. His body was emaciated but his legs and the lower half of his face were monstrously swollen with water edema. His back was against a wall and he was sitting in slush and snow on the sidewalk as if impervious to the wetness and cold, which showed how far gone he was. He had apparently traded for food his fancy garments, a richly checkered sports coat and blue woolen trousers, and he was now wearing a ragged and soiled gray jacket with all its buttons missing, tied with a string at the waist, its lapels held together with a safety pin but still revealing a bare chest lacking a shirt. What looked like a cleaning rag was knotted around his throat, and his feet, no longer ensconced in elegant oxblood-red Oxfords, were wrapped in more rags from which peeked dirty bare toes. His jaws were moving in a chewing motion, too long and too mechanically for any real food to be in his mouth. He resembled several other unfortunates propped up against building walls on the same block. I stopped uncertainly in front of him but he paid no attention to me.

I saw him but mercifully he did not see me. Behind his cracked lenses his eyes were wildly unfocused. What could I say to him, given that I was deaf and he, a foreigner, would not understand me, and anyway, clearly, his mind was gone? I did not tarry. I had seen too many living dead like him already. He was one of those first people to become "goners," because as a so-to-speak civilized German Jew he could not accustom himself to the overcrowding, filth, and poor sanitary conditions in the ghetto and, a foreigner stranded and alone in an uncivilized east European country, he knew no Polish and lacked local connections and relatives.

Would I have saved his life if I had not played hooky on that summer day a few months earlier? Of course not. The lessons he gave me took place only once a week anyway. He would sooner or later have succumbed to starvation, and the miserable weekly wage, equal to a crust of bread, that my parents paid him would not have made a big difference. All the same, I felt guilty seeing him in that condition. I averted my face so as not to have to look at him. Not that it mattered to him anymore whether I stayed or left: he was too absorbed in his inner turmoil. Walking on past him as if I had not seen him was a decision I had to make as part of my instinct for self-preservation. When I think of that poor crazed wretch bereft of his dignity as *Herr Professor*, I feel such sorrow and compassion for him and all those others.

That was the last time I saw the professor. Either next morning or soon afterward his naked corpse would be found lying on the sidewalk and stripped of its rags, one of a dozen or more picked up at dawn from the sidewalks every day. Some collapsed of hunger on the street and others expired, also of hunger, at home, where their corpses would be deposited furtively on the street to be buried at the expense of the Judenrat. As usual in such cases, their ration cards would be kept by their families. The corpses would be stripped naked, because even the rags and the sorry semblances of shoes they wore were needed by others to protect themselves against freezing to death. They were covered with a sheet of paper. In the morning the professor's naked corpse would be picked up along with other such cadavers by black-clad functionaries of the Pinkiert Funeral Home after they checked for a pulse. It was then transported on either a man-drawn or a horse-drawn cart to a mass grave in a pit in the Jewish cemetery.

My experience with the German tutor left me firmly averse to learning how to speak and lip-read, and no amount of arguing by my mother could persuade me otherwise. Still, my parents did not give up on my education. They hired a girl to teach me how to write a better Polish. She was thin and had a birdlike face. Her name was Regina. I would bring to her essays that I wrote in Polish decorated with fanciful curlicues. She would smile at my amateurish curlicues, correct my mistakes, and hand the essays back to me. I would at the same time bring her pay in the form of a quarter-loaf of bread. Once, for a change, instead of bread I brought her a herring wrapped in paper. It must have been quite a treat for her, because she seemed to accept it with pleasure as if it were a box of chocolates. But why do I remember her smile when she unwrapped that herring? It must have been ironic and wistful as well.

## My Father the Smuggler

As to how my parents could afford to be generous with the luxury that even herring then became, that is a story in itself. As I mentioned, while in Lodz, my father obtained an I.D. card in the name of Feliks Krawczyk, identifying him as a Christian Pole, and when it was announced that the Jews had to move into the ghetto in Warsaw in November 1940, he decided to use that card to establish legal residence for himself on the so-called Aryan side. He already knew what the Lodz Ghetto was like and had no illusions about its future Warsaw counterpart.

He had time to explore this issue all summer in 1940 while we were living with Aunt Dreizel's family; the Warsaw Ghetto was not formally established until November. The imperative need was to support his family and he was aware that in the ghetto he would have little if any chance for doing so. He must stay on the Aryan side in order to have the freedom to move around. In the circumstances, living with his family on that side would be too dangerous and hamper his activities. He discussed this with my mother and they agreed that he would stay on the Aryan side while we would move to the ghetto.

Judging from the privations imposed on Jews in Lodz, Tatus felt that food supplies to the Warsaw Ghetto would be deliberately reduced once it was established and sealed off. He was right about that, of course. That was where his opportunity lay: He would become a food smuggler. He found it no problem to acquire the persona of a Pole, even though at first he spoke Polish with a somewhat suspicious half–Yiddish accent. But he was a quick learner and had excellent visual and aural memory, in addition to being careful not to speak too much. The anonymity of a capital city like Warsaw also helped — my father was not likely to encounter and be recognized here by Poles who had known him in Poznan, although he did meet them on a few occasions — and wriggled out of it, I do not know how.

The location of the ghetto next to Warsaw's downtown area, just two blocks from Marszalkowska Street, the city's main artery, was also helpful to smuggling, because the buildings around it were left intact, unlike in Lodz where the houses around the ghetto were demolished and the city itself became thoroughly Germanized, thus causing the Lodz Ghetto to be guarded and "sealed" much more tightly against the smuggling of food, let alone medicines and other necessities.

My father's decision to stay out of the Warsaw Ghetto proved prescient and ultimately led to rescuing his family from death by starvation or by the bullet and worse. He had rented a partitioned-off half a kitchen in the "Aryan" part of Warsaw, which he used for sleeping and as his base of operations on weekdays. On weekends he would visit us in the ghetto. His favorite mode of entering and exiting was at first through the Grodzki Courthouse, which stood athwart the ghetto border and which Jews and Poles having court business or on the pretense of that business could enter from opposite sides. On entering the courthouse he would take the stairs up to the third floor, as if he had court business, then furtively descend through side stairs back to the first floor and, on giving a 5-zloty bribe to the coatroom attendant, emerge on the other side of the wall. On Friday afternoons he would bribe a Polish cop guarding the Aryan entrance to the courthouse, walk through the courthouse and emerge on the other side where he would enter the ghetto. Sunday evenings he would retrace his path to the courthouse and the Aryan side.

Every Friday he brought us food in a burlap sack or a satchel. Since he obviously could not carry too much of a load without staggering or injuring his back, he focused on stuffing the sack with small parcels of expensive delicacies such as sausage, butter, cheese, smoked fish, and meat, covered in wrapping paper and tied with a string, bought on the black market in the city. Selling these dainties to his contacts kept him busy all weekend, even on the Sabbath — he no longer prayed.

In the ghetto, where most people went hungry and even bread was a scarce luxury, only the very rich and the smugglers could afford such gourmet foods. He sold them to fences at precipitous prices, giving to my mother some of the proceeds to buy staple foods for our family and pocketing the difference for operating expenses and a rainy day. These staples, such as bread, potatoes, beets, and kasha, were our daily diet. It was also the diet of most ghetto dwellers, except that in my family it was more plentiful thanks to Tatus. Sometimes, as a special treat, my mother would smear for me a slice of bread with chicken-fat dripping. That was it. Vegetables and fruits were rare delicacies in the ghetto and at most my mother gave me a carrot to chew now and then. It was supposed to have vitamin A and be good for the eyes.

For nearly three years, from the establishment of the ghetto until the first deportation in July 1942, Tatus would thus regularly, like clockwork, come home to us every Friday and return to Aryan Warsaw every Sunday. That sounds easy, yet every time he did that he risked being caught and shot dead. But then if his true identity had been discovered as Bergman, not Krawczyk, he would also be shot. He was breaking so many German prohibitions, all bristling with expressions like "will be executed" or "will be punished by death."

Tatus as a smuggler was no criminal. Such were the inverted ethics of those times that smuggling was his way not only of rescuing his family from starvation but of resisting the criminal policy of the state. The Germans were deliberately starving the ghetto by gradually tightening access to food, and he did his little bit to stave off death from starvation for his family and some other people.

My father was not part of an organized large-scale smuggling gang.

These gangs were formed by the dregs of society, scum that now floated to the top — lowlifes, criminals, crooks who thrived in the hothouse atmosphere of the ghetto and established highly profitable alliances with their Polish and German counterparts, policemen and soldiers. They amassed fortunes with ease and, by their very nature, given the uncertainty of wartime, spent them just as spontaneously by carousing in the high-priced dives which they frequented together with their Polish and German partners. Yet, it was these gangs that kept the core of the ghetto's population alive. If not for them, it would have died en masse of starvation within just one month. After all, it was impossible to survive on a weekly ration of one pound of bread or less.

All the same, these underworld figures were too unsavory for my father. If he were to join these wolf packs, it meant having to associate with shady characters who could not be relied upon in an emergency and taking risks too high even for this risk-taker. He liked to have a drink now and then and eat in moderation, but with these Jewish mafiosos it meant having to swill vodka and pig out on fancy food to prove that you were a regular guy — and demonstrating contempt for the starving masses loitering in vain hope for a scrap of food outside the ghetto restaurants at which even caviar and champagne were available for the right price. Belonging to these gangs would also have meant being chummy with the Germans who cooperated with them in return for bribes but on a whim might (and did) turn on them and shoot them up like pigeons any time.

Being a naturally cautious man, my father preferred to operate as a lone wolf. He might not amass a fortune that way but he felt safer, and uncontaminated.

Once he entered the ghetto, on the way to our apartment about three blocks away from the courthouse, Tatus would pass entire families wearing scruffy gray rags and lying apathetically on the sidewalk, next to the curb or huddling against the walls, their eyes black-rimmed and faces black with dirt, scrunched up from lack of nourishment, extending their hands in the universal begging gesture, and crying and singing monotonously. They sensed there was food in the burlap sack, the kind normally used to transport coal and now serving to disguise its real contents, that he happened to be carrying. But they did not importune him because they were too enfeebled by hunger and awed by him. (By that time, many Jews had lost their self-confidence under the relentless German psychological browbeating.) He looked so well-fed and confident, in his neat clothes and with his thick Sarmatian mustache, that to them he was a being on a higher plane. This impression was magnified because, trusting his forged Aryan papers, he did not put on the Jewish white armband with blue Star of David once he was in the ghetto, even though he knew perfectly well that being caught without that armband and found to be Jewish meant an immediate death sentence. But then that was just one of his many "offenses."

One time in the early days, entering the ghetto from the courthouse, Tatus relented and distributed to the homeless on the street a little of the food destined for us. They laughed with delight and called him in Yiddish *Der gute Goy*, which means the good goy or Gentile. But he realized he had made a big mistake when the next time he took the same route he was beset by swarms of beggars. They surrounded him, clamoring and stretching piteously their hands. He had a hard time escaping them.

Worse even, this also meant attracting the unwelcome attention of stool pigeons or robbers by falling into some kind of routine that meant becoming noticed. From then on he kept changing his modes of egress into the ghetto, and the only routine he followed was to visit us every Friday afternoon and stay with us until Sunday. Regretfully, he had to abandon the courthouse, his favorite route, also because the noose around it tightened and only people with valid court papers were admitted by the guards.

Henceforth, he would prowl around the wall girdling the ghetto and, with the help of his numerous connections, choose different exits and entrances — through a cellar with the wall knocked down or via another ghetto entrance that was guarded by a gendarme known to take bribes or by getting off an Aryan trolley that crossed the ghetto via Chlodna Street — until the Germans had walls erected on both sides of Chlodna. If one exit was blocked he sooner or later found another, and this continued until the fatal date of July 22, 1942, when the cordon around the ghetto was reinforced and the deportations to Treblinka started.

## The Real and Unreal Worlds

I led a sheltered life. Schools were closed, though of course Dadek attended underground university courses, but there was nothing to do for deaf boy like myself except to play on Tlomackie Square or in the courtyard of our apartment building. (For some reason I was no longer tutored in Polish by Regina.) Besides, my mother did not want me to go outside, not even to Tlomackie Square, as it became too unsafe, what with the occasional shootings of pedestrians for sport by Germans.

In this situation, I became a passionate reader of books, which I could easily borrow from the neighborhood library — the Germans permitted the libraries to operate while shutting down schools and universities. Since I could not learn about the bigger world outside by hearing human speech, books provided a window into that world for me. At the same time, Dadek, an avid reader himself, began to form my taste as, by default, I read more and more the same books he read.

I needed heroes, paragons of virtue, who would inspire me and who I could look up to, and the characters in Dadek's favorite books provided such models to me. I admired the saintly charisma of Prince Myshkin in *The Idiot*, the nobility of soul in Andrei Bolkonski and the radiance and impulsiveness of Natasha in *War and Peace*. I was carried away by the fierce, romantic rebels in Panait Istrati's novels and by Jean Christophe, Annette, and other sensitive idealists in the works of Romain Rolland. Plutarch's lives of the noble Romans transported me into a world of manly virtue. I did not understand half of what I read, but it was enough for me to absorb the spirit, if not the nuances, of such books. I lost myself in this radiant world of superhuman noble-souled characters, so different from the somber and frightening world outside.

In the evenings, given the lack of electricity, I read these books in the bluish unwavering flame of a carbide lamp — the only illumination we had. It consisted of two small cans, one atop the other. The upper can contained water which slowly dripped onto a lump of calcium carbide in the can below, releasing evil-smelling acetylene gas that served as fuel for the flame. It stank of sulfur like a rotten egg but we had no alternative other than stumbling in the dark and candles were a rare luxury. The wonder of it was that my eyesight was not markedly ruined.

Only now, in retrospect, I understand how blind, perhaps mercifully, was my response to the horrible events going on around me. That outside world represented by the ghetto was the real, the terrifyingly real world I lived in, not the imaginary world of novels. What did the refined esthetic feelings and nuanced ethical qualms of Jean Christophe and Prince Bolkonsky matter compared with the real, immediate brutish misery and suffering of the ghetto dwellers? Did not the injustice depicted in Hugo's *Les Misérables* pale in comparison with the thousandfold more horrific injustice of life in the ghetto?

The novels were paper cutouts that served to shield me from the three-dimensional world of real people, the world of the ghetto I had been living in. This real world was beset not only by starvation and cold but also by unbelievable overcrowding, dirt, stench, the heartbreak of seeing one's parents, brothers, and sisters grow emaciated, ill, lice-ridden and ultimately expire of malnutrition, the doomed bleakness of everyday life. Above all, it was beset by pervasive fear of the Germans.

At any moment a German in uniform would be strutting on a ghetto street and expecting the passersby to take off their hats and bow to him. Those passersby who were slow to respond were punished with blows and kicks or even shot, just like that. Or he would shoot out windows on both sides of the street for target practice or if he perceived blackout violations.

Compared with the tragic dilemmas of the ghetto dwellers, the characters in novels lived in a world of fantasy. I cannot even imagine Tolstoy's Andrei Bolkonski facing the dilemma of whether to look on passively while a German is raping his wife or felling his child with a whip or to intervene and expect to be shot down like a dog. The equally tragic thing is that if Bolkonski were not to intervene, he would be merely be buying time for his family and himself because they are anyway doomed to die sooner or later. This kind of dilemma did not happen in novels but could and did happen in the real everyday life of the ghetto. It is easy to predict with what sadistic joy would the Germans of those days respond to fictional Prince Myshkin and the real-life Gandhi. The prince would be dog meat in a jiffy. As for the Mahatma, the Germans of those days were no British with their concern for the high moral road and niceties of law when handling him. The temerity of Gandhi's passive resistance would only amuse and mildly amaze these professional killers, prompting them to guffaw and grin evilly before they would sic their dogs on him.

The stark truth that there was no hope of salvation was ultimately recognized by the young people in the ghetto who rose up, in defiance of their elders, against the Germans in the spring of 1943: if they had to die anyway, let them at least die fighting.

A salutary thing about living in bookish fantasy worlds was that my willing submergence in them shielded me from full awareness of that real bleak world of deprivation, misery, and lurking death, which otherwise would have crushed me psychologically, I suppose. This and the natural resilience of youth helped me become inured to the sights of pitiable begging families living on the streets with no place to go, alongside naked corpses half-covered by sheets of paper. If I were to see these sights today, I would no longer be inured to them. I would become heartsick. I suppose my carapace of toughness is no longer as hard.

This literary escapism may have applied to Dadek even more than to me. He was eight years older than I and grasped many more of the nuances in what he was reading. He, too, had, perhaps to an even greater extent than I, lived in that bookish fantasy world. To him, even more, that world provided a way of escaping the sinister reality of the ghetto.

The protective cocoon of book-reading, separating me from the world of the ghetto, was bolstered by the care shown by my parents in keeping me confined to the interior courtyard of our tenement so as to preserve me from the violence that might erupt at any moment outside. After I broke my arm I spent much more time in that courtyard. There were several other boys and girls my age living in the five-story quadrangle that framed the courtyard and, day after day, we would run around it and play cops and robbers with pieces of wood serving as our rifles and revolvers, or cowboys and Indians riding on sticks as horses. We would also play hopscotch and watch little girls skip rope.

My mother insisted that I did not venture outside the arched tunnel connecting the courtyard to the street, a tunnel wide enough for a team of horses pulling a carriage. It was too dangerous and she wanted to spare me the distressing sights outside. I disobeyed her only on rare occasions, but on those occasions the scenes I witnessed outside were something I have carried with me all my life. They were the scenes of a world out of kilter, an apocalypse.

When the TV shows a horror flick I shrug my shoulders and switch the remote to another channel, knowing that nothing can compare with the real horror of what the Germans did to Jews. When the TV or a cinema shows a murder mystery with the suspected murderer being civilly interrogated, fed, and imprisoned in a warm and comfortable cell with all the amenities, the TV, the sink, the cot with its inviting pillow and cozily folded blanket, the three meals daily, and so forth, I cannot help but think how can such a life be so terrible compared with the tormenting and starving of people during the war and exposing them to dirt, disease, and cold, let alone affording them the luxury of a trial. Does this mean that I am psychologically scarred? Probably. Only an idiot would emerge unscathed from such an experience.

## Vignettes

One time when I happened to be on a sidewalk fronting Tlomackie Square I saw a young man crossing the square. Suddenly, a pack of boys in their low teens surrounded him. They began to pummel him until he kneeled and fell in slow motion. They then stomped on his body. This happened in broad daylight on a crowded street, yet the passersby averted their eyes and gave it a wide berth, with no one trying to help the victim. The strange thing was that, although this young man's height was some six feet and these boys were at most only half as tall, he did not defend himself and meekly lay down without moving on the pavement. That was hardly the outcome that Swift had imagined when he conceived his story of Gulliver lying motionless while the Liliputs swarmed around his body. The urchins went through his pockets and seized his wallet, watch, and some other things and then scattered. The young man remained lying for a while and then calmly got up, patted his clothing free of dust, and walked away as if it were the most common thing in the world, except that his legs wobbled a little and he looked a bit disoriented. What strange apathy or despair moved him not to resist? But then this was a derailed world.

Of the passersby who witnessed this incident not one came forward to protect the victim. What made it particularly surreal was that no one had bothered to stop either. They just kept walking as if the whole thing were totally ordinary. I myself observed that whole scene from a block away.

Then there was the episode with the snatcher. I was walking on a street, which was thronged as usual — thronged because the ghetto dwellers needed to breathe fresh air after being cooped up in their stifling rooms from curfew hour, usually nine, until dawn, and the ghetto itself was being continually reduced in size by the Germans and was simply too small to accommodate all these hundreds of thousands of people. As I was moving along with the crowd and passing a deli store, open only to the fortunate few who could afford its prices, a woman carrying a small package stepped out of it. What happened next took place in a flash. A thin young man, about seventeen, who lurked outside the store, lunged at her and grabbed that package. In seconds, while falling on the pavement, he tore the wrapping off and greedily stuffed the contents, some smoked fish, into his mouth.

As he lay prone, the shocked passersby kept kicking his prostrate body. When those preteens on Tlomackie Square attacked and robbed the tall young man, the passersby made no move to help him. This time it was different, because theft of food was such an outrageous crime in the ghetto. One man even tried to grab what was left of that food in the snatcher's fist but the boy was faster and crammed its remaining contents into his mouth, chomping greedily. The robbed woman kept lamenting and cursing. There was such a blissful expression on the snatcher's face as he was swallowing and chewing the food while enduring the kicks and blows. That blissful sensation can be understood only by those who have suffered the pangs of hunger for a long time and suddenly have a taste of heavenly real food.

These were some of the scenes I witnessed on my forays into the ghetto street. Usually, the sidewalks were lined with the homeless. Lying on the sidewalk, entire families, fathers and mothers and children, with hollow-eyed and begrimed faces, some wearing only blankets and bed-sheets, lay next to the curb or propped against a wall and kept crying and lamenting. Huddled against the wall were scruffy old people and, at a distance, vendors peddling everything and anything — candy made of flour and saccharin, single slices of bread, single cigarettes, matches, buttons, boiled potatoes kept in water to prevent discoloration, oatmeal cutlets, rutabaga cakes, and, in winter, single lumps of black coal, along with displays of worn shoes, shoelaces, buttons, needles, ragged used clothing, old pots and all the like junk that would not pass muster at any normal flea market but that they would gladly barter for a crust of bread or a potato. Some even tried to sell pitiful stacks of old books. Barefoot, half-naked hirsute men were searching for cigarette butts in the gutters. And in between those huddling against the walls and those lying on the curb surged and eddied crowds of pedestrians who seemed to fill every empty space.

From dawn till curfew hour of nine, these streets were much more congested than Times Square. The crowds not only thronged on the sidewalks but also on roadways, which were anyhow empty most of the time except for an occasional bicycle rickshaw, to which they slowly gave way, or a German car before which they panicked and parted like the Red Sea. Most of the passersby had nowhere to go and were just pacing back and forth within the cage of the ghetto. They were in the grip of a mass psychosis, moving with a febrile energy, like people at the verge of a nervous breakdown, which they indeed were. Little wonder, since they were subjected to continuous psychological terror, living from day to day in dread of Germans who might suddenly show up riding in a rickshaw or taxi and beat or shoot them like rabbits for target practice.

The Germans were like Golems but Golems turned against Jews — broad shouldered, robotic in a nightmarishly sinister way, striking mortal terror in the hearts of the Jews they met on their path. The Golem, that prototype of Frankenstein fashioned by Maharal, a Prague rabbi, to protect Jews against pogroms, now had its purpose perverted. In hindsight, this makes perverted sense: A legend says that Rabbi Maharal created the Golem by putting in its mouth a card with the Hebrew word *Amet* (the truth). *Then the Lord God formed man of the dust of the earth and breathed into his nostrils the breath of life.* After the clay hulk had accomplished its job, Maharal decided to uncreate it by deleting the initial letter, aleph, from the card, thus changing the Hebrew word into a very different one: *Met*, or death.

It seems that the creature was not really laid to rest. For it arose from the mud, still with that word of nihilation in its mouth instead of the holy word, and became the German Golem. It became a symbol of arrogance, brute might, and evil. In particular, this Golem was incarnated in the notorious gendarme whom the ghetto dwellers had nicknamed Angel of Death or Frankenstein, because he looked like Boris Karloff in the film of that name and had the same lumbering gait. This Golem regularly stalked the ghetto to kill or maim each time at least a few of those who had the misfortune of catching his eye.

This Golem was born and lived only to take the lives of others. This undisguised serial killer is said to have vowed to kill a thousand Jews. (His name was Josef Blosche. He was the soldier pointing a rifle at the little boy in short pants who is looking at the camera with his hands in the air in the famous Warsaw Ghetto photo. After the war he was recognized by a survivor in 1967 in East Germany, tried, and hanged.) To attract the Golem's attention was risky; to ignore him and walk past him with the eyes averted was to court doom or at least a blow on the head. The passersby chose the middle way: they would take off their hats, bow humbly, and stand like frozen statues whenever they saw that uniformed member of the master race striding with a gun in his hand. When he approached, the whole street was turned to stone. Everyone was petrified with fear, everyone shudderingly watched him pass, and he walked on, contemptuous and disdainful of the subhumans cowering before him until one or another caught his attention and met his fate. But once he disappeared the frozen figures resumed their motion and the street again surged with restless crowds.

Our home was on the first floor in a building whose entrance on Ogrodowa Street was located only about two dozen feet from the wall which blockaded its intersection with the streets of Aryan Warsaw. On the Aryan side of the wall at one corner was a German military hospital, and on our side of the wall there was a pile of garbage thrown out of the windows by the hospital patients. One day I loitered near that pile and out of curiosity I picked up a small can still containing the remains of bacon. There were some bugs inside and I threw the can back onto the pile. When I returned in the afternoon, the pile swarmed with emaciated scavengers.

Another scene I had witnessed happened in the winter of 1941–42, when Ogrodowa Street was coated with ice and slush. Not far from the same wall, I saw a German gendarme stand behind a humbly bent old woman wearing a thick plaid shawl, the kind worn by peasant women, that covered her head and body. She was kneeling in the slush and ice while he grimly kept cursing and pummeling her back with his fists, his breath clouding his face. He was methodically belaboring her with his fists like a boxer hitting a punching bag in slow rhythm as she, with a face of stone, slowly took out, one after another, a loaf of bread and some potatoes from inside her shawl and dropped them onto the pavement. How could a strapping young man like him be beating a feeble old woman? Much later, after the war, I saw a photo of a smiling German turning the chin of an old woman with the tip of his whip and it revived my memory of that scene. The only difference was that, in the photo, the German was using a whip while the other, the one I saw personally, used his fists.

Another time, as I was walking down Leszno Street, a main ghetto thoroughfare, I saw that it became in just an instant completely emptied, with masses of panicked people ducking into doorways. I could not figure out why. There was probably shouting and sounds of a gun firing, but being deaf I could not hear all that. I just sensed danger and decided to run along with the others and take shelter in the nearest doorway. A moment later, around the corner a German command car appeared. The car was being driven at breakneck speed toward the ghetto barrier and the Aryan quarter behind it. Standing in the car, a fat, red-faced officer was laughing gleefully and firing a handgun wildly at the people taking shelter. He hit a few, who keeled over, and he still chortled as the guard raised the barrier and the car left the ghetto. So that was why the passersby were fleeing: they heard him shooting, which I could not hear.

With the car's departure the street again became crowded, as if that random shooting were an everyday happening, which it lately had become more than ever.

These are my most vivid memories of the ghetto, and they are curiously few, although on my occasional walks I must have seen many more scenes of this kind and after all I had lived there for more than two years. Yet, my memory of them seems scant: it must have been repressed if I was to stay sane passing from the world of random shootings and sidewalks on which lay naked corpses covered with sheets of paper to that of the relative normalcy of my home where Mamusia was bustling in the kitchen and a pot was boiling on the stove, spreading a pleasant aroma and warmth even if it was only potatoes or kasha. Tatus was somewhere outside the ghetto, Dadek was poring over pages copied from a textbook used an illegal university course, and Bronek as usual was away all day, mostly at the apartment of his buddy Dudek Klepfisz where he played bridge with other teenagers or in a place on Leszno Street where he played ping-pong.

The ghetto, now that I look back at my life in it, resembled a sinister version of *Alice in Wonderland*. "Off with their heads!," the favorite phrase of the Queen of Hearts, was embodied in real life by the Germans when they shot people with abandon, right and left. If they visited the ghetto after sunset, they would shoot out any windows which they thought were not properly blacked out. The ghetto gate itself could be likened to a looking-glass, a passageway to a world in which values and appearances were warped and upended, with the dregs of society floating to the top. Since the laws and regulations governing the ghetto were intended to terrorize and starve it into non-existence instead of promoting common welfare as in a normal society, to survive meant disobeying them or circumventing them by means of widespread bribery, with almost everyone enforcing them — Germans, Blue Police, Jewish police — on the take.

The ghetto did not just consist of ragged wretches. They happened to be the most visible because they lived on the streets. There was no room for them even in the schools and synagogues, which were filled to more than capacity. The overflow slept on the sidewalks, drenched by rain in summer and, if they survived till winter, shivering in the harsh wind and extreme cold, such as is common in northern Europe, day upon days, night in the outdoors upon night, slowly dying of hunger, pneumonia, dysentery, typhus, and bone-chilling cold.

These homeless and uprooted unfortunates came from the provinces or were forcibly resettled from Germany and Austria to a totally strange and barbaric environment which left them bewildered. It goes without saying that they had no relatives or connections to rely on in the ghetto. They presented a growing and ultimately catastrophic dilemma to welfare organizations in the ghetto.

Jews have always paid special attention to caring for their own poor. The small and hardly prosperous Jewish community in Poznan with its roughly 2,000 members in the 1930's had funded as many as twelve or more charitable associations for nursing the sick, sponsoring vocational training, distributing lumber and coal allotments to the indigent and handicapped, paying for the health care of those unable to afford it, helping widows, and so on. Even earlier, the influential Jewish historian Simon Dubnow arrived at the conclusion that Jews owe their survival throughout history not only to their culture and religion but also to their communality. The major purposes of that communality also include charity, helping their own poor.

But in the Warsaw Ghetto, as in the other ghettos, these good intentions did not prove enough. There were simply not enough resources for helping the poor, given the tight and tightening grip the Germans held on food supplies. A major catalyst worsening the food supply situation occurred in 1941 when Germany attacked the Soviet Union and later declared war on the United States. This cut off the inflow of aid from American Jewish charities and food parcels from both countries. The poor became doomed when even the soup kitchens providing them with bread and soup daily became gradually closed to them.

These soup kitchens had originally been established for the poor by a network of organizations of civic-minded people and activists from various political parties. Once there was not enough soup for all applicants, its distribution became restricted to members of political parties and their families. When the supply of free soup ran out completely, House Committees were set up. In our building, too, members of one such committee would rap on the doors and ask tenants to contribute a spoonful of flour or groats or its equivalent each.

Still, the ghetto was no concentration camp or a scene of unrelieved misery as in Lodz. It did not contain only emaciated adult and child paupers with gaunt, dirt-encrusted faces, their clothing in shreds, who dragged their feet until they fell to the pavement from exhaustion and gnawing hunger. Nor was this ghetto a vast, drab sweatshop like the Lodz Ghetto. On the contrary, it was studded with deli stores, cafés, and restaurants in which the most expensive and scarce gourmet foods — lamb, duck, pot roast, lox, pastries, champagne — could be bought if one had the money, as a small elite of big-time smugglers and their Polish and German pals did. At the same time, outside these places milled crowds of beggars and starvelings.

In between these two extremes, the rich and the paupers, there was the majority of ghetto dwellers who continued to tough it out by selling off their assets — hoarded coins, jewelry, rare china, precious mementos, and the like — bit by bit but not yet reduced to total destitution.

The ghetto dwellers also resisted German terror psychologically by attending concerts, seminars, literary evenings and cultural festivals in honor of writers and poets like Peretz, Bialik, and Sholom Aleichem. The rich cultural life of the ghetto reflected their desire to preserve and sustain spiritual and moral values and avoid demoralization. The Judaic Library was the site of many such artistic and intellectual activities.

The ghetto was not after all a reservation for the illiterate uncultured. It was also the compulsory home of some of the country's greatest artists and a place where Jewish culture flourished. At least half a dozen theaters were open, offering a variety of operettas, comedies, concerts, skits, satires, and ballet performances, along with literary gatherings. There was even a Jewish Symphony Orchestra, which gave a concert at the Judaic Library on Tlomackie in November 1940. More than two score underground periodicals were published in Yiddish, Polish, and Hebrew by competing political parties and movements. There were many eminent scientists, sociologists, economists, and literati living in the ghetto, and Dadek benefited from their lectures while taking clandestine university courses.

On still another level, through community efforts, clandestine classes were set up at high school and university levels, such as the ones Dadek attended, where he formed friendships with like-minded idealistic young people. The lecturers at these classes were among Poland's foremost intellectuals.

Above all, the ghetto, that mosaic of sharp social contrasts, was the scene of a miracle, like a flower growing in the mud — the resurrection of Zionist youth movements, such as Hashomer Hatzair used to be in Poznan, with their high morale, bonds of personal comradeship and shared faith in a new, better world where social justice would reign. On these young people the German terror tactics produced a contrary effect: instead of crushing their spirit they actually bolstered it and nourished their desire for revenge. All this happened in defiance of the attempts of their elders to reconcile them to their enslavement in the futile hope that a remnant would survive and be saved.

The very existence of these young idealists was a miracle. Historically, young people are the most vulnerable generation in times of war, unrest, and moral degradation. In a might-makes-right atmosphere, which encourages them to develop the worst sides of their nature, their family ties loosen and they turn into thieves and hoodlums, packs of jackals and, like their role models the Germans, sadists. They become demoralized, callous, and lose moral inhibitions. Not so the members of Zionist youth movements. They proved impervious to this corrosion of values. They were the kind of youths I had admired and remembered from my life in Poznan and whom I had seen in the ghetto when now and then when they came to visit Dadek. What I remember most about them was the controlled intensity of their feelings, the calm and determination with which they moved as if in the possession of a great secret.

With their strong sense of solidarity, these young people knew and trusted each other totally. The war and the ghetto experience forced them to reorient their goals and no longer believe in a halcyon future, in a new, better world in Israel. As a martyred Jewish girl, a member of a youth movement, put it, "They, the young, the strong, who had for years been educated in the spirit of building a new life, a new society based on social justice, now had to crown their lives with bloodshed, sabotage, destruction."[5] They realized that their promising lives were over and now they desired only a worthy death, and leaving a memory that some day would be honored. As Adolf Liebeskind of the Krakow youth movement said, "There is no turning back. We stride on the road of death. Let him who wants to live stay away. Death is at the end of the road and the strong go forward to meet it."[6]

The enormous physical and moral stresses these youths had been subjected to only strengthened their spiritual stamina and desire for revenge. Three years of maltreatment, humiliation, and persecution could not suppress their vitality. They kept up their morale and organization by attending clandestine meetings at which they practiced their Hebrew and sang

Hebrew songs. They took such delight in each other's company, feeling dear to each other, feeling themselves to be better, stronger persons for being in such company. Having in most cases lost their families to the deportations, they each contributed what was left in their homes — bed linen, clothing, valuables, all that became common property. Family ties were replaced by bonds of camaraderie. These youths became attached to each other. They slept together, ate together, trained together in the use of the miserable few weapons they had, and fought together. What joy it was to have their own weapons, even if they were only handguns that could shoot 20 yards at the farthest, against tanks and armored vehicles. It was these young people, the finest flower of Jewish youth, who had revolted against the Germans and died honorably in combat rather than let themselves be enslaved and slaughtered. But that came later, the following year, in 1943.

## The Siege and the Escape

Then came July 22, 1942, a date that has a special meaning to every survivor of the Warsaw Ghetto, including myself. Before that date I could still live a somewhat normal life as a boy, however fraught with danger. It was normal in the sense that I belonged to a loving family and led a fairly sheltered life. After that date, my family and I potentially became part of a mass of hunted animals driven through ghetto streets to deportation trains and death past a gauntlet of beaters.

In the morning of that memorable day, while out for a walk I happened to see a crowd reading a big red wall poster glued to a Morris column. It announced in German and Polish that all the inhabitants of the ghetto regardless of age and sex would be deported east. "East" was, of course, mainly the Treblinka death camp, because it was located nearest to Warsaw. With its recently built gas chambers, this gruesome charnel house was ready to begin functioning, only at the time no one in the ghetto knew it. The poster prescribed special categories of those who were exempt from the deportation, such as the Jewish police and members of the Jewish Council along with their families. Fat chance: later those and other categories turned out to be not exempt either. It was part and parcel of a satanic deception plan, intended to quell active resistance among the victims. The Jewish fly was now firmly trapped in the German spiderweb, and the life of the Jewish population and culture was being throttled to death.

The poster threatened, as was now standard, death to anyone who disobeyed. Operation Reinhard, the code name of the plan for the biological extermination of Jews in Poland, was being implemented. Under this plan the death camps in Treblinka, Belzec, and Sobibor were built, as were the railroad sidings leading to them. Now it was time to cram their gas chambers with victims plucked from the ghettos.

In the afternoon on the same day after these posters had been put up, adult and child beggars were rounded up and placed in carts and wagons along with occupants of refugee shelters in former synagogues and school buildings. It was a frighteningly efficient operation, designed to cram thousands into the waiting trains. In the days following, patients were picked up from hospital sickbeds and orphanages and homes for the aged emptied. There was something about it that did not make sense: how could these sick and old people as well as children be made to do hard work in the East? The ghetto dwellers no longer trusted German promises and began to hide themselves. Finally came the time to deport most of those able-bodied adults who had until then been lulled by German promises of exemption owing to "productive" work.

With the sealing off of the Warsaw Ghetto Tatus was no longer able to visit us next weekend. The remaining four ghetto gates were blocked with reinforced sentries and the ghetto itself ringed with roving German patrols, motorized and on horseback, cutting off the usual smuggling routes.

Tatus and Mamusia conferred by one of the few telephones in the ghetto, in an office to which she had access, and decided that we should leave the ghetto. Bronek was to escape first, and we would follow later so that if one were to be caught the rest might have a chance to survive. Dadek and I needed Mamusia to take care of us. Dadek, while the oldest brother, lacked what Bronek had — robustness and street smarts, while I was too little, so it was just right for Mamusia to lead Dadek and me out and for Bronek to manage on his own and escape by himself.

Bronek may have quaked at the idea of going it alone but with his usual common sense, he understood and accepted the decision of his parents. An opportunity arose when shortly afterward one of our Poznan landsmen, a Mr. Hutoran, said that he knew a work detail foreman who for a bribe would include one more laborer in his detail scheduled to leave the ghetto for the military airfield in Okecie, where it was to carry sacks of cement and barrels of tar.

The work detail with Bronek in it trudged to the ghetto exit in a loose military formation, with Bronek and Mr. Hutoran marching in the last row. At the ghetto exit the foreman deliberately miscounted the number of men in his detail. In the prescribed manner, he snapped ramrod straight at attention, clicked his heels, took his cap off, and declaring "*Melde geho-ersamst*," (reporting most obediently), reported that number to the gendarme on duty, with whom he was in cahoots in return for a fat bribe.

By prearrangement, once they were out of the ghetto and on the Aryan side, as the column was approaching a corner Mr. Hutoran and Bronek started to lag behind the others. Finally they stopped and bent down, pretending to tie their shoelaces very slowly so as to give the marching column enough time to vanish behind a corner. Then they quickly took off their white celluloid armbands with the blue Star of David emblazoned on them, stuffed them in their pockets, and ran in opposite directions. They were seen by the Polish passersby, who observed the whole happening passively.

Bronek proceeded to 58 Towarowa Street, where Tatus was renting half a kitchen, and joined him there. He never saw Mr. Hutoran again. Together, father and son now lived hoping that we would join them.

The gas chambers of the German Moloch in Treblinka needed to devour the lives of at least 6,000 to 10,000 people daily, that being the capacity of the trains and the chambers. The shelters the hospitals, the orphanages, the homes for the aged, and the like were emptied, with their inmates seized and deported to the killing camps. Then it became progressively more difficult to fill the freight trains. The Germans tried a new ruse: they announced that three kilograms of bread and a kilogram of jam would be offered to those willing to show up. Earlier, they had stopped the usual shipments of the measly rationed food to the ghetto so as to starve the inhabitants totally and spur them to report for deportation. With so many people having nothing to eat, this ruse worked for a while, luring those driven by hunger, despair, and despondency. But afterward once again the Germans found few takers for the *Umschlagplatz*, the railroad spur just next to the ghetto from which trains proceeded to Treblinka. After that, units of German soldiers commenced their dragnets by surrounding individual apartment buildings and rounding up all the tenants to pack them into the trains. This meant immediate danger to my family and me.

These units were accompanied by Jewish police who served as their guides and by the Askaris. That was the monicker which the ghetto dwellers gave to the Ukrainian, Lithuanian, and Latvian auxiliaries of the Germans, by analogy with the name of the African colonial troops formed by the Germans during World War I in southwest Africa. They used that monicker since they never knew until the last moment whether the auxiliaries showing up in their courtyard would be Lithuanian, Latvian, or Ukrainian.

These combined squads would blockade successive apartment buildings, storm inside, shout commands for everybody to assemble in the courtyard with 15 kilograms of baggage in hand, and threaten instant shooting of anyone who stayed in his apartment. After the tenants, carrying suitcases or satchels with their belongings, assembled in the courtyard, the soldiers would search all the apartments for those still hiding, hacking open with hatchets any doors that might be locked. They would shoot on the spot the tenants whom they found hiding or hurl them from the windows if they were too feeble or crippled to move, together with their crutches and wheelchairs.

After nearly two months, between July 22 and September 6, what remained of the Warsaw Ghetto could never be the same. A once vibrant and lively community became reduced to a smoldering remnant. Its core was destroyed, and with that destruction Polish Jewry was no more. Even then its embers lived on and flared up memorably in the revolt of 1943, that awe-inspiring drama, the first Jewish revolt in 2,000 years since the Bar Kochba uprising. It was also the first revolt to occur in any city in German-occupied Europe and it set aflame revolts in other ghettos — Bialystok, Bedzin, Sosnowiec, and elsewhere. That was the other meaning of the Holocaust.

But that was yet to come. In August 1942, stores in the ghetto were shuttered for lack of supplies, and no food was available for those whose homes were as yet left intact, except the slave workers in the German factories. In my family all we had left to eat was a handful of groats but for others in our building it was much worse. They were dying of hunger.

Among them was my best playmate, Mietek, the companion of my courtyard games, a boy of my age, about twelve, who habitually wore a pilot's leather cap with ear flaps raised. It covered his shaved pate, even in summer. His hair had been shaved following an attack of typhoid fever, to protect him from lice. After July 22 he no longer shoved up in the courtyard and, as I missed him, I visited him at his home. He lay stretched on his bed in a state of apathy, his face haggard and his scrawny arms covered with boils. On the table next to his bed lay an uneaten half of a loaf of brown bread with runny insides. For a change it was adulterated not with the usual nodules of white talcum but with some wet brown clay that made it look and taste like mud and feel leaden in the stomach. That was probably why even he, whom hunger was gnawing, had no appetite for it, just as shipwrecked sailors prefer to die of thirst in the midst of an ocean rather than to drink the saltwater and expire in agonies of pain. When he saw me he turned away as if having nothing to say anymore. Was Mietek dying because that bread was well-nigh indigestible or because already at twelve years of age he had lost his will to live? I would never know. In normal circumstances I would have been shocked and sickened at this sight, but my recent experiences had hardened me, as it were. I had nothing to give him and left soon.

Olek, the super in our building, supplemented his income by selling candies from a large cigar box suspended with a string around his neck. These candies were made of flour laced with saccharin. On the first day the ghetto was locked down, July 22, he still sold candies for the equivalent of 50 cents apiece. On the second day their price went up to 5 zlotys. On the third, 50 zlotys. To get some idea of what this meant, a loaf of bread in the ghetto cost some 20 zlotys on the black market before July 22 and the daily wage of the laborer was less than 5 zlotys.

On the fourth day the super had no more candies left to sell. This experience left me, unfortunately, for a long time with distrust of money and unwillingness to save. What good was money if it could not buy food?

Any day now our turn would come and a roving squad of Germans and Askaris would raid and round up the tenants in our building. They would be accompanied by Jewish guides who had been lured to cooperate as pathfinders by the false promise that their own families would be spared.

Mamusia had anticipated this raid, and for the last couple of days she woke Dadek and me just before dawn for a practice drill, making us dress quickly and run to hide in the basement of the outhouse in the courtyard.

Like most apartment buildings in Warsaw, ours consisted of four housing blocks surrounding a central courtyard. There was a fairly large stone outhouse in the middle of that courtyard. Groggy with lack of sleep, we followed Mamusia to that outhouse, where a few other tenants having the same idea were already raising the slab in the cement floor next to the urinals and descending by ladder to the cellar underneath. There we waited for a couple of hours. Nothing happened. Since the Germans were methodical, showing up for their raids regularly at seven o'clock, by nine everybody felt that they would not come. We clambered up and returned to our homes.

We repeated this drill on the following day. None too soon, because the real thing happened the very next morning. As before, at dawn we ran to the outhouse and descended to the cellar along with a dozen or so others. Somebody replaced the trapdoor. After we huddled for an hour in the cellar below, I could see in the semi-darkness that the others adopted tense postures, raising their faces, which told me that the Germans had arrived. I could not hear anything, being deaf, but from the tensed, swiveling faces of the others I could guess that this was no drill and this time in all seriousness the Germans had entered our building, and right now were in the outhouse and tramping with their jackboots the floor above us. When the others finally stopped raising their faces, it was a signal to me that the Germans had finally left the outhouse.

But they had not yet left the building, and we waited some more hours or longer in that big dark cellar, in the gloom pervaded by the stench of urine until all noises died down and it was safe to ascend the ladder and raise the trapdoor. To me, with my deafness, sitting in the darkness, this succession of scenes was like a silent movie being unspooled very slowly, with long periods of blankness broken now and then by frames showing someone shifting their position in the semi-gloom.

Only now I can imagine what kind of noises were made above our heads while we were cowering in that basement — the shouts of command for everybody to go down into the courtyard, the sounds of the shooting by the pursuers of those who stayed in their apartments or refused to go down to the courtyard, the shrieks and screams of their victims and the noise of doors being broken down with axes and crowbars and windows being shattered. These noises must have been nerve-racking to my hearing companions in the cellar. I was spared hearing them because of my deafness. Even so, the toll on my psyche, the terror, the panic, must have been terrible and it probably accounted for my break-down in Czestochowa.

When we finally came up to the surface and left the outhouse, it was late afternoon and the sun illuminated the courtyard, which looked like a hurricane had swept through it. As if in the aftermath of that hurricane, white feathers were swirling in the air. They came from the down comforters and pillows that the Germans and Askaris had ripped open with bayonets and knives in search of hidden valuables. Half-open suitcases and scattered piles of clothing covered here and there by broken glass littered the pavement. Shards of glass crunched under my feet. In one corner lay an overturned wheelchair, or what was left of it after it had broken up on impact after being hurled from a window, and next to it lay the mangled figure of its occupant, Pan* Leichendorf, in a pool of congealed blood. Because he was wheelchair-bound, he had been evidently unable to come down to the courtyard and instead was dropped onto it from the second floor together with his wheelchair. A few other bodies lay here and there in unnatural postures, like dolls with broken arms and legs. I looked up and saw that most of the windows were broken, with the half-curtains, customary in Poland, swaying in the breeze.

When we reentered our apartment we found it ransacked. Chests of drawers were hanging open, with clothing strewn on the floor, and mattresses were upended.

After a hurricane people clean up the trash and rebuild their lives, but like everyone else still alive in our building, Mamusia no longer had any motivation for it. We just slumped around. There seemed to be no future for us other than being caught up in the next raid and either killed on the spot or seized to face a hideous future. We did not bother to rearrange the overturned furniture. For the first time even the always optimistic and iron-nerved Mamusia seemed to lose hope. Despair was etched on her careworn face.

Suddenly, a parcel tied with a string was thrown through a window into our home, which was on first floor. Mamusia unwrapped it and found a loaf of bread inside. It was real bread, dense, fresh, and smelling wonderful, not like the gluey obscenity I saw at Mietek's. When she sliced that loaf open, we found a note from Tatus. It said, "Sara, leave the ghetto with the children. The Germans will come to kill you. Do not go to the wagons or the railcars — that's certain death. I cannot enter the ghetto. Get out as soon as you can. You know where to find me." It was signed "Pawel." That was Tatus's Polish name when he did not call himself Feliks. His real name was Pesakh (Passover) in Hebrew, Pawel in Polish.

We felt safe to venture into the street since the Germans settled into a routine, blockading the buildings only until the early afternoon. That was still in August 1942, before they lopped off big parts of the ghetto and

*Pan, Pani and Panienka translate to Mr., Mrs. and Miss.

turned the remaining ghetto into a closely supervised forced labor camp. We all put on the best clothes we could find that were just right for the summer, abandoning everything else, all our other belongings, since even carrying a suitcase would make us look suspicious. The three of us, Mamusia, Dadek, and I, without Bronek, left our home. Other people too began to emerge from their hideouts and filled the streets, though no longer to any jam-packing extent as the ghetto was then starting to become depopulated, with most of its dwellers expiring in agony in the gas chambers. Ultimately, between July 22 and September 6, some 300,000 of the 350,000 ghetto dwellers were deported to Treblinka. The historians agree, but did they not also say that at its peak the ghetto's population reached 450,000? The missing 100,000 apparently died of hunger and disease in the nearly three years of the ghetto's existence.

As for Mamusia, Dadek, and me, we proceeded to the nearest ghetto gate. It was manned by a German gendarme along with a Polish policeman and a Jewish policeman. The German's green uniform alone was enough to strike terror. The Garnetman, or Blue, as the Polish policeman was called because of his navy-blue uniform, also looked fearsome in his hat with its unusually long visor that looked like a duck's bill edged with a metal band. The Jewish policeman wore civilian clothing, but his coat was girdled with a leather belt and he wore riding breeches, high boots and a visored, blue-banded hat. It was he also whom Mamusia first approached and, after a whispered conversation, handed a thick wad of banknotes along with some papers that appeared to be forged Polish I.D. cards. I had not even known she had them. That wad with the bogus I.D. cards was then passed on to the Polish "Blue" policeman, who took a cursory look at the cards presented to him by his Jewish assistant. He deftly pocketed the money, passed on the cards to the German guard and motioned for us to approach him. The German also did not bother to scrutinize our I.D. cards closely. He handed them back to Mamusia and just let us pass. Later, the Garnetman would probably share that bribe with him and give a lagniappe to the Jewish policeman.

We were on the other side. Entering the Aryan quarter from the ghetto was like emerging from the underworld to the earth's surface. It seemed as if we passed from a black-and-white movie to a Technicolor one. The calmness and normalcy of the sunlit street were blinding to my eyes. Even the air was easier to breathe, being no longer filled with terror and dust.

Just a moment ago we had been on that other, nether side of the world, streets filled with milling, panic-stricken inhabitants in the hours after the morning raids, caged behind walls and barbed wire, guarded by armed sentries. There, the sun shone through a haze of dust, the sidewalks were treeless, the streets were strewn with trash, their roadways empty, the stores were shuttered and their shelves empty. Here, the sun shone brighter and harder, the sidewalks were swept clean, and the roadways bustled with cars, *droshki* (four-wheeled horse-drawn cabs), and red-painted streetcars. Here, trees were covered with green foliage, stores were open, their modest window displays dazzling to someone used to living in penury like me, coffee shops and restaurants abounded, and women, men, and children wearing clean, unpatched clothes were strolling peacefully, without terror in their eyes. They walked with a sense of purpose, knew where they were going — home or shopping or to a theater or cinema. This was such an unaccustomed strangeness to my eyes. I felt like I was transported to another world.

I saw that Mamusia and Dadek had altered their gait and walked like the Poles, with a sense of purpose. I too adapted my gait to theirs.

Of course, I was not aware at the time that the Poles were not living in a paradise either. A subjugated people, they were living at the occupier's mercy and eking out a subsistence living, for the Germans had a special animus against Poles.

The Germans considered Poles subhuman, just a notch higher than the Jews. They were treated like dirt, and their food rations were only half as high as those received by the Germans, just enough not to starve, though still much better than the miserly starvation rations of one-sixth of normal assigned to the Jews until July 22, when they were suspended completely. These outwardly normal, bustling streets and people of Aryan Warsaw were in reality also gripped by an atmosphere of terror, with the Germans conducting daily roundups of young Poles for forced labor in Germany or as hostages to be executed in hundreds for one German, whenever a German was attacked by the Underground.

Once we passed from gloom to light, from the ghetto to this other, "normal" side of the looking-glass, Mamusia, Dadek and I made our way through a little crowd of curious Polish onlookers. And there lurked the danger. Among the gawkers there must have been the *szmalcownicy*, the "greasers," informers, depraved men and youths who would want their palms "greased" by waylaying the Jews in hiding and demanding, "Hand over your *szmalec*" — literally, "fat" or "dripping." They would tell their victims to enter the nearest doorway and order them to drop their pants for signs of circumcision. Thereupon they would extort from them money or valuables under the threat of betraying them to the Germans.

Once we were past the gate, at any moment anyone, not even a German but just a Pole, could stop us by pointing at us and shouting "Jews!" to the nearest German or Polish cop. Then it would be all over for us. That is what I learned much, much later, because on that momentous day, I did not see or was aware of any such vermin. Or could it be that they were there but left us alone for some miraculous reason? We three wore clean and decent clothes, unlike the shabbily dressed ghetto inhabitants, and did not look Jewish, so we might have been taken for Poles who happened to be trapped in the ghetto. I shall never know.

The onlookers parted before us. After we walked for about a dozen blocks with no one following us, Mamusia stopped an old lady and asked her for directions to the address where Tatus would be. Following these directions, we finally reached a cavernous tenement and ascended the dingy stairs smelling of urine, so unlike the clean outdoors, to the fourth-floor apartment where Tatus was renting half a kitchen. Mamusia rang the bell and Tatus opened the door.

His short, cropped hair had turned gray. Only two or three weeks ago, when I had seen him last, it was completely dark. What agonies he must have experienced worrying about our fate, feeling so totally helpless and having to stay in that kitchen all the time in case and in the hope that we would yet turn up right there, since he was not certain from which one of the four ghetto gates we would emerge, if we would emerge at all. He stood rooted to the spot. After a while he smiled that sweet smile which was peculiar to him alone and opened the door wide for us to enter.

# III

# Dodging the Predators

## *Rescued by Dadek*

My father opened the door wide. As soon as we entered he closed it and we hugged.

While he held a hurried conversation with my mother I kept looking at him. His face did not change. He looked just as I remembered him during his last visit to us in the ghetto, two or three weeks ago — a stocky man nearing forty, with an aquiline face and a well-trimmed mustache. But there was that one big change: his grayed hair. And the sight of that grayed hair moved me inexpressibly. It was the outward sign of his worry and anxiety about us, of the agony he had been experiencing in his uncertainty about our fate.

I looked around. There, in one corner of that dingy kitchen, next to the window, stood a cot and a chair with my father's jacket on it, half-shielded by a partition fashioned from a bed sheet. On the floor next to it lay a crumpled blanket and a pillow made up from a folded jacket. Bronek had probably been sleeping on it but he was not in.

The bedding on the cot was unmade. Apparently, given his rumpled hair, Tatus had been lying on the cot and had gotten up on hearing my mother knock. He had stayed there in that small and dark kitchen, day after day, feeling powerless to rescue us and longing to at least go outside and join the crowd of gapers standing at the ghetto entrances and trying to catch a peek past the guards at the scenes of misery and desolation inside. Yet, the only rational course of action for him was to do nothing and force himself to stay where he was and wait for us, aware that my mother knew his address in Aryan Warsaw and desperately hoping she would show up here. Now that he saw us, the grimness on his face vanished. He began to look composed, more like himself. He had to resume this role, to look and act confident in front of us, to bolster our morale.

He listened intently to Mamusia's hurried explanation and thought for a while, then, glancing at us with grave and loving eyes, said, "You all can't stay here in this half-kitchen with me. I'll take you to Kielce. Let's go."

There was not a moment to lose while the day was still young. We had to leave at once before Tatus's landlady came back and discovered us. But before we left Tatus left a short note for Bronek informing him in coded language that all was well and he would return in a couple of days. That was fortunate, because the longer my brother loitered near the ghetto gates in the hope of seeing us emerge from that place where all hope was abandoned, the greater the danger of his being noticed by the blackmailers. Now finally he could stop doing so.

We followed Tatus, I holding Mamusia's hand with Dadek a few paces behind us, to the main train station whence he took us by train to Kielce, a town about 120 miles south of Warsaw. We carried no baggage and, in this summer weather, no double or triple layers of clothing, so as to remain inconspicuous. Already then I had unconsciously mastered the art of conspiracy on my own: I walked with my eyes straight ahead, trying not to stare at the passersby, however novel in their normalcy they looked to my unaccustomed eye — no corpses, no families dying on the sidewalks, stores open and displaying what seemed to me an abundance of goods. Actually, they were shoddy wartime goods but at that time I did not know better.

The richness of the new visual impressions was too overwhelming for me and whole journey passed in a blur. We got off the train in Kielce.

Apparently, Tatus had been hoping to leave us in the Kielce Ghetto for the time being, but we arrived too late: it was already *Judenrein* in Nazi newspeak, denuded of Jews. Just a few days earlier, the Jews of Kielce had been rounded up, with some executed and the rest freighted to their death in boxcars. Of course, there was no mention of it in the official press, so Tatus had been unaware of it until we arrived.

The Kielce deportations took place in August, just a couple of days before our escape. There was not yet a break in the wave of mass deportations to the killing camps from the Warsaw Ghetto. What happened was that, under Operation Reinhard, the Nazi planners assigned additional German troops with their Askari escorts to the towns around Warsaw and farther afield, such as Kielce, where they carried out their macabre work.

We ended up in the wrong place. By the time we arrived in Kielce the local ghetto was no more. The executioners had been here and departed, leaving behind them a trail of devastation. The doors and windows of most of the houses inside the ghetto gaped open as they did in the Warsaw Ghetto, except that here the houses were mostly wooden one- and two-story structures and the streets were unpaved, like in Lodz's Baluty.

Instantly taking in this new situation, my quick-witted father found and rented for us in the emptied ghetto a small crooked shack with a door that was partly torn off its hinges. It had obviously been abandoned under duress by its Jewish occupants very recently. One wall of this shack was charred as if after a great fire. The air inside reeked of smoke. The floor was littered with broken dishes and pieces of torn clothing and the interior was looted of all its furniture except a broken-down cot. Like Lodz's Baluty, this section of Kielce was a slum. This rickety section of the town was a way station into which the city's Jews had been herded before being taken to Auschwitz, Belzec, and Sobibor.

Once we settled in that shack, Dadek retreated into a corner on the dirt floor and sat there brooding. I have already mentioned that he was in frail health and subject to occasional fainting spells. As the oldest brother, he was supposed to lead and guide Bronek and me, but he showed no interest in playing that role, which as if by nature fell to the more robust and outgoing Bronek. After Tatus had sent us that note inside a loaf of bread telling us to escape from the Warsaw Ghetto, Dadek behaved apathetically, letting Mamusia take the initiative in talking to the guards at the ghetto gate and leading him and me to Tatus on the Aryan side. Now that we had escaped from the Warsaw Ghetto, Dadek could easily go outside, given his appearance: his nose was straight and he was blond and blue-eyed like a true Aryan according to Nazi ideology, or rather to Nazi mania. Yet, he consistently refused to leave the house. It was not just that he had this panicky fear of the Germans: if that were the only reason, he would be flinching, trembling, and hanging his head like a whipped dog as I had seen some ghetto dwellers act in the presence of Germans after they had become demoralized by their privations. Owing to the deportations, he had lost high-minded friends whom he cherished and admired, and he became separated from his studies. His hopes for a bright future were gone. What did he have to look forward to these days, in the late summer of 1942 when the dark stain of German victories spread as far east as Stalingrad and as far south as North Africa? At best he could look forward to years of living underground like a mole until not so certain liberation. And that was only at best. He was turning inward. Looking back, I can see now that this prospect combined with his esthetic disgust at a world ruled by pig-dogs and ravening wolves, for that was indeed what the Germans of those days were like, was chiefly responsible for his attitude. Rather than adapt to this repellent new world, he retreated into himself. Only his loyalty to us as a family kept him from giving up completely. In these crucial moments he could not let us down by an act of desperation such as giving himself up.

Since Dadek shrank from going out and clearly needed companionship, Mamusia stayed with him while Tatus asked me to accompany him on a shopping expedition to a nearby flea market. We walked past stalls and carts displaying mounds of used, unpressed men's coats, pants, shirts, and women's dresses and nightgowns, along with piles of cooking pots, cutlery, and crockery. Remembering what kind of broken-down shack we had settled in, even I at twelve could tell from the abundance and charred appearance of these remains of ruined lives that they could only originate from Jewish dwellings that had been looted after their occupants were ordered out of their homes and taken away in sealed freight cars to destinations unknown.

I observed my father keenly and saw how matter-of-fact he acted when bargaining with the Polish vendors for lower prices for these discolored forks and knives and pots and soiled blankets. Once again I noticed with what dignity he acted in contrast to the smirking manner of the vendors. He would pick up a pot or a spoon and on hearing the price put it back and turn away without saying anything. Then, after the vendor shouted after him, quoting a lower price, he would return and pay for it. I could not hear him, of course, but I saw that he was saying little.

That was a lesson to me in how to remain pragmatic: not to mourn in face of tragedy, such as the one that befell the Kielce Jews, but instead to utilize their former belongings for personal survival. It served me well afterward. Later the mystery of my father's reticence was partially cleared up for me by Bronek, who told me that he avoided speaking too much in Polish because of his faint but gradually disappearing Yiddish accent. But I don't think that was the only reason for his being so laconic. There was also his natural dignity. Ultimately, Father bought a cooking pot, three spoons, a chipped white-enameled mug, a knife, and three blankets, which I helped carry to our new home. Mamusia used the pot to cook groats and the knife to cut slices of bread for us. The following day my father left for Warsaw to look for an apartment for us.

After the war, in 1946 Kielce became the site of a notorious pogrom, the slaughter of forty-two Jewish men, women, and children by a Polish mob armed with axes and knives, prompting many of the survivors throughout Poland to emigrate and give up the thought of resuming normal life in this country. The ostensible reason for the pogrom was blood libel. A Polish boy was missing and a rumor spread that he had been kidnapped by Jews who wanted his blood to bake matzohs with. He later turned up safe and sound — he had been playing hooky. But by then it was too late and the massacre had already taken place.

This kind of ritual murder accusation is millennia old and of a surprising origin. According to Christian apologists such as Justin Martyr, Minucius Felix, and others who mention these rumors only to deny them, pagans believed the early Christians to be vampires who celebrated the Eucharist by drinking the blood and eating the flesh of non–Christian children. That was while the Christians were still an island of aliens and strangers in the pagan sea. Once their faith spread throughout that sea, the blood libel was shifted, by a kind of transference, from their shoulders onto those of the Jews, probably because the early Christians were viewed as a Jewish sect. So now it was Jews who were accused of butchering little babies to use their blood in baking matzohs. That is ironic, considering that Jews are prohibited by their religion from eating blood of any kind, and the principal reason for kosher slaughter is to drain animals of blood before they can be eaten.

I wonder if another reason for that pogrom was the resentment, however unfair, masking a guilty conscience, of many Kielce Poles who had profited from the destruction of their city's Jews to occupy or loot their homes and now saw the few surviving former owners return and claim ownership of their possessions. But of course the principal reason was that after years of witnessing German atrocities and becoming demoralized themselves, the burghers of Kielce thought they could kill Jews with impunity. Besides, benighted as they were and running amok with bloodlust, they sincerely believed that every Jew had personally crucified Christ and that among the apostles Judas was the only Jew. That is what Tolstoy would call the power of darkness.

There, in that rickety shack, we stayed, with Dadek and me sleeping on the dirt floor under our blankets and Mamusia sleeping on the cot under another. There was nothing else inside that shack other than a caved-in stove, not even a sink with water. We could get some water from a well outside, and there was an outhouse. Our stay there was to be temporary while Tatus returned to Warsaw to look for a less primitive place for us to live in. Returning to Warsaw, that big city, would offer us a better chance to remain submerged. He was to visit us again the day after tomorrow to see how we were getting on and hopefully bring the good news that he found a place for us in Warsaw. Meantime we were to sit tight. But in his absence a crisis arose and our lives were again directly endangered, because of me.

As it happened, a day later we were out of food and I went with Mamusia to shop for it. We entered a neighborhood grocery. For the first time in years I found myself in a normal food store and I was overwhelmed by the sight of all that lavish variety of foods. In reality, not much was available in that wartime grocery in a provincial town — some loaves of black bread, sacks of rotting cabbage, beets, turnips, potatoes, jars of ersatz jam, a display case with penny candies, and that kind of stuff. Anything better, such as white bread, sausage or butter, was either strictly rationed in tiny quantities for Poles or available only on the black market. After the privations of the ghetto, though, to me the interior of this store looked like a fabulous horn of plenty.

In particular, my gaze was attracted to the sweets display case. It showed an array of candies in multicolored wrappers. *Krowki* (a kind of caramel with a fat dappled white-and-brown cow pictured on the wrapper), sesame candy, rock candy, and similar cheap candies that to me looked like jewels. At twelve I was dazzled by this heavenly sight and devoured all these sweet goodies with a greedy gaze. My eyes shining with desire and hope, I pointed a finger at the display and looked up at Mamusia. But she would not look at me and her face wore such a distracted expression, so disturbing to me in its novelty, that I instantly sobered up, sensing that an acute crisis had arisen. I looked around to see what had caused it and noticed that the other shoppers, several elderly women in flower-patterned headkerchiefs, were watching me and — I could see — at the same time whispering about me. But what shook me above all was the discovery of how severely, with what tight lips and hard eyes, they looked at me. They were watching me with the appalled curiosity of a scientist examining a weird specimen. They started to cast suspicious glances at Mamusia as well. Their faces simply screamed "Jew! You don't belong. What are you doing here? What gives you the right to be still alive?"

Where was the maternal instinct of elderly women seeing a boy eye sweets with longing? The Jews were supposed to be dead and here I was still alive. How could I be still alive, their expressions asked, their lips moving primly? It was as if a pail of cold water were thrown in my face. I lost all desire for the candy and was burning to leave the store.

Mamusia, who observed it all, did not panic. She calmly completed her purchases and, carrying them in a netted bag, took my hand and walked out of the store with me without looking right or left.

At the door I looked at her guiltily and saw how pale she was, her face staring ahead as she grasped my hand firmly.

A few dozen paces outside, I glanced back and saw that no one was following us, but faces behind the glass door were staring at us. Something had changed in the air. Mamusia looked sad and I felt guilty for having exposed her to this suspicion just by casting such a greedy glance at that candy, a voracious facial expression that could only come from a Jewish boy immured in the ghetto and not accustomed to such a cornucopia of sweets. I would have also exposed Dadek to danger had someone from the store been following us. And were we caught, what would happen to Tatus when he returned to look for us?

When we returned to the shack, Dadek turned away without saying anything after Mamusia told him what happened at the store. It was as if he lost all interest in what was going on, not even caring to blame me. Mamusia, too, did not reproach me. That made me feel all the more guilty. To be sure, given the kid that I was then, my sense of guilt had quickly evaporated. Mamusia shared with Dadek and me the loaf of bread and radishes she had bought in that cursed store and in the meantime darkness had fallen. We got some water from the pump outside and, after drinking it, I was still so exhausted by the last few scary days and nights I had spent in the Warsaw Ghetto and my new experiences since then that I quickly fell asleep.

The following day, when Tatus returned from Warsaw and learned what happened, he acted quickly. He had not yet found a place for us in Warsaw but he could no longer leave us in Kielce now that we were recognized, as it was too small a town for us to hide there safely. We were marked people. If just one of those crones in the grocery store gossiped too freely, the wolves with human faces would not have to look far for us. Mamusia, who had kept up the pretense of nothing unusual having happened, practically broke down in front of Tatus. I and Dadek saw her, who was so good at keeping her anxieties to herself in front of me, unburden herself to Tatus. Tears were trickling down her cheeks but her face remained as if carved in stone. To see it pierced my heart. Tatus held her in a soothing embrace. He too did not reproach me. On witnessing this scene I felt guiltier than ever. What made it all the worse was that I was too young and too inarticulate to express to them my feelings of guilt and regret. Well, once again my family faced a full-blown life-or-death crisis and once again the burden of rescuing us was on Tatus now that Mamusia had, however temporarily, reached the limit of her endurance. Our lives depended on him. What iron nerves he must have had not to break down under this weight of responsibility for our lives.

Tatus judged that it was too early for us to return to Warsaw. We could not yet hide ourselves in the anonymity of that big city, not until he met the challenge of finding a safe apartment there. In the meantime, owing to the near-disastrous outcome of the visit to that grocery store, it was just too dangerous for us to stay any longer in Kielce. He faced the urgent dilemma of where to find shelter for Mamusia, Dadek, and me. He opted for Czestochowa, a town about 70 miles southwest of Kielce, because when he had been there on a buying trip a month ago the local ghetto was not blockaded yet. He gambled that it was still intact. Our going there was to be temporary, until he found that place in Warsaw for us all to live in. That half-kitchen he had been inhabiting with Bronek was obviously out of the question.

His on-the-spot decision to take us to Czestochowa turned out to be near-disastrous. It was a desperate gamble because now that the Kielce Ghetto was liquidated and the Warsaw Ghetto had largely undergone the same fate, it was logical for the Czestochowa Ghetto to be axed next. But Tatus felt he had no other choice than to take us there. He may have had good business connections in Warsaw, Krakow, and other cities of the General Government, but ironically enough he knew no Pole whom he could trust sufficiently to leave us with him, even if just for awhile. As with any other nationality, there were both swine and good people among Poles. Yet, the good ones were very hard to find. Even if they were found, there was an almost insuperable problem: the Germans imposed the death penalty on any Pole who sheltered or assisted a Jew. There was Zosia, whom we all loved and whom he trusted, but she was living in Poznan, now annexed to Germany. Then, too, we would be staying in Czestochowa only for a few days as Tatus expected to find a new home for us in

Warsaw soon. As it turned out, finding it took a great deal of time and effort and we had to stay in Czestochowa for weeks on end until it was almost too late.

We left in that shack in Kielce the cooking pot, mug, blankets, and other junk and took a train to Czestochowa, still wearing only our summer attire. When we arrived in Czestochowa the ghetto there was still intact and the fence was so laxly guarded that we had no problem crossing it.

For some reason, unlike in most other ghettoes, the Jewish inhabitants of Czestochowa were not evicted to an outlying slum and continued to live in their homes of brick and stone rather than in shacks without water supply and sewers. Tatus rented for us a room in the ground-floor apartment of the Milsztejns, a middle-aged couple with a nineteen-year-old daughter, that had windows facing the street. Then he had to leave us there and return to Warsaw to resume his search for an apartment before coming again to bring us back with him.

The Czestochowa Ghetto was little, composed of a dozen or so streets, unlike the big Warsaw Ghetto. Like the Warsaw Ghetto and the ghettoes in all other cities and towns of Poland, however, it shared the same history of initial confiscations and robberies of Jewish assets followed by the imposition of levies, induced food shortages, conscription for forced labor, and a hail of other restrictions, all leading to the ultimate end: massacres and deportations. But it was still fairly peaceful at the time we had moved there in late August; its elimination and the deportations had not yet started. There even was more food available, because the guards were not very strict and smuggling across the fence was so much easier and less dangerous than under, above, and through that ten-feet-tall brick wall encircling the Warsaw Ghetto.

But that seeming idyll proved short-lived. Now that the Jews of Warsaw and Kielce were deported for extermination, under the inexorable sweep of the "Final Solution," the turn of the Jews of Czestochowa came. Once again Tatus almost lost the race with time.

With the lull in the deportations from the Warsaw Ghetto, a special unit of SS and Ukrainians was diverted to Czestochowa where it replaced the lax local guards and tightened the cordon around the ghetto. At the same time empty freight trains were dispatched to the local train station to carry off the inhabitants to the killing camps, an operation efficiently coordinated by some perverted master planner. These trains consisted of two dozen or more empty boxcars each. Each train made at least two round trips daily to Auschwitz or Sobibor. A hundred or more people could be and were forcibly crammed into each car. The floors of the cars were covered with lime and chlorine and their narrow window slits barred with barbed wire. I did not know all this at the time, but after my recent experiences in the Warsaw Ghetto no atrocity would have surprised me.

The assault started about three weeks after we had arrived from Kielce. One day in the early autumn (22 September 1942, as I later established), as I was taking a stroll through the ghetto, the street lanterns suddenly were turned on although it was only early afternoon, in broad daylight. People looked puzzled and cast uneasy glances. What happened next was even more mystifying: soldiers in black uniforms began to wander through the streets. Green-uniformed Germans appeared as well and began to daub white paint on cellar entrances. The soldiers in black and green uniforms began to cordon off a section of the ghetto, not yet the one we were living in.

After the war I was unable to find out why the street lanterns were turned on in broad daylight, but I did find out that the reason why white paint was daubed on cellar entrances: it was to find hidden Jews more easily. The soldiers in black uniforms were Ukrainian auxiliaries of the Germans, the so-called Black Battalion.

The inhabitants of the surrounded section were summoned by loudspeakers to report for deportation on pain of death. In all, it took the Germans about six weeks to deport 300,000 Jews from the Warsaw Ghetto, since their trains had a capacity of about 8,000–10,000 victims daily. Given that the population of the Czestochowa Ghetto, about 40,000, was also too large to be deported all at once, the Germans decided to cordon off and depopulate it section by section within a few days. The loudspeakers proclaimed in German and Polish that the Jews living on specified streets were to report for deportation "to the east," as the now usual phrase, so damning in its connotation, ran.

It is hard to tell whether rumors of Treblinka and its gas chambers had reached the Jews of Czestochowa but most of them reported willingly for deportation. The few who tried to hide themselves were for the most part tracked down and shot dead on the spot.

We were in the ghetto quarter that was left intact for the time being. Its turn was to come either tomorrow or the day after. The familiar story of the Warsaw and Kielce ghettos was about to repeat itself, as Mamusia and Dadek realized.

They also realized that we had to get out quickly. But where would we go? We knew no one among the Poles in Czestochowa or anywhere else. Our only hope for rescue reposed in Tatus, and he was in Warsaw and unaware of what was happening here. He could not learn about it from the censored press, of course.

It seems the ghetto dwellers in Czestochowa still hid their heads in the sand and refused to believe the rumors about the suffocating conditions in the freight cars, not to mention the gassing chambers. But apparently some people who had heard the cries and moans of the resisters who were being tracked down in their hideouts in the liquidated one-fourth of the ghetto, decided after all to take precautions against being caught and deported. Among them was Mr. Milsztejn. When I passed through the living room I saw him standing next to an open trapdoor leading to the cellar below. Next to it lay a rolled-up rug that he was obviously going to camouflage that trapdoor with — a witless ruse, easily noticed by any experienced Jew searcher, but then Mr. Milsztejn was obviously an amateur. He was flustered to see me and angrily waved me away. So far as he was concerned, I was a deaf and dumb moron. I descended the stairs to the cellar and saw that the door to a closet just under the living room was already painted over so as to blend, not very well, with the surrounding wall. It was a tiny closet, with just enough room inside for Mr. Milsztejn and his wife and daughter. So that was why he was annoyed when I saw what he had been doing.

When I returned to the room I shared with Mamusia and Dadek, from a window I observed a lone soldier, apparently a Ukrainian since he was wearing a black uniform with yellow collar and cuffs, standing at a street corner by himself. I also saw Mamusia emerge from the doorway below and approach him. She talked to him with urgency visible on her face and offered him her watch. What did she hope to accomplish by this act of desperation? It was so purposeless. He inspected the watch with a detached curiosity and then returned it to her as if saying no, he would not be able to help. He was young, hardly more than twenty, and apparently still had some civility left: another soldier in his position would have pocketed the watch and pushed Mamusia aside if not worse. After all, in those days Jews had no rights, and anyone who was not Jewish could do with them as he pleased, kill them, rob them, beat them with impunity if he was a German or by working for the Germans as that Ukrainian was. I saw my mother walking back dejectedly.

Dadek and I watched the conversation between Mamusia and the Ukrainian. When she returned home, Dadek talked with her, his face grave. I had never seen my shy and retiring oldest brother looking so alert and determined. His jaw was set and he pleaded with her but she shook her head, at first firmly then hesitatingly. I could not hear, of course, what they talked about but I found out in the evening. He argued that to escape meant the risk of being caught and killed, yet to remain in the ghetto meant the certainty of being killed. The risk was preferable to the certainty. What happened was that, after witnessing the scene between Mamusia and the Ukrainian, Dadek reached a decision. He told her he was going to Warsaw to Tatus for help. She pleaded with him to stay; it was too dangerous. But he firmly said there was no other way to get out of this trap and she had no choice but to agree to his decision. I had never before seen my gentle brother act so full of resolve.

On the same day the inhabitants of another ghetto section were summoned by loudspeakers to report at the ghetto square for deportation tomorrow. After that it would be our section's turn. We were trapped. Had we escaped from the Warsaw Ghetto only to die miserably by being stuck in this new ghetto? Our food ran out and there was nothing to buy.

To Dadek and Mamusia the signs were unmistakable: What happened in Warsaw and Kielce was going to be repeated in Czestochowa. They already knew about the gas chambers of Treblinka. They spent the day looking out of the window at the deserted streets. In the afternoon Dadek ventured outside and scouted the boundaries of the ghetto, looking for a less guarded place. Dusk was falling as he finally found a promising spot. It was a walled-off segment of the ghetto border with a Catholic convent on the other side. Elsewhere the border was marked by a wire fence with guards posted at intervals along it, but here the wall segment offered a kind of concealment from sentries at night and a chance to escape, because it was not too tall. About six feet high, the stone wall had fortunately no crushed glass on its top and could be easily surmounted, unlike the ten-foot-tall brick wall topped with broken glass that encircled the Warsaw Ghetto.

Standing on a couple of bricks, Dadek peered over the top and saw on the other side a deserted convent garden, dimly illuminated by a blue-shaded streetlamp. He heard the approaching tread of the jackboots of a German sentry pacing along the wall and ducked. After the noise of his tread disappeared, Dadek checked his watch. A moment later the sentry reappeared, having turned back in the other direction. My brother kept looking at his watch but waited patiently. After ten minutes he heard again the approaching tread of the sentry's hobnailed jackboots and tucked his head down. Listening to the noise made by the jackboots revealed to Dadek that the sentry would reappear at ten-minute intervals. He timed it twice more to make sure these were the right intervals.

Returning to Mamusia, Dadek explained his plan to her. He would climb over the wall to the other side while the sentry was away, take a train to Warsaw and return with Tatus the following night. It sounded so simple, but in reality he was taking terrifying risks. My mother reluctantly yielded to his pleading.

As in the Warsaw Ghetto and Kielce, we were ready to leave as we were, once again without extra clothing or suitcases as it was summer and we had to appear casual and dressed lightly to avoid notice. When it grew dark, Dadek took Mamusia and me to the same spot near the convent wall. We all sat down on the steps leading to a cellar.

Dadek and Mamusia kept whispering. I could not hear them, of course, but in the semi-darkness I could see that they looked both resigned and determined. We stayed like that for hours as Dadek wanted to wait far into the night, when the sentry would be tired, before crossing over to the Aryan side. Finally he got up, kissed Mamusia, gestured goodbye to me in a man-to-man fashion and approached the wall. He peered over the wall and waited for the sentry to recede in the distance. There was no time to lose as the sky was about to brighten in the east. He could hear the sentry go past with his heavy tread; he waited until the sentry was gone and then climbed the wall. Straddling it, he took a last look at Mamusia and me. We stood up and looked on anxiously as he took off his shoes and, holding them in hand, he jumped down in his stocking feet so as to muffle any noise.

He was now on the other side. He found himself in a deserted convent garden dimly illuminated by a blue-shaded streetlamp, like the night before. He breathed heavily and crossed the convent yard, past the columned arcade of the convent, toward a postern which he found unlocked. It was apparently used regularly by the German sentry.

The first of a fearsome series of obstacles was overcome. He walked down a silent street. He came to a park and sat down on a bench under a tree, waiting for the sun to rise.

As the sky lightened, passersby began to appear on the street, and the grinding noise of the first trolleys shook the air. He arose from his bench and, as casually as he could, walked in search of the train station, taking in the sights of normal life. The birds sang, the sun shone, people were hurrying to their jobs, and the iron shutters of the stores were being unlocked, while in another, cordoned-off part of the town people were milling about in their homes, uncertain what to take and not to take along for the journey into the gruesome unknown, and for the most part unknowingly preparing to report for the trains taking them to the abattoir.

He encountered the first passersby coming from the opposite direction on the sidewalk. A man and a woman. Their suspicious stare pierced him to the quick and stiffened his spine. All at once, he realized that he was dragging his feet and avoiding looking at them. He passed them and looked back but found they were not watching him. But this encounter gave him a big scare and he realized he had to do something about his gait and posture. He straightened his back and, emulating Tatus's self-assured gait, began to walk with a firmer and more elastic step and hold his head high.

Czestochowa was not a big town and by just reaching a street with taller buildings and more stores and pedestrians he was able to locate the train station.

Like some men who disrobe in their imagination every desirable woman, there were many pedestrians in those times who in their imagination "disrobed" every person encountered for suspect Jewish traits — anxious movements, uncertain steps, hunched shoulders, the look of a hunted animal. It seemed as if every passersby looked at Dadek, always sizing him up, but he struggled not to avert his eyes and defiantly engaged in wordless eye-to-eye confrontations. To walk on those streets was to run the gauntlet of intrusive basilisk stares and to coldly repel them, keeping his head high. The worst part was seeing an oncoming German or Ukrainian. It took such strenuous effort to resist the inclination to lower his eyes or let his steps falter. He had to steel himself to look at them directly with a faint smile on his pale yet resolute face and maintain his stride when passing them.

The Germans in their green uniforms whom Dadek encountered now and then swaggered on the sidewalk, with the Polish civilians parting to let them have the right of way. The black-uniformed Ukrainians looked less sure of themselves and walked in pairs. They knew they were not just resented but despised by the Polish population.

Dadek, who had such a panicky fear of the Germans and kept so much to himself, save for a few equally idealistic soulmates he had had in the Warsaw Ghetto, now ventured outside into a hostile world with the mission of saving Mamusia and me. To this day I wonder how my shy egghead of a brother managed to accomplish such a heroic feat, truly against all odds.

It required another strenuous effort of will for Dadek to enter the train station and purchase a ticket to Warsaw without showing any agitation. The worst part so far was passing the ticket collector who was accompanied by a German gendarme. He had never before been so close to a German. He forced himself to make eye contact with the gendarme and did not flinch. The gendarme looked him over but said nothing. Fortunately, he was not asked for his papers. He then eyed the ticket collector, who read the ticket and handed it back to him. Once admitted to the platform for the departing trains he elbowed his way through the throng pushing to board a coach. He was learning fast, copying the behavior of others. In normal life he would have waited patiently until everyone else had entered the coach, but to do so now would have attracted unwelcome attention. He sat down on a slatted wooden bench. He had faced the first test and passed it so far. He wondered if his courage would have failed him it if it were a question of his personal survival alone, and he knew the answer. What steeled him was the burning desire to rescue Mamusia and me; for our sake he had overcome his panic and terror. I know this for certain and could identify with him, because much later, in 1944, when I was a slave laborer in a German factory, when I faced a similar but ludicrous plight, my resolve not to betray my family was my only idée fixe as well.

The floor of the rail coach David traveled in was strewn with torn pieces of paper and hulls of sunflower seeds. It smelled of soured milk, unwashed human bodies, and *makhorka*, cheap tobacco. He ignored the smells and closed his eyes as if napping, which also saved him from having to talk with his fellow passengers. He was too keyed up to sleep, even after a sleepless night.

Hours later when the train reached Warsaw's Central Station, Dadek got off. Walking through the terminal with an unconcerned air he saw two men in leather coats and Tyrolean hats stop a wild-eyed young man with a shock of black hair. As they asked the man for papers, he suddenly bolted. They chased him. Everyone gaped, Dadek too, looking on as if he were a curious bystander. One of the Gestapo fired, and the man fell. Profiting from this commotion, Dadek stepped out of the terminal. Outside, he was uncertain which way to go find Tatus and stopped an elderly woman, asking for directions. A few blocks later, he stopped another woman and, with her advice, he reached the intended address, 58 Towarowa Street.

As it happened, Tatus was just then leaving the tenement on his way to the train station and Czestochowa. He saw his son approach and instantly halted. To see his son there in broad daylight on an Aryan street, his boy who was usually so shrinking, so afraid of the hostile outside, was a stunning surprise, and it heralded another crisis. The father's face showed no emotion; he had trained himself to be impassive, but inwardly his heart contracted with apprehension. Their eyes met and he turned away and walked toward the corner with his hands casually clasped behind his back, so as to keep a distance from the tenement doorway where he might be observed talking to Dadek. He glanced over his shoulder to see if Dadek was following and catching up with him. For the benefit of any onlooker, he shook hands with Dadek as if he were a casual acquaintance. "What happened?" Tatus asked, and Dadek described to him the whole situation. How the Germans and Ukrainians surrounded and were eliminating the Czestochowa Ghetto, how he had left Mamusia and me on the other side of the wall and came here. "We must get back together and save them," he concluded. "I have to come with you. Only I know where to find them."

How do I know all this? Dadek never shared with me the feelings and sensations he experienced while running that savage gauntlet of stares and confrontations. But like any other survivor in occupied Poland I shared the same feelings and experiences when walking outdoors. Later, of course, I became inured to them and more fatalistic, but those first impressions upon my escape from the ghetto I never forgot and I knew exactly what my brother must have felt.

"We're leaving right now," Tatus said. Even though his own heart was harrowed by grief and worry about his wife and me, he could not but feel pity and admiration for his son as he looked at his pale face drawn with fatigue and sleeplessness. It was inexpressibly heroic of this nineteen-year-old youth, who was so frightened of Germans, to venture into this jungle of bloodthirsty beasts for our sake, not for his own.

At the same time, the news about Czestochowa was a shock and Tatus berated himself for having brought us there. The Germans were destroying the Jews of Czestochowa as they had destroyed the Jews of Warsaw and Kielce. He should have known better than to expect them to leave the Czestochowa Ghetto intact. Their lust for Jewish blood was insatiable and they would not rest until they killed all Jews. "Give me a moment to let Bronek know," he said and hurried back upstairs. It took him not more than two minutes to return and walk on, followed by Dadek, but not before his son had crossed glances of silent recognition with Bronek, who looked at him from the doorway of the tenement.

Bronek was now alone. If Tatus and Dadek were caught, that would mean the end of Mamusia and me as well and he would be left to fend for himself, friendless and knowing no one. Even then, his chances for survival were better than even. He was resourceful and quick-witted. He looked Polish and spoke perfect Polish too. All the same, he spent the next twenty-four hours in anxiety, waiting and hoping for us to return.

It was afternoon when Dadek and Tatus took a tram to a suburban Warsaw station to avoid the plainclothesmen always present at the main terminal. The train to Czestochowa was crowded and they separated for safety's sake. With difficulty, Dadek found a seat next to peasant women who reeked of garlic. Tatus was standing on the other side of the partition. Sitting on the hard wooden bench, Dadek gazed through the window, only half-aware of the sparks flying past from the locomotive and the sooty smell of burning coal. Lulled by the clatter of the wheels, exhausted from lack of sleep, feeling his father's comforting presence in the coach, he sank into deep sleep despite all the nervous tension racking his mind, until he awakened by the jolt as the train stopped in Czestochowa and they got off.

There was the old fear of being detected and the burning resolve to reach his goal. In the gathering darkness Dadek walked toward the ghetto, with Tatus following a few paces behind. They entered the convent yard through the still unlocked postern and waited for the sentry to pass, hidden behind the columns of the arcade.

The previous night, after Dadek had left us, Mamusia and I huddled on the cellar steps in the chill of the north European summer dawn. With daybreak and the end of the curfew we walked back to our room. As we entered the hallway, the Milsztejns were already awake. They looked frazzled as if they too had spent a sleepless night and I saw that Mania's face was tear-stained. If they noticed that we came back without Dadek, they did not comment on it, being so entirely preoccupied with their own affairs and fears.

We spent the day cowering in our rented room and watching the deserted street from the window. Once again, as in the Warsaw Ghetto, here the streets became deserted in broad daylight, all the stores were closed, and there was no food to buy. A loudspeaker blared the announcement that ours was the next section of the ghetto to be scheduled for deportation tomorrow. That was it. We were trapped. We had only one more chance left: Last night, on leaving, Dadek said that he would return with Tatus for us tonight.

As the night fell, Mamusia and I returned to the little square in the ghetto facing the convent wall and settled down to wait on the steps leading to the cellar. We were alone. We were tormented by hunger. It was dark and chilly. In that darkness, the scenes I had witnessed in the past piled up and overwhelmed me — the corpses covered with sheets of paper in the Warsaw Ghetto, the sight of a fat, red-faced German officer standing up in a car as it was racing on Leszno Street, laughing and firing at people who were scattering and fleeing, the anguished faces of the ghetto dwellers in their shabby clothing, the German soldier who was methodically pummeling the back of an old woman as she removed from under her coat, one after another, a round loaf of bread and potatoes and dropped them onto the slushy pavement.

These memories of my nightmarish past in the Warsaw Ghetto and, above all, the more recent cold, piercing looks of the old babushka-wearing women in that grocery in Kielce haunted me. Finally, the memory of that incident at the Kielce grocery unlocked the floodgates of utter despondency.

The atmosphere was redolent with the scent of flowers from the convent garden across the wall, yet so oppressive with terror that I could hardly breathe. The strain was unbearable and apparently I experienced a nervous breakdown. It was then that I did something that almost endangered Mamusia and me even more directly, for by that time I was as close to a nervous collapse as a twelve-year-old boy could be. All these nightmarish experiences were too much for me, and that was when my nerves became strained to the utmost. I experienced such a feeling of utter hopelessness that I started to sob and moan. Mamusia tried to shush me but gave up after awhile. In face of my absolute despair she was helpless. I suppose she herself was despairing and near the breaking point.

Suddenly, I was blinded by the beam of a flashlight. It was wielded by the German sentry from the other side of the convent wall. My sobbing and cries must have attracted his attention. He shone the flashlight at me for an agonizing ten seconds or so but finally he turned it off, leaving us again in darkness.

What was that sentry thinking when he saw a sobbing and crying boy embraced by his mother, both sitting on the stone steps? I shall never know, but I was relieved that he did nothing about it, and at the same time the shock of the blinding beam brought me to my senses. When after a moment I opened my eyes and looked in his direction, I saw his helmeted head, framed against the bluish light of the street lamp, descend behind the wall and disappear. The shock I experienced quieted me down. I stopped sobbing and clung to Mamusia as we sat on the steps in the darkness.

An hour passed. Suddenly I felt Mamusia tense as she was staring at the wall. A head appeared above the wall from the other side. It was Dadek. Tatus's head too appeared. They were beckoning to us. We got up and approached them. But Mamusia became terrified. Her oldest son was young and agile and could climb that six-foot-wall but she could not. She just stood there paralyzed, and Dadek himself almost gave way to panic. In desperation, he climbed over the wall to our side and picked up some bricks which he stacked one upon another, for Mamusia and me to climb on. He supported us as we clambered over the wall, and Tatus helped us to get down on the other side. Shoes in hand to muffle our footsteps, we hurried to get away before the German sentry would come back. Through the silent garden, past the columned arcade, to the postern and through it into the street.

I do not remember how the four of us managed to get back to the railroad station and then ride on the train from Czestochowa to Warsaw. On the train Tatus told my mother that he had succeeded in finding an apartment. Actually, he was just leaving for Czestochowa to bring us back with him when, thankfully, Dadek encountered him.

We completed successfully the journey from Czestochowa to Warsaw without being detected and stopped by informers and police agents, with one near miss: we had a big scare after we got off the train in Warsaw. As we were passing through the station building on our way to the exit, a leather-jacketed civilian stopped Tatus and started to question him. But he let him go after Tatus smilingly said something to him. How I wish I knew what he had told the Gestapo agent that made him release my father. The main thing is that we arrived successfully in the new home that Tatus had in the meantime found for us, and where Bronek was already waiting for us.

That was a close call because at dawn the Germans started to evacuate, that is, to evict and deport the last Jews, the fourth and last section of the Czestochowa Ghetto, the one we had stayed in.

## *Fobbing Off the Landlord*

Even before Dadek had come to Warsaw on his rescue mission, Tatus kept scanning the real estate ads in *Nowy Kurier Warszawski*, the collaborationist Warsaw newspaper, as he felt uneasy about our safety in the Czestochowa Ghetto. He finally came across an ad offering for rent an apartment at 6 Wolska Street. He met the landlord, Pan Mieczyslaw Nawrocki, a dapper little man in his sixties with pomaded black hair and a thin mustache whose ends curled upward in the manner of Salvador Dali, though not as long as Dali's. The one-bedroom apartment on the third floor looked ideal for our needs and Tatus rented it on the spot. The six-story apartment building stood at the corner of a busy intersection, which also helped us to avoid detection. Its four wings enclosed an inner courtyard. The windows of our apartment faced the courtyard, but outside the stairs led directly to the entrance facing the street so that I almost never entered the courtyard, let alone played in it with other children.

We settled down there, the five of us in the kitchen of our new home, waiting for our landlord to leave.

Then a problem arose: Pan Nawrocki was supposed to move out as soon as he found a new place to live, but he declared that he needed more time to find it. Father agreed to allow him one month to find another place and vacate his room, that one bedroom.

A month passed and the Pole still remained there, saying he could not find another place. We were stuck with him, for two years as it turned out. After awhile, Tatus stopped pressuring Pan Nawrocki to leave and so our landlord, who was then about sixty, continued the status quo, living in that bedroom at the end of the railroad flat.

It is important to describe this apartment since we stayed there for two years in relative safety. It consisted of a kitchen, a hallway toilet, a living room, and a bedroom at the farthest end. The kitchen was where the five of us stayed most of the time, and fortunately it had a door that exited into the hallway. We kept that door always closed so as not to let Pan Nawrocki peek in. At night, Mamusia and Dadek slept there while

Tatus, Bronek, and I slept on mattresses in the living room. That living room was infested with bedbugs. These cooties had the habit of dropping on our bodies from the ceiling. When, years later in America, I tasted my first whiskey, its odor reminded me of these bedbugs when crushed. No matter how many we found and crushed, every morning we found on our bodies itching red spots where they had sucked our blood.

At the very end of the apartment Nawrocki, the unwanted lodger, occupied the bedroom. Because of him, not wanting to arouse his suspicions, Mamusia and Dadek rarely had a free run of the living room and most of the time stayed confined to the kitchen. He was an inconvenience we had to live with.

The layout of the apartment favored our privacy. Above all, it was fortunate and rare that the kitchen had its own door facing the hallway. It was kept closed so that Pan Nawrocki could not peek in when passing in the hallway. Since that was where the five of us stayed most of the day, and Dadek and Mamusia all night long as well, I must recreate the kitchen's layout from memory. It measured about 11 by 13 feet. Facing the window across from the door was a table with three chairs where we ate our meals and played games. To the right of the door was a cot on which Mamusia slept and, in the daytime, when he was home, Tatus took naps. To the left were a sink and a stove and in the back, just to the left of the door, stood a gray-painted wood armoire.

I do not know what tacit understanding Tatus had achieved with Pan Nawrocki, but the Pole never tried to open that kitchen door when he passed it in the hallway on his way to and from work. He was a man of rigid habits. Regularly, like clockwork, he would leave for work at eight in the morning and return at six. It also helped that Pan Nawrocki was a very private person who always kept the door to his room closed and very seldom ventured out of it other than to leave for work. He was some kind of a municipal employee and left for work early and came back late. He had a stove in his room, and on that stove he cooked his meals and boiled the water for his tea. Bronek would bring him the water for his cooking from the kitchen.

Soon after we moved in we learned his ways and habits and when he was around we tried to be quiet so as not to arouse his suspicions. When he left for work early in the morning, he would pass from his bedroom through the living room and then through the hallway past the closed kitchen door, while Tatus, lying on a mattress next to Bronek and me and pretending to be asleep, listened to his footsteps. In the evenings Pan

Nawrocki retraced the route back his to the bedroom and usually got Bronek to light the stove for him in that room. As my brother told me later, nearly always then, Bronek was the reluctant listener to Nawrocki's repetitious tales about his unfaithful wife and his childhood in the small town where he was born and grew up. Quite often he would talk to Bronek about those spiteful Jews who swarmed everywhere.

Once he told my brother about some nine-year-old Jewish boy with red hair and yellow eyes who sauntered on the town's streets with a gun in his hand and looked for Poles in order to kill them and how he, Nawrocki, outwitted that boy by hiding in a horse stable. Bronek, of course, nodded approvingly and praised Nawrocki's wisdom and courage. One day, Nawrocki told Bronek that, while he was walking near the main train station he noticed a Jew whom he had known well before the war and who had the impudence, as Nawrocki put it, to walk through the streets of Warsaw in the uniform of a railroader. He then said in a whining voice, "I started to scream as loudly as I could, 'Jew, Jew!' but that dirty pig ran away before anyone could catch him. And I was too old and slow to chase him." He cursed, *"Psiakrew!"* Dog's Blood! There was something creepy about that little man with the upturned curling mustache. According to Bronek, he was a born bureaucrat. Being an engineer by profession, Pan Nawrocki must have obviously finished at university but he was not as obviously an educated and intelligent person.

Periodically, Bronek and Tatus would stage a fake dialogue in the living room with Pan Nawrocki listening in his bedroom behind the closed door. One time, Bronek declared loudly that a (nonexistent) acquaintance, Janek, had killed a fourth acquaintance because he did not like his face. "What a guy! Wow!" Tatus would comment. Next, Bronek said Janek liked him so much that he would do anything for him. He had asked him today if there was anyone Bronek did not like. If so, then he would wipe the floor with him or thrash him black and blue. Tatus and Bronek acted out similar charades from time to time in order to intimidate Pan Nawrocki and show him that they were genuine Poles, as he saw it. These charades reflected the low esteem they had for him and the warped values prized by people like Nawrocki. At any rate, this seemed to work and the little man never did anything to harm us.

There was something strange about this situation. Nawrocki was a declared anti–Semite, yet in the two years that we had lived at 6 Wolska Street until the very end he never once tried to open the door to the kitchen where Mamusia and Dadek stayed hidden. It would be only normal for this Jew-hater to suspect that someone was hiding behind this closed kitchen door in a city where the discoveries and denunciations of Jews were a daily occurrence, yet he never did anything about it. I shall never understand it, and neither did Bronek when I asked him about it — he denied that Nawrocki had known who we really were, but I find it hard to believe. My father may have known the answer, but he is not alive any more to provide it.

## Mysteries of Mimicry

Just in case, Tatus obtained new Polish identity cards for us, the family of "Feliks Krawczyk." Except for me — legally I did not need one, being under age fourteen. Instead, he had the building super sign a photograph of me certifying that I lived at 6 Wolska Street. Dadek became Tadeusz; Bronek, Bronislaw; Mamusia, Zofia, and I, Eugeniusz. These cards were not expensive and fairly easy to obtain because of the extensive document-forging network operated by the Polish underground for many of its members who were in hiding, which as a corollary also became more readily available to Jews as well.

Now, the Jews living on the Aryan side could be divided into two groups: those in hiding, living "on the bottom," who feared that their Semitic looks might give them away and those living "on the surface," in the open. Those living "on the bottom" stayed day and night in claustrophobic hideouts provided by their Polish hosts, usually for a price. Their situation was deplorable. They had to live most of the time in darkness, in broom closets, cupboards, or other cramped spaces, subsist on a Spartan diet provided by their hosts, and their toilet needs had to be accommodated to a strict daily schedule. This life in self-imposed confinement caused them to become listless, pale, and in poor health. Still worse, they were and felt completely at the mercy of their hosts. That exacted a psychological price even if they were sheltered by altruistic hosts, but especially when the hosts treated them disrespectfully or just used them as cash cows — until their money ran out and they were turned out into the street. Yet, amazing as it sounds, many of them did survive the war without serious aftereffects. That says something for the natural resilience and toughness of Polish Jews considering that the German Jews deported to the ghettoes died en masse like flies.

As for those living in the open, they looked more "Aryan," spoke good Polish, and exuded sufficient self-assurance to "pass." "Aryan looks" are hard to define. Being blond and blue-eyed helped but was not enough. One's Polish had to be free of the thick Yiddish accent, and one had to look people straight in the eye. It was important to avoid looking like one had a chip on one's shoulder or indulging in those telltale emotive Italianate gestures that brand one as Jewish in Poland. Mamusia and Dadek were neither "open" nor "covert," for while they did not look Jewish and could if they wanted venture outdoors, they chose to stay in the kitchen, small as it was, to isolate themselves from an outside that, like a jungle infested with crawling snakes, rats, and spiders, may have seemed too repulsive to these pure souls. This self-seclusion did not damage them psychologically, for, secure in self-knowledge and in the knowledge that a loving and caring being, Tatus, was their protector, they did not have to feel dependent on the good graces of some stranger. Also, the kitchen was spacious enough for them to feel comfortable and move about freely.

To be sure, it may have been a cramped space judging by normal standards, but it was infinitely better than living in a closet or a pantry. Relatively speaking only, I suppose, because after the war I was diagnosed with tuberculosis owing to years spent in cramped spaces. This must also have affected my mother and Dadek. Most importantly, they basked in the warmth of a harmonious family — harmony to which they themselves greatly contributed by their poise and calm.

That is all the more remarkable as regards Mamusia in particular. Behind those calm airs of hers she must have been suffering the torments of anxiety every time any one of us left the apartment for the perilous outdoors. And indeed, after the war, safe in America, when she no longer had to rise to the challenges of wartime, she became much more outspoken about her fears and dependent on Bronek and me for calming her anxieties, such as her worry that we should not be out late because of muggers in the streets in Queens, New York City, where she lived. Still, she always retained that essential goodness and warmth of character.

Incredible as it may seem in retrospect, we managed to remain in that apartment at 6 Wolska Street for as long as two years, from September 1942 until August 1944, while, as I learned later from Gunnar Paulsson's book, *Secret City: The Hidden Jews of Warsaw, 1940–1945*, during that period practically all the other still surviving Jews in hiding, whether "on the bottom" or "on the surface," in the non–Jewish side of Warsaw had to move from one refuge to another every few weeks or even more often to escape detection and denunciation.[1]

Our survival as a family is even more incredible considering that we never got any help from anyone. During those years two different secret institutions operated to help people like us: Zegota, or the Council to Aid Jews, formed by sympathetic Poles, and the Jewish National Committee, representing the Zionist parties and the Bund (socialists). Bronek tells me that we never received any help from either of them, either in the form of financial aid or forged documents, and I myself never heard of them until years after I had arrived in the United States. They kept lists of Jews in hiding, and their representatives periodically brought the Jews funds to tide them over and false identity papers as needed. But we were not on their lists. We had no trusted Polish friends to rely on for help and support either. Even if we had, we would have been very hesitant to ask them for help since the Germans executed any Pole who gave shelter to Jews, and besides such Poles were in danger of denunciation by their anti–Semitic neighbors.

Nobody helped us. We were entirely on our own and we all in the family were dependent on just one person, Tatus. Without him we would have been dead long ago, as simple as that.

A year passed and it was now 1943. We still did not have to move to another hideout and still remained undiscovered and untouched where we were living. That in itself was something special, as I realize now.

As Jews living in the open under false identity, Tatus and Bronek had the compelling psychological urge to assume as fully as possible the persona of a non–Jew, to identify strongly with the internal motivation of the character being portrayed, generally that of a pious Catholic who knows how to cross himself, remembers to take off his hat when walking past a church, and is given to exclamations like *psiakrew*, or "dog's blood," a curse that is as uniquely Polish as *caramba* is Spanish or *merde* is French.

That went for Tatus and Bronek, I suppose. As for me, a deaf boy, I veiled my identity at a more primitive level. I could not say *psiakrew* but I did learn how to cross myself, which I practiced with Bronek, and acquire the habit of taking off my flat cap when walking past a church, a national custom in strongly Catholic Poland.

Willy-nilly, like most Jews in their position, Tatus, Bronek, and apparently I, had a compulsive need to block knowledge of our own identity, to adopt the Stanislavsky method of acting, to get under the skin of the role played, to live out that role fully as a way of getting relief from the grip of that terrible tension. All this is far from having been merely passive victims during the war. This dissembling, this enacting of type-cast "character" roles, required a tremendous and active will and determination. By saying that I am also doing justice to all those other crypto–Jews living "on the surface" in "Aryan" Warsaw who had courageously bested the overwhelming odds against them and lived or did not live to see the war end.

The tension was sometimes unbearable, and I personally know of instances, a very few, of my fellow survivors who as a result became unhinged during or after the war. After the war this condition became known as posttraumatic stress disorder. For some other survivors that I have met, also a very few of these, this dissembling, this utter self-absorption in an assumed role led to another extreme: they ended up in self-denial and even after the war continued to live out their assumed roles all their life long and became self-hating Jews. A majority, however, have thrown themselves with gusto into a new life in a normal world to the extent that to them the past is merely a bad dream or, in worse cases, a nightmare from which they, however, wake up in the morning and pursue their normal lives.

We lived in complete anonymity and only once did we give shelter, albeit very temporary, to anyone. That was when Mr. Hofnung, a lawyer friend of Tatus from Poznan, whom he had encountered on a Warsaw street, brought to us a little girl, his daughter, and left her with us overnight. He did not show up the next day to reclaim her, nor in the following days. After a week, Bronek took her to a convent on Hoza Street and left her there in care of the nuns. Like so many other Jews, Mr. Hofnung disappeared without a trace but at least he provided for his daughter to have a better chance to survive. The daughter now lives in Israel, has married, has a family of her own, and still remembers Bronek with affection.

At that time, most other crypto–Jews used to change their hideouts often so as to obscure their trail when recognized or to avoid suspicion among neighbors. How then was it possible for me and my family to stay at the same address undetected for two years, from September 1942 to August 1944? To be sure, we lived in the dense downtown area of a cosmopolitan capital where most neighbors minded their own business, but even there, as anywhere else, there must have existed some prying neighbors.

As well, there was always the building superintendent, whose business it was to know the identity and pursuits of every tenant.

It cannot have been pure luck that we remained undetected, because living in wartime brought the tenants closer together. Being confined inside the building after curfew, the tenants would meet on the stairs and in the courtyard for company and gossip. Besides, owning a radio was forbidden by the Germans and there was no television in those days, so the tenants were all the more anxious to stay out of their cramped quarters as much as possible.

How then was it possible for me and my family to avoid denunciation for two years? A major reason may have been, as I established after the war, that the headquarters of the district command of the Polish underground was housed in our tenement. This seems to have accounted for the ostensible lack of curiosity by our neighbors. Incidentally, not so long ago I learned that at one time in 1943 a surviving ghetto fighter, Kazik (Simcha Rotem), together with his renowned comrade-in-arms Antek (Yitzhak Cukierman), had been hiding out for a month in another apartment at 6 Wolska Street.[2]

Oddly enough, in the fall of 1940, before the establishment of the Warsaw Ghetto, 6 Wolska Street was the address of a Jewish orphanage, according to the historian Emmanuel Ringelblum. It must have been, of course, moved to the newly established ghetto in that same year.[3]

At any rate, there was at least one person in the building who must have known about us in some detail — Lednicki the super, if only because he had signed his name to a photograph showing my face and certifying that I was indeed a tenant of 6 Wolska Street. That was the only proof of identity I needed since, in 1943, at thirteen legally I was not yet required to carry an I.D. card. My father must have bribed him to sign that photograph. In those times in occupied Warsaw a super was endowed with far-reaching powers, probably more even than those of a Paris concierge. He kept a registry of all tenants. He was supposed to keep the police posted about tenants and their visitors. This was in addition to his regular duties such as sweeping the courtyard and at night locking the entranceway, opening it after the curfew hours to illegal latecomers in return for a tip. Unlike most of his confreres, Lednicki seemed an educated man and not a drunkard. That made sense, since the underground staff was housed in our building and he was probably a member and a lookout. He never showed any curiosity about us.

It also helped to obscure our identities that we lived near the city center, on a busy street where pedestrians kept coming and going from dawn till curfew.

During those two years that we lived at 6 Wolska Street Mamusia and Dadek almost never went out, with the exception of one evening in the winter of 1943–44 when Dadek, his face half-hidden in a muffler as if he had a toothache, was taken out for an evening stroll by Bronek and me. That was not a smart idea, as we realized quickly — even in the semi-darkness of the evening, hiding half of his face under a muffler merely aroused the curiosity of the passersby, who stopped and scrutinized Dadek with narrowed eyes, only to avert their gaze and hurry on. That gave us a good scare and we rapidly and — thankfully — safely returned inside the apartment building.

That was the last voluntary foray in Dadek's life. Otherwise, he, like Mamusia, stuck to the kitchen except in the daytime when, with Pan Nawrocki away, now and then they joined Tatus, Bronek, and me in the less cramped expanse of the living room. It was a hard life but Dadek and Mamusia at least had enough room in the kitchen to get up, sit down, and walk around in that confined space compared with the lot of, say, Jonas Pasternak, a relative of mine and a distant relation of the Russian poet Boris Pasternak, who had to hide together with three others in a hole dug under the floorboards, directly under a bed. They wore only undershirts and trunks but still they perspired freely as there was hardly any air to breathe except through chinks in the floorboards, whenever neighbors would be visiting their Polish host. During such visits they had to struggle to hold their breath, not to sneeze or even clear their throats while listening to the neighbors curse the Christ-killers and say how glad they felt that they were meeting their just punishment at the hands of the Germans, with their host also perforce voicing his satisfaction about the extermination of the Jews. Their vile joy at the killing of children, women, and old people made Jonas's blood boil — he had just recently lost his family to the execution-ers, and it required a superhuman effort for him to contain his outrage. His companions also felt the same way. When the neighbors finally left and the hostess let Jonas and his companions out of their crowded coffinlike space, she apologized to them for having to express sentiments she abhorred in order to deflect suspicion. It was like that all the time: some Poles were good people and some were not. It was sad that it took the test of war to see what a person was really like.

In comparison with Jonas's experience, that kitchen of ours was a spacious heaven. None of us looked particularly Jewish and we all had the choice of going outdoors. Yet two of us, Dadek and Mamusia, preferred to immure themselves in that kitchen. With his blue eyes and blond hair, Dadek looked the opposite of the anti–Semite's image of a Jew. Yet, aside from that winter evening, he never again ventured outside — until that fateful summer of 1944 when he was forced at gunpoint to leave the cellar for the outdoors and saw the expanse of the blue sky for the last time. It was not out of fear that he preferred to stay in the kitchen all that time: he had proved his steely courage and sangfroid when, alone, he climbed the ghetto wall in Czestochowa, took a train to Warsaw, found Tatus, and returned with him to safely rescue Mamusia and me against crushing odds. He was no coward, as he had proved by his heroic feat. His reluctance to go outdoors was due to not so much to fear as to ethical and esthetic disgust. The outside world, a haunted forest peopled by humans with faces of boars and hyenas constantly on the prowl, was simply too sordid for him and running the gauntlet of suspicious stares of passersby was unbearable to a young man of his refined sensibility. It appears that Mamusia also confined herself to that kitchen for the same fastidious reasons, as she too could have ventured outdoors if she wanted to, since she did not look Jewish either. After all, she used to be a teacher of Polish in Lodz before she had met Tatus. Her Polish was more fluent than Tatus's, who had until the war preferred to speak Yiddish and thus spoke Polish with an accent. During the war, however, being a quick learner, he had improved his diction to a point at which his Yiddish accent became very faint if audible at all. This contributed to his successful survival as a Pole.

The kitchen was a safe haven guarded and tended by Tatus, with all our lives depending on his. It was a miracle that he did not buckle under the enormous strain of providing for and protecting his family in this spectral world. In former times he was able to unburden himself to my mother, and she to him, but now that kind of intimacy was no longer possible in the continual presence of their children, all cooped up in the same small kitchen, who perforce listened to their every word. Instead, a deeper intimacy developed between my parents, with my father saying little and my mother trusting him boundlessly.

This self-immurement may have worked better for Dadek than for Mamusia, who lived under a constant strain of anxiety for our lives. Having faced and bested the all-or-nothing challenge of rescuing my mother and me, he gained in self-knowledge and confidence. This experience rescued him from his depression. His interest in life was reawakened. My sensitive, highbrow brother, with his intellectual detachment, plunged once again into reading books that I brought him from a neighborhood lending library. He also acquired a new occupation, that of marking with a red pencil the advances and retreats of the front lines on a map of Europe and the Soviet Union pasted to a kitchen wall. As 1943 went on, these advances were grudgingly revealed, one after another, by the *Nowy Kurier Warszawski*, the German-sponsored reptile Polish newspaper, according to which the Germans were conducting "strategic retreats" and killing countless numbers of Russians on the way. But we, reading between the lines, knew better.

After Stalingrad, in February 1943, the front line steadily shifted westward toward Poland, as even the lying newspapers with their claims of "strategic withdrawals" had to admit, and this is what inspired us with fresh hope for liberation.

For Mamusia, the situation was more equivocal. Every waking moment she lived in fear that Bronek, Tatus, or I might be recognized and caught outside, or that any time now there would be footsteps on the stair landing and rough knocking on the door and extortionists or, worse even, Germans would barge in. And indeed, that fear of rough knocking was once translated into reality when a Polish "Blue" policeman once invaded our home. The door opened and there he stood in the hallway, tall and frightening in his navy-blue uniform and a hat with a long silver-banded bill. For all that there was something slimy about his smile. Tatus negotiated with him, handed him some money, and the strange thing is that he never came back to keep blackmailing us.

Stranger, even, that was the only time during those two years that we had been detected where we lived. It is beyond my understanding how Mamusia in particular as a mother could bear to live thus all the time in an agony of dread about her family without ever breaking down. The burden must have been greatest on her because she almost never ventured outside, was not a reader of books and hardly participated in the pen-and-pencil games Dadek invented to play with me. Just about her only occupation was cleaning, washing laundry by hand, sewing, scouring, and preparing or cooking our meals.

Our diet was now somewhat more varied than in the ghetto. Kercelak, Warsaw's famous, bustling open-air market, was nearby. It occupied an entire square, and one could buy practically anything there, even, later in the war, firearms from German soldiers and deserters. Bronek used to shop there almost daily. He would bring home fresh fruits and vegetables in season, and now and then some chicken. Basically, though, we still subsisted on potatoes, kasha, and cabbage. We also used to drink hot water with ersatz coffee.

As I look back on that period of time, it seems to me as if, for the sake of keeping my brothers and myself mentally stable under these abnormal circumstances, my parents made an unspoken pact never to reveal to us their own fears and anxieties, to live as normally as was then possible. Yet, how much anguish and arduous effort this pretending for our sake must have cost my mother! For my father it was easier; he could always find relief and forgetfulness in his activities, whether traveling and outwitting the gendarmes and police or selling and buying bicycle parts, flashlights, and other stuff in demand on the black market, but there was no such outlet for Mamusia. Outside our warm and cozy kitchen, flames of racist hate raged and beasts of prey prowled the streets looking for people like us, but inside Mamusia kept busy doing household chores, while Tatus, when he was home from his buying and selling trips, was calmly taking a nap on the sole cot in the kitchen, his face covered with an unfolded newspaper for a shade.

One might think that he had not a care in the world, sleeping so peacefully, the very picture of a paterfamilias dozing after a meal, but we all knew better. He was like some forest animal and we were his young, huddling in a cave while he foraged for food in a hostile jungle and brought it to us, every time evading the beings with the faces of tigers and rats and snakes prowling for him. The sight of his relaxed body on the cot, his very equanimity, though always combined with watchfulness, the newspaper hiding his face as if all was right with the world, was a boon to our morale. To my morale in particular, even when a look at his hair reminded us how it had suddenly gone gray when we were trapped in the Warsaw Ghetto after the deportations began. We boys sat around the table and talked in whispers so as not to wake him while Mamusia was sewing up a tear in a shirt or a sock.

My father may have been reassuringly calm but he was never falsely cheerful after the war began. I rarely saw him crack a smile or make a joke, not even when he haggled with his Polish customers. To this day when I think of him I am perplexed. No man is hero to his valet, they say. Yet, I, his son, can only think of him with awe. I asked Bronek, because after all, being five years older than I, he knew Tatus much more intimately and spent much more time with him, but he too could not remember anything dragging down Tatus from his pedestal and he said he considers him a hero. Sure, my father acted like a fool when he involved himself in that altercation with Mrs. Grosberg in Poznan, but that was before the war. Apart from that I cannot think of any single incident that detracted from my regard and respect for him. He was a remarkably self-controlled man to whom displaying negative emotions, such as anger, was a sign of weakness. Perhaps he knew that his sons were always watching him to see how he behaved, and that may have also spurred him to become what he was. I keep trying hard to visualize him as a human being and not a hero, but all I can think of is that when he was with us in the kitchen he ate with appetite and occasionally coughed, belched, wiped his nose and lips, and grimaced, thus demonstrating, as it were, that he was human too.

## The Ghetto Revolts

At night in the early summer of 1943 I watched from a window the flames of the burning ghetto rise above the roofs. The once populous Warsaw Ghetto was decimated. Even before July 1942 starvation, cold, and disease took away 100,000 of its inhabitants, and in just eight weeks, between July and September 1942, the ghetto's population shrank by an additional 300,000. After most of the ghetto's Jews had been transported to Treblinka and gassed within those eight weeks, the tempo of the deportations markedly slowed down. Those remaining were almost all of able-bodied age, not counting the few old people and children in the hideouts. About half of these 40,000 proles labored all day long in fenced-in factories set up within the truncated ghetto converted into enclaves of forced labor. They slept in the adjoining housing blocks, also fenced in. From dawn till evening they toiled making wood and leather products, brushes, and other supplies for the German army. In return, they received soup, bread, and the right to live — or so they hoped, with growing uncertainty.

This Jewish manpower was relentlessly exploited under slave-labor conditions while Jews en masse were being gassed and Jewish property looted. Of the other 20,000 in the ghetto, many worked for the *Werterfassung*, a huge German enterprise for organized looting. That happened after the hundreds of thousands of ghetto inhabitants had taken along to

Treblinka the permitted 15 kilograms each of their most precious belongings. Once their trains arrived in that killing camp, these belongings were seized and they were subjected to dire torments and finally gassed. Behind them, they left in the ghetto numerous empty apartments that could be stripped of their furnishings. The *Werterfassung* was set up for just this purpose. Inside the ghetto, a large city in itself with more than 100 street blocks, these empty apartments were stripped of whatever fine furniture, valuable porcelain and pictures some contained. Nothing of any value was left in them, not even chandeliers, bedding, mattresses, cutlery, or kitchen sinks. All of this the Jewish slaves were required to transport to the warehouses where they would be evaluated and processed for shipment to Germany, along with scrap iron and plumbing fixtures.

The slowdown in the deportations in mid–September 1942 was no longer interpreted by the surviving ghetto dwellers as meaning that the Germans would spare them. By then they had already heard rumors about Treblinka's gas chambers and knew that their days were numbered.

It was a time of reckoning for the ghetto's leaders, both those in the Jewish Council and those heading the political parties. Some, not all, realized too late that their policy of appeasement was bankrupt. It was an age-old policy of saving the community by bribing its enemies, except this time it was different: the bribes were in the form of human beings and not gold. That was a difference these public figures had overlooked, to their grievous regret, as they tried to placate an implacable foe, until it was too late. They could hardly be blamed — they meant well and that policy worked in the past, before the rise of Nazi Germany. Besides, they were intimidated. In the past the Germans would routinely execute at least a hundred Jews for every German killed. That was a foretaste of things to come, and it was enough for the community leaders to fear a bloodbath in response to any show of armed resistance. Not even Czerniakow's suicide disabused them of their belief. He had killed himself rather than accede to the demand of the German Moloch for victims on July 23, 1942. Symptomatic of the attitude of these public figures was the conduct of the industrialist and major Jewish Council figure Abraham Gepner a few weeks later. When the Germans arrived to seize more victims for Treblinka from the building where he had his office, in response to their command to descend to the courtyard for a bogus inspection of papers, Gepner, instead of going into hiding, descended first and ordered his assistants to follow him only to be seized too.[4]

It is said that wisdom comes with age, but that is not always true. People like Gepner, the respected big businessman and philanthropist, were supposed to be wise and cunning beyond measure. But in the end they turned out to be fools.[4] The old become ossified in their ways of perceiving reality and their responses become mechanical. They are like generals who fight the last war's battles. The unimaginable bloodbath which they had so feared and tried to avert did come anyhow.

It was the young, the members of idealistic youth movements like my admired Hashomer Hatzair of Poznan, and now also of Warsaw, who first recognized much more clearly than the old the fate awaiting them all at the hands of the Nazis and resolved not to submit to it meekly. The elderly and the middle-aged, brought up to consider the Germans as embodying human culture, at first found it hard to acknowledge that they were dealing with a Genghis Khan maniacally bent on turning them into mountains of bones, and it was only toward the end, in the beginning of 1943, that bitter experience taught them to finally mistrust German promises and support the young. But by then it was too late and they became pariahs of public opinion in the remnant ghetto. They were shunned and abused. They were blamed for mindlessly executing German orders ever since the ghetto was established far back in 1940 and for the tragedy that befell the ghetto when the Germans wrecked it by shooting and gassing 250,000 to 300,000 people during the Great Deportations, July through September 1942.

The numbers of Jewish fighters in the early summer of 1943 totaled about five hundred. They could have been 5,000 or more dedicated and idealistic young people had not it been for one of those orders that the Jewish Council had so mindlessly executed since 1940. In compliance with German orders it organized young people for transportation to forced labor camps where they lived under appalling conditions, and were tortured and compelled to do back-breaking work that most did not survive. The few survivors were emaciated and tottering like old men when they returned to the ghetto.

With the discrediting of the Jewish Council, the five hundred fighters left in the ghetto won the support of public opinion. Volunteers flocked to join them, but most could not be accepted owing to their lack of weapons and training. The fighters, those eighteen- and nineteen-year-olds and those in their early twenties, the flower of Jewish youth, were more clear-sighted and had abandoned all hope much earlier, in September

1942. These striplings dared what their elders shrank from: They ignited a revolt that spurred uprisings in Bialystok and smaller ghettoes. They determined at least to face death with weapons in hand instead of meekly exposing their throats to be slit by the German executioner. Utilizing the pause in the deportations after mid–September 1942, the adolescent pioneer movement members, now having mostly lost their families to Treblinka, formed communes within which they practiced using the few weapons they had, until finally they were ready for organized armed resistance in January 1943.

The uprising they started has hardly any counterpart in history. Normally, a revolt breaks out when an oppressive regime relaxes its hold on a people by tolerating a limited reform such that people finally are emboldened to hope for liberation from oppression. The French Revolution did not break out until after King Louis XIV allowed some measure of freedom by permitting parliament to meet. The summer 1944 insurrections in Paris, Slovakia, Warsaw, northern Italy, and elsewhere were triggered by the retreat of German armies and the attendant awakening of hopes for liberation. But no such prospects and hopes attended the Warsaw Ghetto uprising. It was the desperate response of people who knew they were doomed to die but at least they were resolved not to die on their knees.

When in January 1943 armed ghetto fighters for the first time fired on German troops trying to round up more Jews for deportation, the Germans were so shocked that they left the ghetto alone until April, when they launched concentrated artillery attacks on the ghetto fighters and gradually razed the ghetto to the ground, setting fire to and dynamiting building after building so as to smoke out the fighters hiding in the attics and underground bunkers.

That spring and summer of 1943, in April and in May, in the daytime I watched from a window a pall of smoke spreading from the ghetto above the city and breathed in its bitter reek. At night, plumes of flames from the blazing buildings illuminated the sky. For two months these youngsters, armed with revolvers and grenades, tenaciously battled seasoned German troops equipped with automatic weapons, tanks, field guns, and flamethrowers who were dynamiting, shelling, and razing, one after another, the ghetto's buildings until only the smoking ruins were left. It was a losing battle, but at least these brave and desperate youths died with honor. For them, becoming armed was happiness and to fight was "a last desire in life," as their commander, the twenty-three-year-old Mordecai

Anielewicz, put it.[5] As it was, they had fought the Germans longer than the Poles did in 1939. In this kind of house-to-house and street fighting, ensconced in fortified positions inside buildings they could have lasted much longer and turned the ghetto into a miniature Stalingrad from which to stage raids and breach the ghetto walls — if only they had weaponry to match that of the Germans. That was not to be. When I think of these doomed fighters, I feel such burning rue.

## Forays from the Kitchen into the Jungle

As time went on, I became used to leading a double life to such an extent that I contracted cabin fever and began to take almost daily walks in the city despite Mamusia's fears and grudging opposition and Tatus's unspoken but visible disapproval.

Staying in that kitchen all day was just too stifling for a boy like me. At thirteen I was too big and too immature to listen; my parents could not keep me home by force as they prudently realized. I had already rebelled earlier, in the ghetto, when I sometimes disobeyed my mother's injunctions and ventured outside onto the streets, even if risking sudden death.

I needed new sights and exercise through walking. I did not look particularly Jewish. My hair was then blond and my eyes blue, as they still are. My being a boy, too, helped me to escape notice. I must have had more guts than brains. If I had to do it all over today, it would be too scary for me and I would just stay home all the time like Anne Frank, but in those times I was a kid and stupid — and lucky — and treated my excursions as a challenge, as an imperative need to breathe new air. I did not realize I was courting death with my bravado and, worse even, endangering my family every time I went out because the identification I had on me gave the same false Polish surname, Krawczyk, as they, and the same 6 Wolska Street as my address. I suppose it was in the same foolhardy spirit that Bronek attended parties at the homes of his newfound Polish fellow teenage friends, playing games with them and flirting with the girls as if he had been one of *them* from birth. Of course, it was all a sham, as he knew inwardly, but he tried and succeeded in forgetting it at times.

Tatus himself in his early forties was no spring chicken, yet he took even greater risks than Bronek and I. He traveled a lot by train to Krakow and other cities, in search of merchandise which he could sell at higher prices in Warsaw. Bicycle parts, carbide lamps, and whatever brought a higher price in Warsaw than in Krakow, and vice versa — it was black-market merchandise and therefore there were no uniform prices for it, depending on where it was available and where it was most in demand and thus brought much higher prices. That was a very dangerous occupation because of the German emphasis on weeding out smugglers, and because every time my father entered or exited a train station he faced scrutiny by the Gestapo and its agents. Even on the train itself he had to face frequent inspections by gendarmes. I just cannot understand how he survived these hazards so often and so regularly. As a result of his many travels, he was home only about two or three days a week, and that lessened the congestion in our kitchen, though we missed him whenever he was away and felt so glad whenever he came home. He certainly braved death even more constantly than Bronek and I and as an adult he was much more aware of the risks he faced, yet he took these extra risks in stride.

As for myself, in those times I left home on long walks almost every day when the weather permitted. I wandered in the parks and on the Vistula riverbank, window-shopped the stores, and walked across Kierbedzia Bridge to the Praga suburb on the other bank of the Vistula. Acting natural was my camouflage. I developed the trick of gazing blankly and unconcernedly at whoever happened to come from the opposite direction, whether it was a Pole or a uniformed German, and only afterward shifting my gaze. To match stares too long or to shift my gaze too quickly would have betrayed me as someone who did not belong and was not supposed to be alive. At times I witnessed German patrols stopping passersby and checking their papers, but they paid no attention to a boy of thirteen like me.

Now and then I encountered anti–Semitic posters pasted to the walls. They portrayed a top-hatted, paunchy, and fat-lipped Jewish plutocrat in a frock coat with a nose that looked like the number 6 or was curlicued in the manner of a snail's shell. He was shown lugging money bags conspicuously marked with the dollar sign. For a change, other posters showed a devilish, skull-faced Jew, an old-fashioned spiked cloth helmet marked with a big red star on his head, wearing a Red Army uniform and wielding a whip with which he scourged shuffling ranks of humble, downtrodden people walking with bowed heads, but he too was shown with a nose like a figure 6.

These posters often were affixed to the walls near the guarded ghetto gates above which hung signs saying "Danger — Epidemic" and *Seuchen-sperrgebiet*, or "Plague-Infected Closed Area." "Plague" had a broader resonance in the demented German mind. It was construed as the infection of a Nazified European "civilization" by cunning Jews.

The people living inside that decimated and truncated ghetto in the spring of 1943 were also Jews, but they were destitute and starving Jews, lacking the money bags of the plutocrats and the brute nihilistic power of the Soviet commissars attributed to them in the posters. Moreover, in reality they were naive and gullible, unlike the image of the sly and devious Jew in Nazi propaganda, since they let themselves be so easily duped by the Germans into believing that they would be spared and survive until the war's end if they only obeyed every German decree and order. This only tightened the garrote more and more as the community elders surrendered unresistingly, one by one, the weak, the ill, the aged, and the children, to save the "core," which too finally was destroyed — but not before it staged an armed uprising in the late spring of 1943.

As if to compound this dichotomy between the all-powerful Jew of the German propaganda and the browbeaten Jew of the ghetto, I also saw posters at this time portraying the Jew, with lice, roaches, and rats shown crawling all over his face and body, as a filthy carrier of typhus and other epidemics. His nose was similarly drawn to resemble the number 6, an idea concocted by some devilishly sick-minded Nazi to distinguish Jews from the hundreds of thousands, if not millions, of so-called pure Aryans in Germany who had long, aquiline, crooked, broken, tapir, knife-edge, or beaky noses. That "number 6" nose was ostensibly the only thing common to all these caricatures of Jews, as contrasted with the potato-shaped proboscis of the true Aryan.

So those supposed Jewish masters of the universe were also depicted in other posters as breeders of lice and roaches. I suppose this illogic in demonizing the Jew can be only explained by the Nazis' obsessive viewing the Jew as their ideological antithesis, their archenemy with ridiculous ethical constraints, their supposed rival for world domination. Even depicting them in Nazi propaganda as carriers of infection that threatened civilization made sense, since this kind of infection by normal human decency was by its very nature a mortal threat to Nazi civilization (an oxymoron if there ever was one).

The supposed Jewish puppetmasters turned out to be the helpless victims of the Nazis. They could be plundered with impunity, toyed with like a cat with mice, and liquidated. No matter what his multiple guises, whether as Mister Moneybags or Red Death or a filthy bacillus carrier and useless eater or a degenerate artist, behind all these guises, the Jew embodied what to the Nazis were primitive notions of conscience and morality as opposed to the brute power of the gun.

I mentioned family harmony as reigning inside our kitchen but, of course, I don't mean that we were a totally harmonious family. This enforced proximity was sometimes too much, especially for us three brothers. We engaged from time to time in spats and quarrels inside the kitchen, but they always petered out soon. Once, for some stupid reason I cannot remember, I got so mad at Dadek that I kicked him in the crotch. He was bigger than I but he did not retaliate and this lack of response drained me of all anger. To this day I feel heartsick when I recall that scene and how he doubled up and grimaced in pain.

My parents for their part, though, never quarreled; they lived in total concord, and that in itself was a benign and lasting influence on us. To this day I guide myself by the perhaps odd and snobbish notion that quarreling is low-class. As my mother once said, when you are angry, talk to the wall. This precept has served me well.

My two brothers were not much alike. Dadek was a very conscientious young man. In 1942 when we first moved into 6 Wolska Street he was twenty. He read books all the time now that he no longer could enjoy the company of his like-minded idealistic friends from Warsaw Ghetto days. I used to procure these books for him from the local library. Physically he was weak and sometimes, Bronek remembers, he used to faint during prayers at the synagogue before the war. But he would recover quickly. At school in Poznan he passed exams with such high grades that, despite being Jewish, he was admitted to the College of Commerce.

Dadek was three years older than Bronek and eight older than I. In the ghetto he had found friends among youths as idealistic and pure-minded as he. He was a handsome young man. He seemed to be destined for higher things. Given his quick intellect and keen perception of nuances, had Dadek survived he would of a certainty have given much to the world, to say the least.

It was a boon for him and me that, soon after we moved to 6 Wolska Street, I registered with a nearby public library and began to borrow books whose titles he had specified to me. Because of his refined taste I learned how to distinguish between quality books and trash. I remember in particular that one of his favorite writers was a Romanian, Panait Istrati, whose novels abounded in fiery romantic heroes. He is undeservedly forgotten these days. Another favorite writer was Romain Rolland. The Germans turned him and Knut Hamsun into supposed supporters of a German-dominated Europe, but that was unfair to them. I remember in particular Rolland's comparison of Jews to yeast that stimulates and provokes the growth of European dough, meaning culture. The novels of Istrati and Rolland perhaps best illustrate Dadek's tastes, and what he read he usually passed on to me during those two years when he secluded himself in that kitchen. I owe him, among other things, saving my life in Czestochowa and my good taste in literature.

I too was an avid reader, but for different reasons than he, to whom the characters in these novels appealed because, like he himself, they were idealistic and sensitive young people. For me, books were a lifeline. Because of my deafness I could not benefit from conversations with others and from comments voiced by others. All my impressions of the outside world were filtered through the eye. It was as if I was enclosed in a bubble of soundproof glass that isolated me from the larger hearing world. I tried and failed to imagine the noises surrounding me — the clanking of trolleys riding on metal rails, the cries of street vendors, the high-pitched voices of women and the bass or low-pitched voices of men, perhaps also some unseen music from a guitar.

I could only conceive these noises in the abstract, from descriptions in literature, and that was not enough. What could high-pitched or bass voices mean, for example? These noises of everyday life were abstract ideas to me, just as colors are abstract ideas to a blind man. I knew them only from reading about them. Like the proverbial elephant whose shape cannot be ascertained by a blind man feeling its legs, to me, a deaf boy, the world around me would have remained an unplumbed shape to me had not books enabled me to understand its workings, opening ever new nuances of comprehension. Even so, to me the Prophet Ezekiel's and Flaubert's injunction to read in order to live is too extreme. To me, the purpose of reading is not just to live but to live more fully. Ah, those public libraries, in the ghetto and on the Aryan side! The Germans may have banned schools but they were not thorough enough to burn books in Poland as they had done in Germany itself and to close libraries in Poland. They would probably have done so if given enough time anyway. Without those libraries I would have remained an uneducated clod.

Of course, even the most passionate reader needs a diversion now and then, and in those long evenings Dadek and I used to play games like chess and checkers as well as a game called Words in a Word, for which all that was needed was pen and paper. The object of that game was to find the largest possible number of words that can be made up from the letters of a particular word, and Dadek was usually the top scorer. Bronek sometimes joined us when he happened to be home.

Bronek on his part was always attracted to street life and partying with his peers. He was the most practical of us three siblings and had the street smarts that Dadek and I lacked and socialized much more easily than we did. Now, "socialize" is a word that hardly applied to Dadek and me, for different reasons. If absolutely necessary, Dadek could socialize with outsiders but he preferred to live in that kitchen in voluntary isolation. As for me, socializing was something alien. Isolation was forced on me by my deafness. I could not even engage in conversation with other people because of my unaccented "deaf" speech that most could not understand. I had to limit myself to the unsatisfactory means of pen and paper. What of it if I rambled through the city unlike Dadek when there was no one I could talk with or play with? In the ghetto, at least, I could engage in games with other kids in the courtyard where we had lived, but once we crossed over to the Aryan side, for the next three years, until Liberation, I was totally friendless. The one time I had thought I found a friend, in the last year of the war, he turned against me once he found I was Jewish.

Now in Aryan Warsaw, Bronek had no problems in forming liaisons with new teenagers, this time Polish ones, playing cards and attending parties with them, because of his easy adaptability. He was away all day long, coming home only just before the curfew. When not socializing with his fellow teens or working as a baker's assistant, he kept busy working for Tatus, peddling carbide lamps and other black-market stuff. These carbide lamps were very popular in wartime Poland, given the frequent power blackouts. They had an unpleasant sulfurous smell but they were cheaper, did not flicker, and lasted much longer than candles. Tatus used to make periodic trips to Krakow to buy dozens of these lamps and, on returning to Warsaw, he passed them on to Bronek for sale.

To me, there was one special aspect about Bronek. I cannot understand or explain why, but I could lip-read him in Polish much more easily than anybody else. In that sense he was my "lifeline" to the immediate hearing world around me by explaining to me directly what was going on within and without our family. That was something that, being deaf, I could not have understood or known from books, without his mediation. He would say, "Quiet. Tatus is sleeping." "Are you tired?" "It is snowing," or even longer sentences and I did lip-read him with ease. Because he was so easy to lip-read, he served as my living lifeline to the immediate world of prosaic daily life in contrast to the abstract lifelines to the world provided by books and newspapers. To make themselves understood when using complex words and sentences, Tatus, Mamusia, and Dadek had to write me, but not Bronek; the way he mouthed even complex sentences was so familiar and easy to lip-read. Every deaf person needs such a "lifeline" in his childhood and I was lucky to have Bronek in mine.

In that summer of 1943, as the battle for the ghetto died down, roving patrols of Germans began increasingly often to detain passersby on streets of Aryan Warsaw and demand to see their *Arbeitskarten*, or work cards. Those who could not produce any such cards were pressganged for forced labor on German farms and factories. Since Bronek at eighteen was in the age category in such demand, Tatus used his connections to get him a job in a bakery for a person named Pan Buze so that he would be entitled to a work card. In the bakery he swept floors, washed baking utensils, and served as an assistant to Pan Domaracki, a master confectioner, who was, together with Pan Buze, more often sloshed than sober. Bronek was paid a pittance but what mattered was that he received a work card and brought some bread and buns home besides. Since Pan Buze was a *Volksdeutsch*, or of German descent, the work card approved by him was more important than usual. After that, at roundups for forced labor, whenever gendarmes would stop Bronek for a document check, he would show them his work card and they would let him go.

A year later, in August 1944, when the Polish Uprising erupted in Warsaw, Bronek was in Mokotow Borough, swimming with his friends from work and unable to return home. This probably saved his life because the German thugs killed all the males at 6 Wolska Street and snatched the female tenants, including Mamusia, for forced labor in Germany. During the uprising, Bronek fought with a platoon, most of whose members got killed. He himself escaped to the woods outside Warsaw where he joined the partisans. He never disclosed to them his Jewish identity after he saw them kill a stray Jew. At one time, he found himself in Piotrkow Trybunalski, the hometown of our cousins who now lived in Israel. After many vagaries he was liberated by the Russians.

While we lived on Wolska Street, sometimes after Tatus returned home from his trips to Krakow carrying packages of black-market merchandise, I accompanied him on walks in Warsaw, such as to a nearby park where I saw him engage in a short conversation with a haggard, shabbily dressed stranger, apparently a Jew and at loss where to go, to whom he gave a banknote before leaving.

That was not the only instance of his generosity. One day, he took me along on a short suburban train trip to a small station deep in the forest. We alighted and spent the afternoon with two Jewish girls, the sisters Anka and Janka, and their uncle, who were hiding there. It was Bronek who, about one year after our escape from the ghetto, while taking a tramway ride, accidentally came across Anka in midtown Warsaw. She had first met him in the ghetto and formed a romantic attachment to him. They were part of the same crowd, teenagers all, and in the ghetto they used to meet in Dudek Klepfisz's apartment, where they played bridge. Sometimes they went to play Ping-Pong to a place on Leszno Street. She told him that she, her sister Janka, and their uncle were hiding in an attic in some small village near Warsaw and were desperately in need of food. The Polish lady who allowed them to hide in her attic was poor herself and they ran out of money. So, on some Sundays, Tatus and Bronek, and sometimes Tatus and I, would take the train to that suburban village, meet them in the forest, and bring them food and whatever else we could. Long after the war, in Israel, I met Anka again and she told me how her parents were seized and transported to Treblinka. Later, in the winter of 1942–43, she and Janka escaped from the ghetto and showed up at the home of their Aryan former maid. The maid let them stay overnight but in the morning, when they woke up, they found that a little sack with their heirloom jewelry that they had secreted under a pillow was missing. They asked the maid about it and, without even bothering to deny the theft, she brazenly told them to leave at once or she would denounce them.

The sisters were now alone and penniless. They left the maid's home hurriedly before she could carry out her threat, and they spent the remainder of the war in the forests together with their uncle, whom they met by accident. Now the sisters and their uncle were desperately out of food. So, on some Sundays, Tatus and Bronek or Tatus and I helped them by bringing them a little food and whatever else we could. Of course, that was not enough but somehow they survived. In time they wandered farther eastward and were liberated by the Russians after the Polish Uprising in Warsaw in August 1944, while we got stuck on the German side. After the war they moved to Israel.

Every day I felt stir-crazy, stifled in that kitchen and living room, with nothing to do except play word games with Dadek or read books. As an added diversion, I sometimes played with painted soldiers cast from lead, each about an inch and half tall. I had a squad of tropical troops in tan uniforms and white cork helmets and another of blue-clad riflemen in kepis, some kneeling and some standing but all aiming their rifles directly ahead. In a separate cardboard box I also had a squadron of English or French scarlet-cloaked horsemen with silver helmets, sabers in hand, bestride steeds that seemed to gallop madly with their hooves in the air.

But, thrilling as it was to plan and execute battles with my toy soldiers, it was not enough to keep me busy. I would wander the streets of Warsaw, absorbing the sights, in my short pants and short-sleeved shirt, looking like an average fourteen-year-old boy and acting like one, as by then I had learned how to be inconspicuous. One day I happened to enter an amusement park and watched some Mongolian or Kalmuck soldiers wearing green German uniforms take joy rides on a carousel. I had never seen Asians before. They looked undersized and wore their uniforms sloppily. Another day, I was taking a free trolley ride, clinging to a stanchion outside, when suddenly the trolley stopped and two German soldiers pulled me off the steps. My initial fright passed when I saw them smile. They said something, slapped my bottom, apparently to warn me against the dangers of clinging to a trolley, and let me go. I wonder how would they have reacted had they known I was Jewish.

Still another day, in the course of my wanderings I entered a park in the suburbs where I was surrounded by a gang of boys my age. They started talking to me, and when I pointed to my ears to show that I was deaf, one of them wrote to me with a stick in the sand, *"Jakiego masz huja?"* (What is your dick?). I calmly answered (as then my speech was more understandable than now), *"Takiego jak ty."* (The same as you), without really understanding what they meant — whether I was circumcised or not — and only moments later the meaning of the slang word *huj* hit me — I had given them the correct answer without realizing it. They smiled at me and let me go. I could have joined them in their games but I did not. I never went back to that park.

Of course, I was not the only deaf person in all Warsaw. There must have been at least a thousand or eleven hundred of them in that city if statistics are to be believed that there is one totally deaf person to every thousand hearing ones. As for me, when I saw them gesticulate to each other on the street, I averted my gaze and walked on. I assiduously avoided all contact with them. For one thing, I still remembered how children in the ghetto chased a local idiot who happened to be deaf. They pelted him with pebbles and he, a retarded deaf man, ran all hunched up and with an idiotic grin on his face. The impression this left on me was such that I was not keen to meet other deaf people. For another, Warsaw was a big metropolis so that in my two years on the "Aryan" side I never had to deal directly with other deaf people. Just once, in a cinema, I saw a deaf couple gesticulate but their signing looked so strange to me that I had no wish to introduce myself. Sign language can be beautiful when used properly, but their gestures looked primitive, further repelling me. I could not find anything in common with these contortionists writhing in a kind of St. Vitus dance, and this further strengthened my low opinion of the deaf.

I was thus unknowingly spared by the fates considering that the Polish deaf community in Warsaw, as everywhere else, was a very small community where everyone knew everyone else and my surfacing in that world would cause tongues to wag — oh, no, I mean hands to flutter — about a suspicious deaf boy who appeared out of nowhere and could only be a Jew, an outcast who had no right to live.

By the way, in Warsaw at Three Crosses Square there was a school for the deaf called the Institute for the Deaf and Blind but I never knew about it until much later. It was a vocational school. There, as in practically every school for the deaf in Europe, the students were taught manual skills like carpentry and metalworking because they were considered not bright enough to attend a university. It was only after the war, in America, that I got to know intelligent, college-educated deaf people and a genuine, advanced deaf culture.

As the summer of 1944 wore on, I found my own source of income and no longer had to depend on the small allowance I received from Mamusia. I fell in with a gang of three or four boys who gathered in front of cinemas such as the Apollo. We would be the first in line in front of the box office and as soon as it opened we would invest in ten or more movie tickets each that we would then sell off at double or triple the price to people who arrived too late for a sold-out show.

Now and then I would take in the movies myself. For the most part, they were cloying filmed versions of Lehar and Strauss operettas. With their actresses wearing bodices, corseted waists, and hoop skirts, flirting and romancing with bewigged cavaliers wearing satin frock coats, these smarmy Austro-German movies were totally unrelated to the reality of occupied Warsaw. Perhaps that was why the film showings were sold out. For the Warsaw public, watching misunderstandings between titled lovers on the silver screen was a good way of forgetting for a while the oppressive atmosphere outside the cinema. Romance between nobles, counts and baronesses was the stock-in-trade of these films and in their focus on song and dance they were precursors of Bollywood movies. That was in line with Nazi film policy in occupied Europe. Were the Germans to show films dealing with Hitler youths, Leni Riefenstahl's cult of the idealized Nazi body, or German victories, the cinemas in Poland would have had to close owing to lack of audiences. So instead the films shown were of the escapist kind, set in a different period of time, such as the eighteenth or nineteenth century, and intended to distract the population.

Once, however, I also saw a different kind of movie, *Jew Süss*, about a scheming, conniving court Jew in eighteenth-century Germany who was hanged for raping a chaste German maiden. As usual, I could follow the plot line by reading the Polish subtitles. I thought this movie interesting but not believable. After all, I had grown up a Jew among Jews and never saw among them such a despicable, falsely humble character as the one shown in the film who was, if I recall correctly, wringing cunningly his hands like — and probably copied from — Uriah Heep in Dickens's *David Copperfield*. It was obvious Nazi propaganda. Even at fourteen I could see how contrived and false it looked. I was struck once again by the intensity of the racial hatred and contempt it reflected and at the same time I sensed how perverted and wrong it was. The Jews I knew were either warm-hearted and caring people or, as in the ghetto, browbeaten, miserable wretches or idealistic young people, totally unlike this odious caricature. It was the Germans and the Polish blackmailers I knew, luckily only at a distance, who were odious characters for whom I could feel no respect. If it only could, a hunted rabbit or other small animal would want to become mighty with powerful claws like the wolf or fox hunting it, so as to avoid being caught and eaten. I was in the position of that rabbit but somewhat more discriminating and I could not conceive surviving by wanting to turn from prey to predator, by envying and wanting to become one of those bestialized German gendarmes or slimy Polish blackmailers, because even at fourteen I could sense that their mentality was repugnant and amoral and therefore too alien to accept without losing what was most precious to me, my core of selfhood.

In our spare time, after we sold off the last of our movie tickets, we urchins would squat in a doorway and play blackjack for hair. Every time I lost at blackjack I would let the winner pull out one hair from my forehead, and vice versa. Good thing my career as a ticket scalper did not continue long or I would have become bald. The Warsaw Uprising of August–September 1944 cut short that career.

I earned a few zlotys from the movie ticket sales, just enough to buy candy. Finally, I made a killing from a different source — I earned 50 zlotys, a fortune for me. This happened toward the end of July, 1944, just before the uprising. I helped a man called Engineer Wojcicki and his family push a handcart with their belongings all the way from city center to a suburban town. ("Engineer," yes, that was how he called himself and was called — in those times and even now people in Poland with engineering or master's degrees have their names prefaced by such honorifics as "Engineer" or "Magister.") He seemed in a hurry to leave Warsaw and as the events unfolded he knew what he was doing.

Actually, the Red Army was approaching Warsaw and the Polish underground was about to commence an uprising in the capital, so the engineer did the smart thing in moving to a suburban area to wait there until the worst would be over, that is, if he did survive the retaliatory German measures. He gave me a 50-zloty bill for my help. To get an idea what it meant, in those times a loaf of bread cost about 4 zlotys and the average official hourly wage for Poles was 1.5 zlotys. I had never made that much money before, and when I came home in the evening I showed it proudly to Tatus. He just looked on without saying a word. I could sense that he both disapproved and was impressed by my enterprise.

The next day, I happened to be near Most Kierbedzia, a bridge spanning the Vistula, and witnessed a long procession of wounded and bandaged German soldiers retreating from the east, from the Praga suburb on the river's right bank. They lay or sat on horse-drawn carts and open truck bodies, their heads, legs, and arms swathed in white gauze. I stood in a crowd of gawkers who could barely suppress their pleasure at this sight of a once mighty swarm of locusts now retreating. I took this spectacle in, sensing that things were coming to a climax with the Soviet armies approaching Warsaw.

I did not realize how soon, two days after, on August 1, that climax would erupt. That climax was the Warsaw Uprising of 1944, staged by Poles, as distinct from the Ghetto Uprising of Jews in 1943. On the very day of its outbreak I left home as usual, this time for a swim in the Vistula because it was such a hot day. That was the last day I saw my father and Dadek.

# IV

# From the Uprising
# to Liberation

## *Saved from Drowning and Shooting*

1944. It was August again, two years after we had escaped from the Warsaw Ghetto. The portents were all there: The Russians were coming. My parents were aware of the ongoing retreat of German troops across the Vistula and through Warsaw and could, I imagine, hear the approaching drumbeat of Soviet artillery from the east. I myself saw flashes of artillery fire at night from the living room windows. Yet, Tatus preferred not to follow Engineer Wojcicki's example and have us leave the city. He expected that it would be easier for us to remain undetected in a swarming big city like Warsaw than in the countryside, and he hoped the Soviets would seize the city by storm as they did many other cities in the course of the mighty summer 1944 offensive of the Belorussian Front which reconquered western Russia and pushed into Poland as far as the Vistula.

Another reason why he may have thought so was because the Germans showed little intention to defend Warsaw. They were not fortifying it apart from sandbagging the entrances to major buildings. To be sure, they appealed to the Polish population to dig some trenches around Warsaw, citing the hokey threat of Bolshevism, but that was a flop since there were hardly any volunteers, not even among the most anti-communist Poles, now that they knew defeat was staring the *Szwaby* or Swabians, as they pejoratively nicknamed the Germans, in the face. Father may also have known that the Warsaw Uprising was about to break out and thought that the Germans, threatened by a two-pronged attack with the Red Army in front and the Polish insurgents in the rear, would speedily abandon Warsaw. That was the logical thing to do, to preserve troops and equipment. Besides, then the Germans would be gleeful bystanders, letting the mostly right-wing Russophobic Poles seize control of the capital and then probably clash with the Red Army so as to save the Germans the trouble.

The problem was that at this stage in the war the Nazis were no longer logical, if they ever were. They changed their mind, gripped by a mad desire to destroy Warsaw, and focused their energies on smashing the Polish uprising while the Soviets stayed on their side of the Vistula and let them do the dirty work of killing off the troublesome Poles. Besides, what tilted the scale was that while the hate the Germans felt toward Jews was obsessional, their hate of Poles was visceral, Teutons against their ancient enemies the Slavs. Acting against rational self-interest they had blindly pursued the goal of the Final Solution even if it meant killing off masses of enslaved Jewish skilled workers who would otherwise have markedly bolstered the German war effort. Now once again to their own detriment the Germans just had to suppress the Polish insurrection, even if it meant withdrawing combat troops and resources from other fronts. They also sicced on Warsaw the notorious Dirlewanger brigade of thugs who would kill all men and rape women. In the end, they turned Warsaw into another Stalingrad and this time they won the battle, leaving the city a smoking wreck.

At any rate, not anticipating this outcome, my father decided to gamble and stay put, unlike Engineer Wojcicki. This was not the time to leave on buying trips either. He remained home together with Mamusia and Dadek on the day after I had helped Wojcicki push his cart toward Otwock, but did not object when, with the weather being so hot, Bronek and I left the house in the morning on our usual jaunts. Bronek left first, to meet his Polish pals at a swimming pool in the Mokotow suburb, and I second, to take a swim in the Vistula and then to scalp more tickets at the Apollo.

There was another aspect of my father's behavior that leaves me puzzled and impressed to this day: he never actively tried to prevent me from going out despite the dangers I was facing. Given that we were illegals and faced death if caught, he acted remarkably poised about my almost daily rambles. This was a matter of life and death to my family, and most other fathers would have been jittery, laying out all kinds of prohibitions, but not he. I will never understand why he was so laid back about it, considering that if I were caught I would endanger the whole family, since my identity-card photograph showed the same name and address as my family's. Yet, by then it had become a regular habit with me to absent myself from home in the daytime. Since the outbreak of the war he never told me what to do. I was free to come and go as I pleased. He never hit me either. If I misbehaved, a glance of reproof coming from him was enough for me to sober up: he had that kind of moral authority.

Would I have listened to him had he actually forbidden me to go out? Probably I would. But I was not mature enough to endure staying cooped up in that small kitchen all day with Dadek and Mamusia. I would feel unhappy, rebel, and poison the atmosphere inside. I think my father realized this and that was why his reproving glance was the limit beyond which he did not go.

As for my mother, she was worried every time I went out, but since my father and Bronek also regularly left the apartment, she could not stop me.

On this particular day, because of the uncertain situation, Tatus might have special reason for insisting that Bronek and I stay home together as a family, but he did not and this resulted in weighty consequences. The climax was in the air: the Germans were retreating and the Soviets coming. Any day now Warsaw would be freed. It was the wrong time for my brother and me to go swimming even though the day was so hot. Yet even on such a day Tatus did not object to our leaving.

When I left home that morning on the first of August, I did not know that my departure would change my life. On that momentous day I was to start living on my own for the next ten months and saw Tatus and Dadek for the last time. If Bronek and I had stayed with them on that day we would probably have been killed together with them by Dirlewanger's thugs.

Once outside, I noticed that the streets were largely deserted, and at a corner I saw a hurriedly walking pair of men casting suspicious glances right and left. One of them was carrying a longish object wrapped in packing paper that even to my untrained eyes looked suspiciously like a rifle. As conspirators they were overdoing it in my judgment, now that I was a seasoned expert at camouflage. I was surprised at that sight, so openly defiant in a Warsaw under a reign of terror, and this intimated to me that this was going to be a special day. But even so, foolishly or not, I decided to ignore it and proceeded to the riverbank.

On reaching the riverbank I noticed that the bridge to the right-bank Praga suburb and the connecting streets was completely deserted. Only recently a flood of cars, trucks, and horse-drawn carts carrying wounded and bandaged German casualties had been rolling westward across it toward Germany. This was strange, since it was broad daylight and even without the German retreat that part of the city was normally bustling with crowds and traffic, but I did not pay much attention to this phenomenon. Yes, there was something odd about it, but so many unusual things had already happened to me and so many times I avoided disaster by acting as if nothing had happened that I decided to ignore this sight. Much later, after the war, I learned that the Germans had through informers learned in advance that the Polish Uprising was about to break out, so they rerouted the withdrawal of their wounded upon hunkering down. As for the Poles, most of them must also have known something since the city looked so deserted.

That was in the morning. The uprising began later in the day.

At the riverbank I tested the water temperature with my foot. It was refreshingly cool. I was going just to take a dip before proceeding to the Apollo Cinema later in the afternoon to make some money scalping tickets, but the sun shone so fiercely that I decided to take a swim in the Vistula for the first time, since I had my swim trunks on anyway. As there was nobody around, with the streets so empty, I decided to shed my short pants and shirt and leave them on the slope where I could see them. I took a calculated risk because wartime Warsaw was a city so full of thieves that, the joke ran, a newcomer exiting from the main train station was bound to lose his suitcase the moment he put it down and turned his head away for an instant to ask for directions. For some reason, because this was such a strange day, my taking this risk was warranted. I waded into the river.

The greenish, murky water was pleasantly cool. I waded a little farther and started to swim. That was my big mistake. Once my feet left the river bottom, I was seized and dragged downstream by a swift and powerful current. This was surprising and dismaying, but then I had never before swum in a river, especially one as wide and swift as the Vistula. Overwhelmed, I reversed my direction and tried to swim against the current to return to the riverbank spot where I had left my clothing.

But the current proved too mighty, despite my beating against it. I panicked. I flailed fiercely with my arms and legs and suddenly sensed cramps in my legs. I could not move them and lost all feeling in them as if they were paralyzed. I began to thrash desperately about with my arms. I was losing strength and felt my body being gradually sucked down to the bottom. I was just about to go under when I sensed someone grabbing me with strong arms and pulling me up onto a boat. I landed in a heap and, with my legs still quivering uncontrollably, I raised myself with difficulty to a standing position. I saw that my rescuer was a scowling middle-aged man with a toothbrush mustache. He fixed me with a baleful glare and was saying something to me and, as I did not answer, he pointed at my swimming trunks and with a commanding gesture motioned to me to pull them down.

That could mean only one thing. I clutched firmly with one hand the waistband of my sopping-wet trunks, in case he tried to pull them down, as if a fourteen-year-old boy could prevail in a contest of strength with an adult, while pointing with my other hand to my ear to show that I was deaf and shaking my head stubbornly.

The boatman's scowl deepened. He glared at me so hard that I quaked and was even more frightened but remained defiant. My heart sank and I felt my end had come. He was bigger than I and could have easily pulled my trunks down with one harsh tug and then — the consequences to me would be unimaginable. After all, this was Catholic Poland where circumcision was viewed as the ringed mark of the Cain, the annulus branding the cursed Christ-killers. But, strangely, after I had gestured to him that I was deaf, he did not approach me. Instead, he turned away and faced the riverbank. Rowing against the current, with one oar he turned the prow of his skiff to bring me back to the quay and, when it touched the ground, he stood by silently. I stole glances at him from a corner of my eye and saw that he was watching me without any expression on his face. I jumped off the boat without even thanking him or looking back — I was in such a daze.

Once on the quay I walked to the place where I had hidden my shirt and short pants and sandals, put the shorts on over my wet trunks, and started to cross the street toward a building on the other side.

There was still no one in sight, which was rather strange in a big city like Warsaw. To a deaf person like me, this absence of visual cues, this utter "visual silence" as if of a city stricken by plague, once more alerted me that something uncanny was going on. I was alone on a vast operatic stage. But I was still too much in shock after my near-drowning and rescue to seriously wonder about this strange lack of visual noise. As I glanced around and up and down, reconnoitering visually the world around me, I noticed sand swirling around my feet. That was odd since there was no wind, but I ignored this freakish phenomenon and was about to cross the street when from the other side I saw a man run toward me while pointing a revolver at me and shouting at me.

Those bullets he fired at me were no BB gun pellets. If he had been a little more accurate as a shooter, I would have been, if not dead, walking with a limp or a prosthesis from then on.

He probably was shouting at me "Hands up!" but to me, seeing that man suddenly appear in the desolate sunlit urban wilderness and point his gun at me was such an astonishing sight that, my gaze riveted at him, in my inexperience I was not even smart enough to raise my hands and just stood there confused. That sight was something I was to see in the movies many times afterward — a revolver pointed at someone — except that this was the first time and the target was I. Before that nothing like that ever happened in my experience since up to then the only movies I had seen were, not counting Jew Süss, those cloying Austrian operettas.

Instead of feeling frightened and raising my hands in surrender as I should have, I stopped in my tracks and stared in wonder at this apparition. He himself looked at me with disbelief and amazement at my lack of response. Then I realized that the man's moving mouth was asking something of me, given the interrogative expression on his face. I gestured at my ears. What he saw was a preteen boy in short pants, sandals, and a short-sleeved shirt, with uncombed and still wet hair, who was pointing at his ears. His wary and suspicious expression gave way to a bitter, half-ironic smile. He must have been perplexed to see me ignore the bullets he had fired in my direction and his repeated shouts and walk wobblingly toward him without raising my hands in gesture of surrender. The gunman's bitter, half-ironic smile was the same kind of smile that I was to witness in my life many times afterward in passersby who happened to stop me on the street, ask for directions, and, after I pointed to my ears in silent pantomime, think to themselves: *Hah, how ironic, the guy is deaf and dumb. Just my luck!* As if I was bringing bad luck to them!

I have always been reluctant to engage in the dumb-show of pointing at my ears unless absolutely and directly asked a question by a stranger. This response establishes a relationship that is more intimate than I would want: the stranger smiles and begins to treat me familiarly, all too familiarly, by engaging in primitive finger-pointing gestures as if I were a child or less than a human being, as if my deafness placed me in an inferior position. Sometimes his initial response is to make a dirty gesture and grin. If I demonstrate my ability to read and write, he gets surprised and raises his eyebrows as if I were a trained circus horse that can add and subtract. If we get to know each other better, he usually accords me the respect that was missing at first. But that takes time. Until then, I dread first encounters.

But here and now, on the quay, after the gunman's smile, at least I was no longer in danger of being fired at again. He tucked his revolver into his belt. Although I could not hear his questions I could easily guess that he wanted to know who I was. So many times in my life since then it has been absurdly easy to guess from the initial expression on their faces what others wanted of me even though I could not lip-read them. All I had to do was to stay alert, as for example in a diner when the man sitting at the counter next to me and eating a hamburger said something to me and I just knew he wanted me to hand him a bottle of ketchup which was closer to me than to him — and I was right. When I am stopped on a street and asked a question, it is just as easy to guess that I am being asked for directions. In the gunman's case, too, it was patently obvious what he was asking: he wanted to know who I was. I pulled out my photo signed by Lednicki the Wolska Street super, from a pocket and showed it to him. He looked at it and, handing it back to me, gestured to me to follow him.

So he had been shooting at me and missed, and that was why the sand at my feet had swirled, from his bullets. He was probably at the same time shouting at me to stop and identify myself, but of course I could not hear him.

Was he a poor shot or did he miss me deliberately? I shall never know. At any rate, within those fifteen minutes the silent reel of my life unwound at a dizzying speed with one cliffhanger succeeding another.

## Inside Insurgent Warsaw

Thus began a new chapter in my life. From then on until the end of the war I lived on my own, separated from my family.

I followed the gunman. We crossed the street together, and in the entranceway of the building facing the quay several other men wearing guns and rifles surrounded me, chattering at me until the gunman explained to them that I could not hear them. It was then that I noticed they were wearing white-and-red brassards, the colors of the Polish national flag, even though they wore civilian clothing instead of uniforms, mostly the gray overalls of factory workers. They were carrying handguns and rifles, and I realized what was happening. They were Polish insurgents and the uprising against the Germans had started.

The nom de guerre of the gunman was Karakul, probably because he wore a Van Dyke beard that was curly black like the wool of Karakul lambs. He was in command of a squad of insurgents occupying the river-bank building. With his manicured beard and distinguished good looks he stood out among the average Poles and, in retrospect, I wonder how was it that he had not been previously caught in the nearly daily roundups for forced labor in Germany, but then Warsaw was a big city that abounded in mysteries.

Now I understood why I had seen a man carrying a paper-wrapped rifle earlier that day and why the streets looked so empty and the bridge across the Vistula, not so long ago crowded with retreating German troops, was so deserted. It was the day the Warsaw Uprising of 1944 began, August 1. The Poles had thought it would be a sure thing to liberate the city now that the Red Army was approaching it from the east. Of course, they were wrong and the Red Army would not cooperate, but that is another story. Warsaw was not Paris, where an uprising also broke out in the same month, and the Red Army was not as cooperative as the Americans in helping to clear the city of Germans.

I wanted to go home but could not. Street battles raged around me. From where I took shelter in a courtyard I saw the insurgents running, crouching and firing past me in the direction of the bridge. Smoke was rising from buildings in the neighborhood. I was stuck and could not go home to be with my family.

As it turned out, the Germans were bent on reconquering the river-bank to establish communication with Praga on the other bank of the Vistula and to resume and protect the withdrawal of their troops westward across the nearby Kierbedzia Bridge and through the city. They brought up artillery and began to bombard the quay. Their shells struck also the apartment building which Karakul and his men were defending and set fire to it. A line of tenants and insurgents passed pails with water to quench the fire started on the roof by an incendiary shell and I joined that line, doing my bit. Nobody asked me to, but when I saw them working together in harmony, I felt I should help them out.

For the first time in my life I took part in a cooperative endeavor, if the games I had played with other children in the ghetto are not considered, after having lived in enforced isolation for years. Strike that! It was not the first time, as before the war, in first grade at my elementary school I remember taking part in a kind of choreographed physical exercise. We little kiddies were standing in a large hall, facing a podium on which stood mock-ups of an anchor, a life-belt, and a three-masted schooner. In tune with the teacher, we were singing a ditty that sounded like this: *"Goodbye land, ahoy sea!/ We brave sailors be!/ We fear no squalls or gales/ Anchors aweigh! Hoist the sails! /Our ship sails on the ocean sea."*

While singing, I turned left and right with arms akimbo and then pulled at imaginary ropes as if to raise the anchor and then to hoist imaginary sails, copying the movements of the teacher standing on the stage. I was aware that dozens of other children were also making the same movements in unison and I was just one element of a choreographic ballet. This memory stayed with me and, I suppose, prompted me to engage years later in another cooperative effort, that of passing pails filled with water from one person to another, in a chain of people attempting to save a building from burning in Warsaw.

It was hard work receiving the bucket with water, hefting it and passing it on to the next person one step higher while at the same time handing down an empty bucket, but I persisted at it until the fire was completely put out. Evidently this burnished my image among the tenants as not just a dumb deafmute and they accepted me as one of them. After we had put out the fire the others smiled and clapped me on the shoulder approvingly. One woman even invited me to her apartment to share a meal with her and two children. Those whitish cubes of meat she served me looked and tasted funny, and only later I realized that they were horsemeat.

But over the next few days the resistance put up by Karakul's fighters proved not enough. They only had rifles and revolvers against the Germans' cannon, automatic weapons and machine guns and artillery. The Germans were determined to seize control of the riverbank and shelled it with growing ferocity, igniting one fire after another until they could no longer be put out and Karakul's men could no longer defend the building I was in. Karakul himself was killed and the remainder of his platoon retreated to City Center, along with the tenants and me.

Instead of seizing the city, in face of intensifying German aggressiveness the insurgents yielded up one position after another and became gradually penned up within several enclaves. City Center, the downtown area of Warsaw, was the largest such enclave and the last to hold out. There, life was for me a succession of narrow escapes from buildings devastated by the "mooing cows," as the Poles nicknamed the German mortar shells because of the peculiar bellowing noise they made as they flew through the air. I learned that nickname from the underground newspapers now published openly by the insurgents, though they were mostly no bigger than in the past, about the size of letter pages, owing to shortages of newsprint. So that was the name of the weapons that were causing all that fire and smoke and those explosions — things I could see but not hear. I suppose that, day and night, the fighting in Warsaw was accompanied by tremendous noises such as the thunder of artillery shells and the explosions of bombs and grenades, but that was all unknown to me. Since I was deaf, I saw only the visible consequences of that fighting — the mounds of rubble on the sidewalks and in the courtyards, the ruins of collapsed buildings, and the occasional sights of people crossing a street at a run, bent over to avoid bullets.

I also learned from these newspapers that the Poles had liberated dozens or hundreds of Hungarian and Greek Jews from prisons in the city in which they had been held when not forced to loot for the Germans whatever of value was still left in the ruins of the ghetto.

What I did not know at the time was that the insurgents viewed those liberated Hungarian and Greek Jews as undesirables and forced them to perform non-combat tasks such as fighting fires and rescuing people from ruins. Damned if you do and damned if you don't — for this led to complaints that the Jews were given cushy jobs. But I did not know this at the time, and I was tempted to join them and start living openly as a Jew. Still, I held back and kept to myself. So long as I pretended to be what I was not, I was accepted as "one of us," a Polish boy among Poles whose only special feature was his deafness. But how would they react if they learned I was Jewish? The memory of that visit to the grocery store in Kielce, of the frosty, disapproving expressions on the faces of those Gorgons in head kerchiefs haunted me. In my imagination, their faces turned into those of hideous, demonic monsters. I could not risk exposing myself and facing those chilly, prim stares again, the stare directed at an undesirable alien. It was a stare of rejection, yet I did not feel rejected. On the contrary, having seen them with a boy's clear-eyed gaze for what they were — provincial, prejudiced, and ignorant old women — I felt like it was I who was rejecting them. That was my gut feeling.

Then one day I saw a newspaper announcing that the surviving War-saw Ghetto fighters had formed their own combat detachment. They were not strangers like those Hungarian and Greek Jews. It was only then, from that newspaper, that I became fully aware of the enormity of the ghetto's tragedy and of the heroism of Jewish fighters more than a year previously. These surviving fighters were my own people, unlike the Greeks and Hun-garians, and with them I would feel free to finally relieve myself of the burden of my secret and admit publicly who I really was. I yearned to join them, but they were fighting in another Warsaw enclave, the Old City, which was separated from City Center by a German corridor. Just as well, since soon afterward the Germans burst into the Old City and killed every fighter they saw except a few who made their way to City Center by sewage canals.

That was in August. I was tempted to look for the Jewish fighters and join them but a strange inertia held me back. That was fortunate because after the war I learned that a squad of the more anti–Semitic insur-gents from the Chrobry battalion massacred the Jews they found. The Jews had emerged from a well-hidden bunker and thought themselves finally safe now that this part of Warsaw was in the hands of the insurrectionists. They were asked what weapons they had, where had they been hiding, and how many were there. The Jews stupidly were happy to answer these ques-tions. The insurgents then exclaimed, "Death to the fucking Hebes!" They shot the Jews and, declaring that there was no place for Jews in liberated Poland, entered the bunker and robbed, raped, and killed the Jewish women. I was lucky then, after all, not to reveal my true identity.

But of course the picture was not uniform as elsewhere the Poles wel-comed the Jews who had emerged and treated them with respect. All the same, I suppose I was right to keep my identity secret.

My family's home at 6 Wolska Street was only a few street blocks away, but I could not reach it owing to the barricades manned by insurgents and the street battles going on. I wandered through City Center like a stray dog, attaching myself to various people and places.

Most of the time I lived in one empty apartment or crowded cellar after another and scavenged what food I could find. I particularly remem-ber one evening when I joined a group of insurgents and civilians in loot-ing a big food store called Julius Meinl that used to sell to Germans only. It was one of a chain of stores from Vienna, and before the uprising it was out of bounds to Poles. We appropriated bags of flour and sugar that were still there after the first comers had taken their pick of the better foods, and I helped carry them to the storeroom of a nearby platoon of insurgents.

In the daytime the insurgents and civilians ran from block to block while crouching to avoid sniper fire. I too wandered from one building to another, always in search of food and shelter. Because of the shelling, I mostly took the underground route through exits hacked into the walls of adjoining basements. The Germans were methodically razing and setting fire with incendiary bombs to one building after another in Aryan Warsaw, just as they did to the ghetto a year ago. It was then that I saw a memorable sight. I had seen dead bodies before, in the ghetto, but there they were covered with paper. Now the body I saw had been crushed by falling blocks of masonry. As I clambered over them I could distinctly see the corpse's exposed, whitish rib cage and red muscles. There was a sickening sweetish smell around it and I quickly moved past it to the next building entrance.

The commander of the platoon to which I helped deliver bags of food from Julius Meinl's, a Pan Szaniawski, saw how helpful I was and kept me on as a kind of sentry. I was ordered to stand guard outside the door to the platoon common room. Most of the time I had enough food, although sometimes I feasted on just one kind of food, as for example, when I found a store of bottles of ketchup and lived off them for a while, sharing them with a couple of teenage girls, scavengers like myself. I must have been a late bloomer sexually because I felt nothing for them other than a mild friendship. At fourteen I suppose I was still too young to experience a sex urge. It did not help that they were so obviously slovenly and plain-looking as to lack sex appeal. Still, it felt good to be in their company after years of not knowing any girls.

I slept in one big room housing the platoon I was attached to. In the daytime I would search abandoned and bombed-out apartments for food. Once I found a hidden gallon-sized jug of fermented cherries and ate and drank so much of it that I became tipsy and slept like a log for ten hours.

Every day there were new sights. As I passed a courtyard I saw for the first time German soldiers taken prisoner. A dozen or so mostly middle-aged men in dirty green uniforms with torn epaulets were apathetically digging graves in a garden under the supervision of some bored Poles shouldering indolently their rifles as if they expected no resistance. To see these prisoners of war was gratifying but also startling. They looked so humbled and humble that my perspective was jarred: they looked so different from their strutting, terror-inspiring compatriots whom I feared like the devil. This image stayed with me to this day, because it was so unexpected. Was it possible that they were human beings after all, or would they revert to type and recover their brutality and arrogance if freed?

So passed August and September 1944. The insurgents were now better equipped with weapons thanks to Allied air drops and some help from the Soviets across the river who had in the meantime wrested the Praga suburb from the Germans and sent to western-bank Warsaw, across the Vistula, boxes of olive-green grenades shaped like pineapples. But that was not enough against tanks, cannon, and aircraft. Besides, while the insurgents now had more hand weapons, their food supplies were running dangerously low, for the civilian population as well. The Germans were furiously shelling and constricting City Center, the only part of Warsaw still held by the insurgents and the part of the city I was in.

As summer turned to fall, the days turned from sunny and warm to cloudy and chilly. The sky was additionally obscured by dust and smoke from shelled buildings. Food was becoming scarce. The uprising could not go on, and finally the insurgents capitulated on October 2, after two months of increasingly unequal struggle.

## I Become a Prisoner of War

The terms of capitulation posed a vital dilemma to me. The Germans would treat the insurgents as prisoners of war protected by the Geneva Convention, while the civilian population of Warsaw would be allowed to march out of the city to a hastily established transit camp in Pruszkow, a town about 15 miles southwest of Warsaw, where they were to be provided with food and medical care and then released.

I faced a mortal choice. I had steeped myself so completely into my role as a homeless Polish boy that I had almost forgotten my real identity, but now I was facing mortal danger again after two months of relative freedom. Should I join the civilians and march with them to Pruszkow or stay with the capitulating Polish troops and end up in a prisoner-of-war camp with them? Where would my chances of surviving as a pretend Pole be greater? Finally, I decided that in Pruszkow I might be discovered and killed more readily because among the Polish civilians there were some brutish and depraved people whom the war had completely demoralized. If I were in close proximity to them, they would detect me with their well-developed ability for rooting out Jews. Poles usually found it much easier to identify Jews than did Germans. One big reason was that 90 percent of Poles were Roman Catholics and had more or less Slavic facial features, that is, they were homogeneous by both religion and ethnicity. This was a country where, as late as in 1965, until the Second Vatican Council, and sometimes even later, the priests on Good Friday still preached sermons against "perfidious" Jews. A shtetl Jew stood no chance in such an environment. If, on the other hand, he was educated and assimilated, he stood out from the common folk by the gentility of his manners. This made him also automatically suspect in a country where the Germans made it their aim to exterminate the intelligentsia and leave only the proles — and to a considerable extent succeeded.

In wartime moreover, to Poles, a Jew in hiding, whether assimilated or not, when he showed himself in public, could easily be detected by his cringing manner, born out of fear, and his tendency to avoid looking others in the eye and by flinching when addressed directly and often looking over his shoulder. These Jews with their wrecked nerves resembled jittery escapees from a prison for whom a manhunt was going on, with the difference that the Jews were escapees from execution. Could I pass the "eye exam" test? Why not — after all, I did pass it daily for two years after my escape from the ghetto and ever since that traumatic confrontation in the Kielce grocery store. But even so, might not the risk of my going with the civilians to Pruszkow be too great? As a prisoner of war and staying with the Polish insurgents who on the whole were subject to military discipline and more idealistic and less corrupted by the war than the civilians, I had a somewhat better chance of not being denounced to the Germans in return for a bottle of vodka or two or three kilograms of sugar. Besides, the Germans promised to treat the surrendering insurgents as prisoners of war under the Geneva Convention. The Germans may have used lies and deceit to lure Jews to the death factories by claiming to deport them to "the East," but toward subhumans on a bit "higher" racial rung such as Poles they acted strict yet fair, "correct," as masters do toward slaves. Gambling on their psychology of such "correctness," I decided that I could trust the Germans more as a prisoner of war and opted to stay with the insurgents and go with them to a P.O.W. camp.

I joined the surrendering insurgents as they marched in a straggling column past smartly uniformed German troops. In contrast, most of us wore either dark-gray mechanics' overalls or civilian clothing, with only brassards with the red and white Polish national colors identifying us as insurgents. Some of the insurgents had, before surrendering, discarded the German helmets and parts of uniforms that they had stripped from German corpses, so as to avoid reprisals.

As we passed, we saluted the Germans and they saluted back at us, keeping up their promise to treat us as regular prisoners of war. Those of us who had surrendered with weapons stacked them on a growing pile in front of German soldiers who inspected them with interest, laughing and exclaiming. These were all sorts of weapons, from long-barreled World War I rifles to brand-new submachine guns and pistols deriving from Allied air drops. Now that I think of it, I am surprised that so many insurgents surrendered their arms so readily instead of destroying or hiding them. To be sure, they had fought bravely.

We were marched to the nearest train station and loaded into cattle cars of the "40 people or 8 horses" kind and actually packed forty to a car, unlike the Jews who would be stuffed a hundred or more to a car on their way to Treblinka. Inside, there was room for the forty of us to lie down on a floor covered with hay.

The train carried us westward into Germany. I did not know where we were going. I tried to peek out to read the names of the stations. Finally, someone told me that we were going to the Muhlberg P.O.W. camp in Saxony. When the train stopped at some small station just before the German border, the local Poles brought us bread, Polish sausage, hard-boiled eggs, fruits, and other foods. To them, we were honored heroes of the Warsaw Uprising and they worshipped us. I personally did not have the opportunity to shoot a German or even fire a gun, but I enjoyed that adulation all the same. For some reason, the German escorts did not bother to shoo these civilians away

During the stopover at that small Polish station I saw that my fellow "prisoners of war" started to write their names and Muhlberg address on scraps of paper and pass them on to the civilians through the open door of the cattle car. I imitated them, handing the scrap of paper with my feigned name, Eugeniusz Krawczyk, and the camp address, to some elderly Polish woman. This move paid off later, as I was to learn.

When we arrived at Muhlberg we were herded off the train and marched to the P.O.W. camp on a muddy road in rainy autumn weather.

On the way one of the insurgents for some reason provoked the ire of a German escort, who struck him with a rifle butt. So much for the Geneva Convention, but at least afterward we were not harassed any more by our captors.

It was still raining when the gates of the camp were opened for us to march in. Coming in the opposite direction was a Russian P.O.W. I had never seen a Russian before but I knew at once he was one. He wore a dirty yellow overcoat and sat in front of a horse-drawn cart hauling what clearly looked like a big barrel of shit. That was the kind of dirty jobs the Russian P.O.W.'s were forced to do around the camp, since the Soviet Union had not signed the Geneva Convention.

We spent the first night on roll call square shivering in the raw autumnal cold. In the still overcast morning, together with a group of total strangers I was assigned to one of the huts. On the train I had plenty to eat — sausage, bread, tomatoes — thanks to the grateful Polish civilians who honored us as heroes of the Warsaw Uprising, but here in the camp I soon began to starve. All we got for food daily was a slice of bread less than two inches thick, a pat of margarine, some tasteless dark fluid, and some watery turnip soup poured into the mess tin I had scrounged somewhere. The bread was apportioned one loaf for every eight men, and one of the older prisoners in my section of the barracks assumed the task of cutting the dark, dense brick-shaped loaf into eight equal slices for the eight of us, each with a pat of margarine. It was not enough. I was hungry before I ate that small piece of bread and hungrier after that. For the next few months I could feel, if not hear, my stomach growl — a condition in which henceforth I remained, more or less, until the end of the war.

From then on until the dawn of liberation, I rarely had a chance to satisfy my craving for food. The first time that chance arose was thanks to Dadek, Tolstoy, and a good-hearted Frenchman.

There was a fence separating the Polish P.O.W. barracks from those of the French P.O.W.'s. In the yard on the other side of the fence the Frenchmen played soccer on days when it was not raining. They looked well-fed, apparently because of the Red Cross parcels they regularly received, wore clean uniforms and — a sight novel to me — acted like they had no care in the world. They laughed, ran, leaped as if frolicking, and kicked the ball with obvious gusto. I had never before in my life seen people as relaxed as they. This was all so eye-opening to me because in the past, ever since I became aware of the world around me, I had been living in a country where people were not given to displays of vivacity and light-heartedness even in the best of times.

We too were slated to receive Red Cross food parcels, but that would come much later. The wheels of bureaucracy had to grind for a long time first.

The months I spent at the P.O.W. camp were among the most vacuous in my life. I was alone. My deafness and tender age prevented me from forming friendships in a barracks where everyone seemed to keep to himself anyhow. My days passed in sleeping, eating those meager rations, waiting for the next time they would be handed out, and idly lounging on the barracks steps when it was not raining, under continually overcast skies. Time seemed to be frozen in place. That is what limbo must be like.

Some time in November, as I was watching those gay Frenchmen kick the ball with verve while ignoring us gawkers as if we, on the other side of the fence, did not exist, I conceived an idea that paid off brilliantly. For a while, my exploit made me famous, I think, in the Polish camp. I owe that idea to Dadek, just as I owe him so much more for saving the lives of Mamusia and myself that nightmarish summer night in Czestochowa. I also owe a debt to Tolstoy and the French language.

I got a Frenchman to throw to me a loaf of bread over the fence. It was the culmination of a long chain of events. All because Dadek had an unerringly good taste in picking novels by such authors as Turgenev, Panait Istrati, Romain Rolland, and above all, Tolstoy ... and passing them on to me to read. Of course, I did not understand many nuances and some of the vocabulary in these novels, but the more I read the more I understood, though never as fully as when I reached manhood years later.

Reading was a habit I continued to indulge in after my family and I had escaped from the ghetto and lived at 6 Wolska Street, when I registered at the local Polish library and continued to borrow books for Dadek and myself. Well, as it happened, one of Dadek's books that I had read back then at Wolska was Tolstoy's *War and Peace* in Polish translation. It contained thick snatches of conversations in the original elegant and courtly French among the novel's aristocratic Russian protagonists.

In those times, in the early nineteenth century, French was the court language of the upper classes in Europe, in Russia too even though France had attacked Russia. It was a language they used not only to sound more refined but also to avoid being understood by the lower classes. To sound authentic, Tolstoy felt duty-bound to reproduce it in dialogue as needed. I do not know about the Russian original, but Polish translations of the French phrases bandied between, say, Anna Pavlova and Prince Vassily Sergeyevich were provided in the footnotes at the bottom of every pertinent page and I read and absorbed their meanings out of curiosity.

What happened next provided a practical example of Flaubert's advice to read in order to live. The result was that I filled my stomach at a time when I needed food very badly.

Here in the P.O.W. camp this was the payoff, and it could not have been more timely: Now, in the late fall of 1944, I remembered the meanings of some of these French words and wrote down in fractured French, *Donnez-moi pain. Je suis faim. Je suis sourd*, on a piece of paper wrapped around a stone that I threw over the wire fence to the French P.O.W.'s playing soccer. It fell on the ground, attracting the attention of one of the players who then glanced at me, saw my finger-pointing gestures, and picked it up. He unwrapped the message, read it, looked at me as I was pointing at my ears with my fingers to identify myself as the hungry deaf boy. He disappeared into a barracks only to reappear after a tense moment with a loaf of that brick-shaped dense camp bread which he threw to me over the fence. I could not be more surprised and waved thanks to him while the Poles on my side of the fence gaped at the whole scene. Thanks to Dadek and Tolstoy this bread from heaven finally satiated, at least for awhile, my gnawing hunger. I borrowed a knife from the guy who was responsible for cutting up the daily loaf of bread into eight slices for us eight prisoners and, after cutting a double slice for myself, I gave the rest to my seven fellow inmates to share among themselves.

That heavy, nourishing brick-like loaf of dark bread made me something of a celebrity in the eyes of my barracks mates. They got me to explain how I winged it and I showed them with pen and paper what I had written in fractured French on that scrap of paper.

The rumor about my feat spread through the Polish section of the camp, and the following day one or two guys tried to copy me by hurling petitions with a similar wording to the French soccer players across the fence and frantically pointing to their ears. But nothing came of it. Apparently the French got wise to these "deaf" guys. And when I myself tried to duplicate my feat, no Frenchman bothered to pick up the rock with the paper wrapped around it. I suppose that, after the isolated burst of generosity by one of their compatriots, the French decided that they just were not going to feed the Poles, deaf or not, all the time. Not that they were starving themselves: They regularly received Red Cross parcels which more than offset their own measly prison fare.

But one of them did share his food with me once more after all, at Christmas time.

For Christmas, the camp authorities let the French prisoners invite the Poles and share their Red Cross food parcels with them. Each Pole was assigned to a different Frenchman. For some reason, I remember my Frenchman's name, Yves de Gall, to this day. We found it difficult to communicate since my French acquired from Tolstoy was just not good enough. He offered me some canned meat, which I chomped down greedily. Then he offered me a small plate of beans in tomato sauce. That was something I had never tasted before and it looked and smelled so different and mouth-watering. I desired it very much, yet I declined it shyly. What came next was frustrating: he did not offer it to me again, to my immense disappointment. The Polish culture I had grown up in considered it polite to first decline an offer once or twice and then let oneself be cajoled into accepting it, but the Frenchman evidently was not familiar with this custom and took back that dish, just like that, without offering it to me again. I felt so frustrated and was still hungry. So much for the oriental intricacy of my Polish good manners. This first direct encounter with the straightforward West was a rude jolt to me.

## My Life Among the Punks

Then it was back to the monotony of doing nothing and subsisting on scanty prison fare as day after dreary day passed. I made no friends in my barracks, where I was anyhow the only boy among adults, and stayed by myself. But it did not last long. The powers that be decided that all insurgents less than sixteen years old were only partly real prisoners of war and could be utilized as civilian laborers. At fourteen, I was in that category and was selected, whether I wanted it or not.

Thus it happened that soon after the Christmas party I was thrown in with a pack of street urchins.

I was escorted from the camp to the train station together with nearly fifty other boys twelve to fifteen years old. I had not seen them before, the camp was so big. So there were that many kids among the Warsaw insurgents. This was not what I expected. Willy-nilly, I was forced to abandon the relative obscurity and safety of life in a huge P.O.W. camp for joining a group of snickering teens whose impudent stares presaged a seemingly quick end to my anonymity.

At the train station I saw an unforgettable sight: a pair of obviously English prisoners of war under escort, wearing brand-new khaki uniforms and carrying tennis rackets and ambling casually, as if they owned the world. In comparison, the middle-aged German soldier escorting them, with a rifle slung over his shoulder, looked more like their batman than their guard. They were about to board a passenger train while we, Polish P.O.W.s, were waiting to be transported in cattle cars. Accustomed as I was to the grimness of people and life in Poland, to me this was another revelation. Like the lighthearted French, these Englishmen seemed superior beings from another world, the Western world, where civility and easy manners reigned supreme. They were treated with respect and circumspection even by the Germans. Moreover, they were playing tennis, that aristocratic game, despite being prisoner. What a contrast to the Poles, whom the Germans treated like dirt! But there were further gradations: in the Muhlberg camp I saw how the Germans treated Soviet prisoners of war even worse than the Poles, made them do the dirtiest menial work and even transport barrels full of excrement.

At the train station I noticed that our group was escorted by not only the German guards but also an adult Polish corporal, Kasprowicz, assigned to supervise us boys by the senior officer in charge of the Polish prisoners of war at the Muhlberg camp, probably because he used to be a teacher in peacetime, as I found out later. The train ride did not last long. After all, Muhlberg in Saxony was not so far from our destination, Brockwitz bei Meissen.

When we arrived in Brockwitz we were marched to a nearby factory and there housed in one large barracks room crammed with twin bunk beds equipped with a straw mattress, a hard pillow, and one blanket each, nothing more. I occupied one such bed and instantly fell asleep. In the morning I had a rude awakening. Somebody smacked my bottom hard. When I opened my bleary eyes, I saw it was Corporal Kasprowicz. All the others were already awake and dressing as I scrambled down from my bunk. The corporal was saying something angrily and pointing at my shoes. It turned out Kasprowicz was punishing me for sleeping in my shoes, a habit I had picked up during the uprising, both out of not knowing better and in order to protect them from being stolen.

From then on in the mornings we were awakened at five, given one hour to wash up and eat the skimpy breakfast of a thin slice of black bread with a pat of margarine, and marched off to work in the factory, which proved to be a secret fighter aircraft plant.

Our work consisted in drilling rivets into airplane fuselages, from six in the morning till six in the evening, with a brief half-hour break at noon. I don't recall if we got anything to eat at noon but I remember passing the factory canteen and peeking longingly through the windows at the German clerks and workers eating their lunch there. In the evening we were taken back to the barrack room and fed a slice of bread and the usual watery soup. Then the door was locked until next morning.

From then on this was the same routine, work six o'clock till six o'clock, six days a week, with Sunday free. Our status was vague, half prisoner of war and half civilian laborer. At any rate we were going to receive Red Cross parcels and clean uniforms as prisoners of war, but that was for the present a distant prospect. In the meantime we were given scanty fare which made us perpetually hungry, the usual monotonous black bread with a pat of margarine. As civilian laborers, we were paid a miserly wage of five or six marks a week. On Sundays we received white bread rolls with a slice of sausage instead of the usual black bread and were free to wander outside into the town of Brockwitz. However, we could not buy anything there with those marks, other than some acid and foul-tasting pickled beet salad, since we had no ration books.

One day soon after my arrival I developed stomach pains. I got no medical attention, but Lutens, the German supervisor, decided to assign me to the physically less demanding job of stoking the furnace in the factory's office building. I was to serve as an assistant to the Polish stoker, a doddering oldster who shuffled rather than walked, with his back bent. He avoided looking at me. For a deaf person like me, eye-to-eye communication was necessary, but I could not achieve that with him as he always kept his head down. Besides, drool kept dripping from his half-open lips and that too made me think that he was partly senile. On his chest he wore a big, purple square patch with "P" on it, branding him a Pole, a civilian forced laborer.

My job itself was a big improvement over drilling airplane rivets. All I had to do was to shovel coal into the furnace now and then and just relax in the intervals. The furnace room was warm, a big plus in the wintry weather, and I got some extra food to keep me from starving because the old man always brought with him a jam sandwich for lunch and passively shared it with me, passively because I simply took it away from him and broke it in half, one half for him and one for me, and the addled guy accepted my decision silently.

I also benefited in other ways. It was warm inside in the winter. Trash from the offices upstairs was brought to the furnace room and it contained cigarette butts. I traded the butts to other guys for food when I did not smoke them myself.

This warm and cushy job was too good to last. A week or so afterward, I happened to leave the furnace room and walk toward the corner bulletin board. As I was standing in front of it, reading the notices, an old German with a face frozen into a mask of dyspeptic disdain like that of a grim tomcat emerged from nowhere and faced me. This was not the first time: people have a habit of unexpectedly appearing in my field of vision. That is because I cannot hear them talking to me or walking toward me behind my back. This old German started to berate me angrily. I did not know what it was all about until he slapped me hard and I grasped from his gestures that I was not supposed to keep my hands in my pockets: that was a flagrant offense here, where everyone was supposed to work hard for the war effort, and slackers were punished. What was I doing there, reading the notices on the board while everyone else was working? Actually, for the first time in months I was indulging my craving for reading matter, even if it was only some notices about factory regulations, blackout hours, and things like that.

The old man kept screaming at me and then Bauer, another German supervisor, a colleague of Lutens, showed up and pushed me down so that I fell in the gutter. Next thing I knew, when I raised my head from my supine position, he was pointing a revolver at me.

That was the second time I faced a gun aimed at me, after the incident with Lieutenant Karakul. I lay on the cold pavement, looking at the black muzzle of Bauer's revolver and at his cold blue eyes, but I felt no fear. I had already witnessed so many unusual sights in my brief life so far that this was just one more occurrence. My only sensations were the icy cold of the pavement seeping into my body and the equally icy cold of Bauer's blue eyes. His mouth did not move — he said nothing as he knew I was deaf.

He stared thus at me but did not fire, after all. He slapped me, straightened up, put his gun back into its holster, and left. All that happened afterward was that I got fired from my furnace-room sinecure and was sent back to drilling rivets with the other boys.

The insurgents in the Warsaw Uprising all used *noms de guerre* because before the uprising they had belonged to the Polish underground army. The boys in my barracks room had copied them in adopting fanciful pseudonyms, mostly referring to beasts of prey, such as vulture, fox, panther, and so on, although they were too young to have taken part in the fighting and at most some served the insurgents as messengers and lookouts during the uprising. Following the fashion, I too adopted a pseudonym, *Zbik*, or Wildcat, though the other boys after awhile nicknamed me Ebe, an onomatopoeic sound that apparently mimicked my funny unaccented babbling deaf speech. It seems that without knowing it they thus also voiced the initial letters of my name, Eugeniusz Bergman.

As time went on, the other boys became to me distinct presences. For the most part they turned out to be youthful hoodlums, homeless orphans who had turned to street crime, as I could already from the outset see for myself from their crude looks and manners. Several, however, stood out radically. Mainly, there was Panienka, or Missy, a boy so nicknamed because of his shy, sweet smile, whose good manners stood out against the background of all these young hooligans. They sensed that he was someone superior to them and some better instinct moved them to treat him with deference. Then there were the Vulture and the Hammer, an inseparable pair sleeping in the same twin bunks, one above and one below. There was something strange about their relationship, with Hammer seeming subservient to Vulture. They kept to themselves as if they were made of a different metal. Subsequent events showed that they were made of the same base metal. The Vulture had a face that, young as it was, looked both delicate and depraved. The Hammer, a boy with the build of a nightclub bouncer and the face of a bulldog, acted as his sidekick and followed him everywhere.

Among those few others who stood out against that background of lower depths there was most prominently a boy with the nom de guerre Miki-Bandyta, for Mickey Mouse the Bandit, as he spiritedly called himself, and he could not have been more different from the others. In another setting, such as a family festivity or a picnic, he would be seen for what he really was — a lively and charming boy with a vivacious mien, sparkling black eyes and a shock of thick black hair. He had a much less conspicuous brother, Sly (Cwaniak), his sidekick, a boy with a crooked smile, who said little and was polite to a fault — also a big mistake so far as the Polish street toughs were concerned. They smelled weakness and pounced on the hapless brothers.

As I recall it, I first became aware of the two brothers on New Year's Eve when Miki and Sly organized a skit for us boys. Unfortunately I could not hear the brothers' dialogue, but it seemed funny and they were laughing a lot. However, their audience of juvenile offenders did not seem to find them funny. Most of them did not crack a smile. It seems that their sense of humor was limited to copulating slang and potty jokes. Because his vivacity stood out so much among these morose urchins, Miki and by extension his brother Sly were also the first Jews to be discovered and hassled in our group. Sly's pickle face did not help either — he was so recognizably Jewish with his crooked little grin. It did not take long for the brothers to have their Jewish origin discovered. Another detail that made them suspect was that they shied from getting involved in fights and arguments. The end was not long in coming.

One evening, after everybody came back from work and the hall doors were locked as usual, keeping us penned in till the morning, the guys were bored as usual and needed a diversion. Miki and Sly were commanded to let down their pants and reveal their circumcised penises to bursts of laugher among the onlookers. I stood among the crowd, a tight little smile on my face as if I too enjoyed the spectacle. Fortunately, because I was deaf, I was not expected to join the others in shouting anti–Semitic comments. That was it. From then on the brothers were pariahs. Afterward, Miki's brightness soon faded and his manner became ingratiating, even wheedling, as if he were begging to be spared.

Soon now they were perforce joined by a third boy, Lynx, who had the most Semitic features of them all. With a face like that it was a miracle that he had not been discovered and caught earlier. But there he was. I was never able to discover how Lynx had survived well into the year 1944 despite his strong Semitic looks. He even still looked and acted innocent, as if he had never before suffered any privations and strayed only yesterday from a warm and normal family home only to land in this snake pit. It was as if he had dropped from another planet. Even his pseudonym, Lynx, did not fit him; he should have been called Rabbit. When addressed, he trembled and looked as if he were going to cry, which only whetted the natural cruelty of the other boys, who enjoyed tormenting him most.

Since we were locked up in our barracks each evening, the toughs had nothing to do before lights out at nine. They devised a game to play in the evenings. They would require Miki, Sly, and Lynx to stand on a table. One or another of the boys would laughingly pound the table with a hammer, making as if they were going to strike the toes of the Jewish boys, who would then jump up and down, and demanding of them that they exclaim, "I'm a stinking kike!" "I'm a mangy Jew," and so on, so on, which they did, cowed and pale, and, in Lynx's case, with quivering lips and tearfully as well.

The Poles particularly enjoyed tormenting Lynx because he cried so easily, which only whetted their enjoyment. Miki and Sly never cried; they were tougher. Except that Miki in particular lost his former dash and cheerfulness. His light had dimmed like that of a guttering candle and he became markedly apathetic. Like certain animals that adopt a protective coloration, he retreated into himself and tried to be as self-effacing as possible. This was not Three Crosses Square where he had wheeled and dealed with German soldiers and, together with other members of his gang, engaged in fisticuffs with Polish boys on the rare occasions when they tried to invade his turf.

Three Crosses Square was a German enclave in the heart of Warsaw. Around it stood a hostel for German soldiers and a cinema and bars that were off limits to Poles. After their escape from the burning ghetto in the spring and summer of 1943, Miki and Sly together with a few other surviving Jewish children gravitated to that square because Poles naturally avoided that neighborhood and Germans were much less likely to tell the difference between Jewish and Polish ragamuffins.

In the ghetto these kids, gaunt, ragged, wearing flat cloth caps that were too big for their little faces, had been the sole providers for their families. They would penetrate the wall by snaking their way through rain gutters if they were small enough or by removing loose bricks or in other ways known only to them, and, once on the other side, beg passersby for food that would save their families from starvation. Those children who were caught by the Germans would be shot on the spot or, while wriggling through an opening in the wall, brutally whacked with a rifle butt on their backs so as to break their spines. Those who survived, some of them little tykes, brought home a loaf of bread and some carrots or potatoes, without which their parents and siblings would have died of hunger. Some even survived the destruction of the ghetto, in particular Miki and Sly, and became marooned on the Aryan side after their families were killed and the ghetto demolished.

"Killed" is such a bland, neutral verb. It conceals so many imaginative — to a killer — ways in which a person can be deprived of his life in the ghetto after first being made to suffer: by being thrown from a window, by being suffocated in a cattle car, by being gassed. But here I must stop. It is unbearable to continue this litany.

To return to Miki and Sly, after the uprising was put down and the ghetto obliterated, they could not return to their homes and so they stayed in Aryan Warsaw. There, they earned a bare kind of living by begging and singing popular Polish songs in the courtyards and picking up coins wrapped in paper that their listeners threw to them from the windows. At the time there also existed many homeless Polish children in Warsaw. Some of them later turned up in our barracks at the factory in Brockwitz, so that Miki and Sly, or Pavel and Zenek, escaped notice. What also saved the brothers was their discovery of Three Crosses Square, where they were able to support themselves in relative safety by selling cigarettes to German soldiers. There, one after another, they were joined by other Jewish children, mostly boys but also a couple of girls, who had gravitated to that German neighborhood because it was ironically enough safer for them than Polish neighborhoods.

One of the busiest places in Warsaw, that square, more like a traffic circle than a square, was also the site of the city's school for the deaf, or rather as it was called anachronically, the Institute of the Deaf and Dumb, as I learned much later. In those times, most of the buildings around it served as rest homes, hostels, or bars reserved for German soldiers. There was also a nearby gendarmerie post and a cinema frequented by Germans. For these reasons, Poles used to avoid that neighborhood.

Thus it was that these Jewish children survived and even disported themselves under the very noses of the Germans, who were not as likely as the Poles to sniff them out. At night, some of the children stayed with Granny, an old Polish woman with a retarded daughter, who let them sleep in the attic, among lumber and rags, for a few zlotys, while others slept in deserted tool sheds on garden allotments. In the daytime on Three Crosses Square, that lair of the beast, the Jewish kids lived in an environment that was fairly free of fear, after they had fought off attacks by gangs of Polish boys, and this encouraged their enterprising instincts. They gradually lost their haunted looks, regained normal weight, acquired neater clothes, and even became cocky — an attitude extremely rare for a Jewish child in those days. In that enclave, Miki was king of the hill. A bundle of energy, he was always hurrying this way and that on some secret errands in his military-style greatcoat with the folds flapping in the wind that was too big for him, but he always kept within the bounds of the square. He would stop passing German soldiers and use his patter to make them laugh and buy cigarettes from him or get them to let him polish their boots for a tip. He transgressed the rules of survival because he stood out from the crowd by having such a bouncy personality, yet he lucked out by living in what proved to be just the perfect environment for him — Three Crosses Square. There, inside the German enclave, he was safe from Polish blackmailers, As for the Germans, they could not tell a Jew from a Pole unless he had that extremely rare Arafat-style "Number 6" nose.

The charmed life led by these children ended when the Polish Uprising of August 1944 scattered them in all directions. And after the insurgents surrendered in October, Miki and Sly had decided, like me, to seek safety in a P.O.W. camp rather than in Pruszkow. Now, like I, they were no longer sure if it was a wise decision.

This life in the factory barracks with Polish street children was a different situation. There Miki's vivacity only earned him slaps and kicks instead of laughter and admiration. Soon, he grew to resemble Sly and Lynx, burying himself in a hollow, trying to become as unnoticed as possible, a bird of plumage that turned into a gray sparrow.

This abuse of the Jewish kids went on. One evening Corporal Kasprowicz summoned all the boys, got them to stand around him in a semicircle and spoke to them about Polish honor and the need to respect Polish citizens of different ethnic and religious backgrounds.

How did I know the nature of his speech without being able to hear it? It was simple to guess from his solemn face.

The Polish boys stood politely and heard him out, but after he finished they went back to their games of tormenting the Jewish boys. That was the only time Kasprowicz tried to assert his authority, other than when he had slapped me on the bottom. Afterward, seeing that his speech had no effect on these youthful hoodlums, he just threw up his hands and simply disappeared. I could never figure how he did that, but I now understand that his superior officers at the Muhlberg camp recalled him.

The Polish boys kept hassling the Jews as if nothing had happened. That was bad enough, but then an unbelievable act of betrayal happened: one or more of the Poles, I will never know who, denounced us as Jews to the German overseer, Lutens. But an even more unbelievable thing happened: For some strange reason or owing to his lack of customary German fanaticism, Lutens did not rush to the Gestapo with that information. Instead, he summoned all the boys and, after asking them to stick together, appealed to the Poles for solidarity with their Jewish comrades, chastised them for their behavior toward the Jews and even threatened to punish them if they kept harassing us. In my singular situation, given that I was deaf, I had not even known that we Jewish boys were denounced by the Polish boys and that Lutens protected us. That was one of those things that I, a deaf boy, could never have figured out for myself. This was very hard to believe: a German protecting Jews openly in Hitler's Germany, but it really happened as I learned after the war from reading the book by Joseph Ziemian, *The Cigarette Sellers of Three Crosses Square*, about the singular adventures of Miki and Sly and others of their group in that square, which mentioned this incident. So that was a danger I had avoided without even knowing about it until after the war.

I was the last Jewish boy to be discovered. It took the other guys much longer, about two months, to find out who I was. I owed this delay to the experience I had gained in acting "normal" and even cocky in my two years in Aryan Warsaw. I did not cringe or act submissive like Miki, Sly, and Lynx, whose behavior only encouraged their tormentor. When the Poles tormented them, I just looked on, not laughing openly like the others but feigning a tight little smile, keeping a poker face, and I remained undetected until March.

Another hazard I faced and overcame, again and again, was participating in the communal shower. On such occasions I acted unconcerned. Since I showed no fear and acted like one of the boys, scrubbing myself openly with the rough wartime soap that produced hardly any suds and taking care not to cover my penis with a hand, no one bothered to take a closer look at it. The other boys were too busy chatting and laughing and the shower room was besides steamy and poorly lighted. That too helped me escape scrutiny.

What also helped delay my becoming detected was a food parcel I had received from Poland sometime in February. It was sent to me care of the Muhlberg P.O.W. camp by that Polish woman whom I had given my name and Muhlberg address on a scrap of paper while the train stopped just before the German border, and it was forwarded to me in Brockwitz. That was a welcome and completely unexpected surprise from a perfect stranger.

The very fact that a Polish woman sent a food parcel to me bolstered my image among the others as a Christian Pole and postponed the discovery of my true identity for a few weeks more.

Not for much longer, though: One morning, in March, on awakening, I saw a sea of grinning faces mouthing "Jew" at me. They found me out! What happened was that during the night, while I was in deep sleep, one guy simply raised the blanket and pulled down my pants to see if my penis was circumcised or not. They guffawed derisively and shouted in my ear to make sure I was feigning not only Polishness but deafness. Since I did not react to what is a painful sensation for hearing people, they had to believe I was deaf. But from then on I had to join the pariahs, the other Jewish boys.

Being German and the supervisor, Lutens had more clout than Kasprowicz and apparently his little speech, or at least his threat of punishment, proved more effective, up to a point, not that I was aware of it at the time. Intimidated, the Polish boys made no further attempt to denounce us. They also stopped harassing us actively. Instead, they turned us Jewish boys into outcasts, as we realized most painfully one Sunday when a Catholic priest arrived to celebrate the mass. The boys lined up in two rows facing each other in front of him as he was going to put communion wafers into mouths. The four of us Jewish boys also joined them out of the automatic tendency to act like the Christian Poles and so remain undetected, but we were rudely shoved away. The priest acted as if he had not seen it, but he did, all right. We Jewish boys were pariahs. Our status was reduced to that of the slaves of slaves. We became the objects of chicanery. When it was time to queue up for our eighth of a loaf of bread, the others motioned to us to move to the end of the line. That was where we were expected to stay from then on. We received the thinnest slices and only half a pat of margarine each. We had to do little chores for the Polish boys like pulling off and cleaning their boots and shoes and endure occasional nose flicks and slaps.

Sometime at the end of February we all received our first and last Red Cross parcels. I do not know why, but some of us received British parcels and others American. They both contained powdered milk, cheese, crackers, canned meat, and cigarettes but the British parcel, while of the same size, had more exotic contents, such as cocoa powder and canned herring, probably reflecting the influence of an empire that then spanned the globe. We all also received from the Red Cross khaki uniforms without insignia. That was the first clean clothing we had since last October and we donned it with relish, replacing the tattered and lice-ridden garments we wore.

Miki and Sly survived the war, and I met them again in a displaced persons camp in Zeilsheim, Germany, in 1947. They were just about to leave in a truck on their then illegal journey to the future Israel when they noticed me. While in that barracks in Brockwitz, strangely enough we never talked with each other. It was as if we studiously ignored each other in the belief that if we were seen together the other boys would torment us more, and apparently the two brothers had thought the same way. Now, in Zeilsheim, I was surprised and pleased when they hugged me and shook hands with me before hurrying to climb onto the truck. I never saw them again and did not even know they were leaving for what was then called Palestine until I read Joseph Ziemian's book.

When my Jewish identity was discovered I was fatalistic about it all. All right, so that was my fate and I had to endure it. I would have been discovered sooner or later anyhow. This torpid mood enveloped me ever since I saw the boys torment Miki, Sly, and Lynx. Still, there was one thing that hurt and outraged me: Maciek's reaction. Maciek was the boy who slept on the bunk below me. When I received my food parcel from that Polish woman, I shared some of it with him. I needed a buddy after being friendless for so long. With Bronek not here anymore, I also needed a hearing friend who could be a lifeline to get out of my isolation as the only deaf boy there.

Before the parcel arrived I hardly ever exchanged a word with Maciek. He was a loner like me, but he was so by nature while my deafness turned me into a loner against my will. He was the kind of person who could not have any close friends if only because of his looks. He had a hollow-cheeked face that made him look perpetually hungry and his pouty lips were frozen in a sour grimace which discouraged others from talking to him. He was habitually taciturn and his movements were deliberate and slow, like those of an old man although he could not have been more than sixteen. His cheeks were hollow and his lips pouting yet tight so that he looked both hungry and dour. Even after I shared with him the tea and rusks I received in that parcel, his attitude toward me, as toward everyone else, hardly changed, but at least he nodded at me in the morning when we got up. That alone made me feel less isolated.

What attracted me to him in the first place was his very lack of emotion, which distinguished him from the other teenagers in the barracks, who were mostly hyperactive bullies. In short, he seemed a reliable person. Well, I could not have been more wrong. When he learned I was Jewish he turned cold toward me, showing no gratitude for the food I had shared with him. He no longer nodded at me, and acted as if I did not exist even though we slept in the same twin bunk beds, I above and he below. I felt betrayed. His dour, pinched looks, the looks of a rat, should have warned me not to trust him but at the time I felt such a need for a friend that I ignored the warning written on his face. He who seemed to be one of those strong, silent persons of whom it can be said that still waters run deep, in whom feelings are too rich and varied to come to the surface, proved to be the opposite: silent, yes, but cold, shallow, and weaselly.

Now I had no friend in the world around me. I hunkered down even more, hibernating spiritually like my fellow Jewish boys, and just ignored with a bland face the slights and maltreatment by the Polish boys.

After the shock I had experienced at Maciek's betrayal I felt more utterly alone than ever. I was sinking into apathy. Then a confrontation with Vulture and his pals faced me with a challenge that brought a rush of new blood to me and shook me alive.

How it happened: now and then, when not tormenting Miki and Sly and Lynx, the Poles had their special sport with me too, especially Vulture, he with the face of a depraved angel. One day he and others questioned me to find out what was my real Jewish surname, Bergman. They slapped me. Vulture struck me in the face with his fist so that I fell down, and then they kicked me but I kept mum while shielding my head with my hands. They had their sport with me but afterward, after Lutens's little speech, they on the whole stopped kicking me and just reduced me to the status of another pariah.

Funny thing, but even if I had told them my real name and, more even, if they had told it to the Germans, my family would have suffered no consequences. For by then, in March 1945, the Red Army had already pushed the Germans out of Poland and reached the Oder River so that they could no longer do anything to hurt my family — if it survived. In these circumstances my silence was misdirected and pointless. But I did not know that, and at the time I was resolved to endure, with my teeth clenched, every imaginable and unimaginable torment rather than to betray them by revealing my real last name.

This was a different kind of choice I was faced with. Until then I had to choose between modes of survival, as when I decided to join the insurgents in the P.O.W. camp rather than go to Pruszkow with the civilians. Now, however, my choice lay between endangering my family and facing personal extinction. This time I violated my own survival instinct and to protect my family I refused to tell my tormentors my real name, even if it meant losing my own life.

I had never faced this choice before. What motivated my decision was also, I realize now, the deep shame I felt then, and the embarrassment I still feel to this day, about my nervous breakdown that night in Czestochowa when I sobbed so loudly that the German sentry shone his flashlight at me. He could have shot Mamusia and me then but he did not. And afterward, when Tatus and Dadek rescued us and brought us to Warsaw, no one in my family ever reproached me for my conduct and the danger it involved to my mother — and this magnanimous silence on their part precisely made me feel even more ashamed of myself. It was this memory also that unconsciously stood behind my decision to bear torture in silence rather than to betray my family.

Years later, after the war, when I finally discussed the Czestochowa incident with Bronek, he admitted how angry and bitter he felt about my brattish nervous breakdown which attracted the attention of the German sentry and almost put an end to Mamusia's and my lives, not to mention the risk to my father's and Dadek's lives as well.

Yet, even if that incident in Czestochowa had not happened, I know there was something in me, a firm resolve, that would never make me betray my family. I told my tormentors nothing. I won a moral victory, and this confrontation wakened me from my torpor and made me feel alive again.

There was an anticlimax. Nothing happened to me because of my refusal to talk. Ultimately, the Polish boys gave up trying to force me to tell them my name. In retrospect, had I told them my real name, even though that would have no longer affected my family by then, in the early spring of 1945, I would have had reason to despise myself to this very day. So it was an issue not just of self-sacrifice for the sake of my family but of self-respect. My refusal to betray my secret bolstered my spirit and helped me endure being treated as an outcast. This awareness that I won a moral victory shook me from my apathy. I therefore just stayed with my Polish name, Krawczyk, and with my pseudonym, Zbik, or Wildcat.

Among that refuse of the streets of Warsaw one Polish boy stood out. He was nicknamed Panienka, or Missy, because of his delicate, gentle face and demeanor. The other boys, those roughnecks, showed an unaccustomed deference to him; he must have impressed them by the saintliness of his personality and an obviously different social status. I took an instant liking to him but once my Jewishness was detected it precluded our getting to know each other and becoming friends. A pity. The times were wrong for forming what might have been a mutually enriching friendship. Panienka's very existence was proof that every nation harbors its share of individuals ranging from the vilest to the noblest.

## The Liberation Comes

One morning in March, not long after the boys tried in vain to force me to reveal my real name, I made a discovery that lifted up my spirits and finally inspired me with hope that this bleak existence would finally end happily. On my way to the airplane assembly hall I picked up a German newspaper that someone had abandoned in a trash can. This was the first newspaper I had the opportunity to read since last October and I greedily absorbed its contents. From it I learned that the Red Army had already conquered Poland and stood at the borders of Germany. The assurances that the German army stood firm and made strategic retreats did not fool me. Now my resolve to endure these privations became strengthened and I felt renewed hope and the first stirrings of joy.

March gave way to April and then the airplane factory stopped operating as supplies to it were cut off. Instead we were ordered to go into the surrounding woods and dig trenches under the escort of a couple of young German privates riding bicycles. The soldiers treated it as a lark and did not supervise us closely, so we did not work too hard with our shovels. One of the soldiers was so friendly as to let me ride his bicycle. I tried it but soon crashed the bicycle as I was too weak to pedal in my undernourished condition.

One morning in late April Vulture and his sidekick Hammer were missing from their twin bunk when we awakened. Somebody had scrawled a swastika on the frame of their bunk. Apparently the two boys were *Volksdeutschen*, ethnic Germans from Poland, and had thought they could ride out the end of the war by pretending to be Poles. But there was something about them that aroused the suspicions of the Polish boys. After that swastika was daubed on their bunk they took fright and decided to make themselves scarce, probably with the connivance of either Bauer or Lutens. That was how I figured it out and I felt relieved, because Vulture was particularly nasty to me, and God only knows what he would have done to me if the war had a different ending.

May came and trench digging was suspended as the Russian armies were approaching. We were confined to our barracks room. The factory was closed. One sunny morning Lutens summoned us and announced that we were free to leave, go back to Poland. He gave a speech to us, which I did not hear anyway, and distributed to each of us a loaf of bread and some sausage. He even took out a knife and demonstrated to us how to slice that loaf thinly so that we would not upset our stomachs by overeating after months of staying hungry. His unaccustomed largesse was probably dictated by the desire of the factory authorities to get rid of us before the Allies arrived so that we would not have a chance to revenge ourselves on the German bosses and vandalize the factory. But of course what mattered to us most was that we were finally free!

This was one of the guys with whom I had to live in the aircraft factory barracks. He is wearing a khaki uniform that we all received from the Red Cross as prisoners of war. The inscription on the back of the photograph reads: "To my dear Eugeniusz Krawczyk, [from] Janiszewski Zdzislaw, Brockwitz a/Mei [am Meissen], 25 February 1945. Fabrikstrasse 1, EL104." Eugeniusz Krawczyk was my assumed Polish name.

We spilled out of the factory grounds. I was walking with Lynx who had earlier caught an infection in his leg and used a stick to hobble along. At this pace we were soon left behind by other boys. When we reached the highway he needed to rest at a bus stop and I stayed with him. There was no movement on the highway until I observed a dot in the distance. The dot grew larger and larger until I could discern the figure of a soldier riding a motorcycle. As he approached I saw that he wore a khaki uniform and a red star on his forage cap. I realized that he was a Russian soldier, probably an advance scout. He stopped and exchanged a few phrases with

Lynx. His face was so expressionless that he could have been a Martian. Then he roared off into the distance. Such was the moment of my liberation.

Now that I knew for sure I was free, I was in a hurry to return to Poland and search for my family. But what to do with Lynx and his bad leg? Caring for him would slow me down.

Lynx begged me piteously to stay with him but I refused. To this day I feel somewhat guilty about leaving him in his condition. It was selfish of me but, now that I was certain I had been liberated, my urge to find my family back in Poland overrode everything else. All the same, I felt sure the approaching Soviet troops must have stopped by and given him help. And indeed, he must have survived because years later I happened to see a newspaper notice mentioning his name as a music conductor in Vienna, of all places.

The highway did not long remain empty. Soon I saw a stream of refugees again, flowing form the nearby town.

So much for the master race: These German refugees humbly and apathetically pulled or pushed handcarts and baby carriages loaded with their belongings, and some were pushing bicycles because that particular highway segment happened to be too steep to bike on.

I stepped to the next man pushing a bicycle, a refugee in his forties carrying a rucksack, and grabbed the bike away from him. He yielded it to me without resisting, his face showing no emotion. It was all done in mime without my saying a word and so ridiculously easy, perhaps because I wore my khaki uniform from the Red Cross. What gave me the guts to do it, right after I abandoned Lynx in his hour of need? Perhaps because for years I had been bullied by Germans and lately also by Poles, so now for a change I became a bully myself.

I mounted the bicycle and pedaled toward the town of Brockwitz. This time the bike did not wobble because, for once, my stomach was full and I felt strong.

In addition to my uniform, I wore a forage cap on which, copying the other boys, I sewed on a little white-and-red flag identifying me as a Pole, and this added to my newfound confidence and made me look terrifying to these German refugees. This role reversal was fun but my overriding desire was to go back to Poland and find my family.

Just when I entered the town's main street, people began to scatter to both sides of the highway, looking up. I followed their example and looked up too. A covey of fighter planes flew above us and a moment later I saw not far away plumes of smoke springing up among the town houses. The planes flew away and I pedaled into town, past flames shooting up from houses and military trucks. My road was barred by a burning army truck with bottles of liqueurs spilling from it. Several bodies sprawled nearby, including a couple of the Polish boys from my barracks who had entered the town ahead of me. They lay in pools of blood mingling with liquors spilling from shattered bottles I picked up a bottle. It was Hennessy Three Star Cognac and I dropped it. If I had been wiser I would have kept it for barter or some other purpose.

Farther on the main street I saw a barbershop that was open. On a chair I saw a newspaper that announced Hitler was dead. So that was it! Good! I was too drained of emotion to react more exuberantly. I had my hair cut for the first time in months and paid for it with the marks I had in my pocket.

On leaving the barbershop I saw a strange sight: a column of Soviet soldiers marching up the main street with rolled up blankets slung on their backs. Only they were not Russian: They were undersized and had bulging cheekbones and slanted eyes. They were Kalmucks, second-line troops from Siberia.

I saw a house with its door open. I peeked in and saw it was empty. On the table in the kitchen there were remains of an unfinished meal. I grabbed a briefcase from a chair and stuffed some bread and a can of sardines into it. As I was about to leave, one of those Kalmucks entered and tried to wrest that briefcase from me, but I resisted. There was a scuffle between us. I don't know what made me resist him. He could have struck or killed me, but all he did was to try and wrest the briefcase from me. Then an officer, a Russian, entered. I pointed to the white-and-red flag on my forage cap and said "Polska." I guess that was enough for the officer because he barked a command and the Kalmuck let me keep the briefcase and released his grip.

Outside, in the street, a few paces away, I sat down on the curb and opened the briefcase. Oh, how I relished that can of— Portuguese, it said on the label — sardines in oil, the first I ever tasted in my life, after I had opened it with my knife! I sopped up all that oil with a crust of bread too. That was a welcome change in diet after that dreary bread with margarine.

When I look back I cannot believe what I did then: In just one heady day I wrested a bicycle from a German, without any compunction, and then I engaged in a tug of war over a briefcase with a Soviet soldier and won. It is to laugh.

As I was chewing on the sardines and bread, I saw trucks carrying more troops, this time real Russians. They were an even stranger sight than the Kalmucks. I saw smiling, happy and singing young soldiers with shocks of hair under their forage caps who looked as if they had not a care in the world. They were so full of life and one of them was even playing an accordion. I breathed in, as it were, the air of a new huge continent where such people could live and grow up normally and happily. I had never before seen people with such joy of life — even though they had grown up under a dictatorship. From the vantage point of the present I wonder how was it possible for such high-spirited young people to live and grow up in a country where it was a crime to speak one's mind freely. Yet this gaiety and devil-may-care air was what I actually did witness and, as I realized later, it was a typically Russian trait. Their high spirits seemed more down-to-earth than the insouciance of those French soccer players.

I made my way toward the train station where I found a train of flatcars. On inquiry with pen and paper I found it was headed for Poland. I clambered onto one, no longer with my bicycle — I cannot remember what happened to it. All these flatcars except one were crowded with slave laborers returning to Poland. The one uncrowded flatcar, next to mine, was occupied by two people locked in an embrace on a huge king-size bed. The male of the couple was a Russian officer, still wearing his blouse with shoulderboards, and the woman whom he was embracing was young and beautiful.

In full sight of people sitting or standing on the flatcars to either side of the one with the big luxurious bed, the couple made love with a passion, naturally and without any embarrassment. I switched my gaze and it fell on a demented middle-aged woman whose whole body was convulsively twitching and who kept mechanically smoothing her hair in the back, again and again. How did she lose her sanity and end up on my flatcar and where did she come from I do not know, and I did not see anyone close to her or talking to her.

In the evening the train finally started. As it moved eastward it made frequent stops in the falling darkness. My neighbors on the flatcar were drinking vodka and eating bread with sausage. They must have been talking a lot, exchanging information and perhaps learning something valuable, but all this was lost on me. Rather than to watch and try to lip-read them — something I was and am not good at — in the gathering dusk I watched the panorama of sights from my flatcar, woods, fields, telephone poles, until, lulled by the clickety-clack of the train, felt not heard, I fell asleep in the night punctuated by clouds of sparks from the locomotive and the sooty smell of burning coal.

Another day and another night, this time already in Poland. At dawn on the third day the train stopped at a suburban station near Warsaw, last stop. It could not enter Warsaw itself because the city was so thoroughly razed.

I got off the train and walked toward downtown Warsaw. Everywhere there were heaps of ruins, with craters filled with muddy water obstructing the roadways. But, as I have always had a good sense of direction, I finally was able to reach 6 Wolska Street, the apartment building where my family and I had lived in hiding for two years after escaping from the ghetto.

I looked up and saw that the upper portion of the building above the third floor was gone, sheared off. I climbed the stairs to the surviving third floor and entered the apartment where my family and I had spent nearly two years. The door was open. There was nobody inside and the dusty rooms yawned empty of furniture. The windows were open and shattered. There was no trace of anyone in the kitchen. I finally came home but it was not home anymore. The landing below looked more normal. I descended to it and knocked on the door, next to which hung the sign, "Block Committee of the Polish Workers Party." The door was opened, but when I asked the people inside if they knew anything about my family upstairs, no one knew the answer. They all were newcomers. My last hope was dispelled. My heart sank like a stone and I started to cry. They asked me to come in and let me use the bathroom and even offered me the luxury of using their soap, towels, and bathtub. I was unused to such kindness. That was the first bathtub I used in years. I still remember how black with dirt my arms were as I soaped and scrubbed my body.

My hosts offered me something to eat, bread with dripping. Seeing that I was now homeless, they gave me a note of recommendation to someone called Comrade Victor and directed me to the headquarters of the Workers Party, which was housed in one of the few intact buildings in Warsaw. I was received by a silent, hard-faced man who called himself Comrade Wiktor. He read the note I gave him and let me stay in a small room in the building. I also was allowed to eat at the communal canteen.

Otherwise, they left me in peace as it was only the early summer of 1945 and Warsaw was just beginning to be rebuilt under the new Polish government.

Having nothing to do, my only occupation was to scan the newspapers, and it paid off. One day I found in a newspaper a mention of a Jewish Committee in Warsaw and its address. Finally, there was a place for me to go to, and perhaps they would help me find my family too. I penned a brief note to Comrade Wiktor expressing my thanks for his hospitality and admitting that I was Jewish. Then I was gone.

Next stop: Jewish Committee. I knocked at the door and it was opened just a little by a man who eyed me suspiciously. I told him I was Jewish and he opened the door wide. After I entered, he asked me to let down my pants, which I did with special relish. What a strange reversal: for years I had to be on guard lest someone might know that my penis was circumcised and denounce me, but now I was elated to display it in the knowledge that it would admit me back into the world of my people and, above all, hopefully provide a clue to finding my family.

The door guard let me to an office where a pretty girl secretary took down my vital statistics. I gave her also the names of my parents and siblings. She checked them against her index cards and — how wonderful!— found one with "Sara Salka Bergman nee Kaganowska." That was my mother. The address was in Lodz. We communicated by writing. She called me *Kochanie*, or darling. When I saw that word, tears sprang from my eyes. I must have been exceptionally sensitive to someone being kind to me after I had been living so long among neutral or hostile strangers. Crying, I told her no one had called me that for a very long time. She too was visibly moved.

I never saw her again but I still think of that defining moment when another human being showed me tenderness.

I was going to leave right away for Lodz to find my mother. But they first got me to sit at a long table together with other visitors to the committee.

They gave me beef stew and a compote, food that was inexpressibly delicious after the bland meals at the Workers Party headquarters. As a finale, they gave me money for the train from Warsaw to Lodz, and wished me luck. I don't remember anything of my train trip; it was a blur since I was so consumed with desire to see Mamusia. Once in Lodz, I went straight to the address given, knocked on the door and, when it opened, fell into Mamusia's embraces.

I shall not go into my feelings on seeing my mother again. Afterward, I asked her where were Tatus, Dadek, and Bronek. She told me she had not yet heard from Tatus and Dadek but Bronek was in Krakow, attending a Polish cadet officer school.

She was living with Mr. and Mrs. Mordkowicz, our landsmen from Poznan. They had survived by escaping from a small-town ghetto to which they had been moved from Poznan and hiding in a forest as well as in cellars under peasants' barns. Their two sons, Zalus and Boris, had survived also but not the third, Szmulek. He had always a half-smile playing on his lips, and he was shot down by a German officer who thought he was smirking. He shot him dead under the very eyes and in the presence of his father, who was so traumatized by the sight that from then on he was no longer right in the head. Zalus and Boris, both tall, strapping youths, fought as partisans in the forest while their parents were hiding in a cave dug under a cattle pen. Zalus had been the head of the Hashomer Hatzair in Poznan and the scouting skills for surviving in the wilderness he and Boris had learned there served them well while living among the trees.

Mamusia herself was almost killed in the first week of August 1944, when the Warsaw Uprising started. The Polish insurgents had maintained a headquarters in the building at 6 Wolska Street but the Germans, after the initial shock, besieged and seized it. The troops that surrounded the buildings were probably from the Dirlewanger brigade, a notorious unit of criminals and rapists, and after they summoned all the residents to come down to the courtyard they segregated the women and children, Mamusia among them and ordered them out.

What happened to my father and Dadek and Bronek? Bronek was alive and in Krakow but Mamusia was not sure where the other two were. She herself, then in her early forties, was transported along with other women to Germany for forced labor as a civilian Pole. That was where she stayed until the liberation. While in Germany, she wrote to our former maid, Zosia, in Poznan and from her she received food parcels and postcards full of sympathy that made life for her somewhat tolerable and allayed the suspicions of her fellow Polish workers about her Jewishness: since these parcels were sent to her by a Polish woman, she must be Polish.

Zosia, of course, was one of those decent Poles that could be trusted. Wonder of wonders, Mamusia showed me some of the prewar photographs of our family that Zosia had saved and returned to her after the war when my mother came to Poznan in search of a sign of life from us but found only one, from Bronek, who had stopped by and left with Zosia a message with his Krakow address. Bronek and I still treasure these photographs, the only artifacts of our past.

Her stay in Poznan upon her return from Germany convinced Mamusia that there was nothing for her there to come back to. All our Jewish friends and all our acquaintances other than Zosia had disappeared and somebody else was living in our old home. She thanked Zosia for her hospitality and left for Krakow to meet Bronek, but he was busy attending an officer school and had no news about Tatus, Dadek, and me. In search of us, she decided to move on to Lodz, which at the time was the largest gathering spot for Jews in postwar Poland. It was located in the center of the country now that Poland's borders were redrawn, and, unlike Warsaw, it was spared the devastation of war because of the overpowering speed with which the Red Army advanced. Besides, the Jewish survivors felt there was safety in numbers as a wave of anti–Jewish violence broke out in small towns and villages, only to culminate in the Kielce pogrom a year later, in 1946.

There was a Jewish committee in Lodz. In an anteroom of that committee, on the bulletin board, Mamusia located the names and address of our fellow Poznanites, the Mordkowiczes, and moved in with them at an apartment left vacant by some Germans.

Mamusia showed me a recent photograph of Bronek seated at a long table together with other cadet officers, celebrating some recent holiday. He was facing the camera and raising high a glass of wine in hand while smiling broadly, as if to say, "Look at me. Isn't life wonderful!?" in such sharp contrast to the expressionless faces and postures of the other cadets staring at the camera as if this were their last supper.

Mamusia called Bronek in Krakow about my reappearance from the unknown. He could not come to Lodz as he was bedridden with sinus trouble, something that has been plaguing him all his life, so we came to him next weekend, by train.

He was still bedridden but, boy, it was wonderful to see him again. After he recovered and we had a chance to talk alone, he revealed to me a secret that he did not want Mamusia to know. When the uprising of 1944 had erupted in Warsaw he happened to be in the Mokotow borough and was prevented by the fighting from returning home. He had fought together with a platoon all of whose members got killed. He himself escaped to the woods outside Warsaw where he joined the partisans. He

**My older brother Bronek (left) raising a toast at a banquet at the Krakow Officer School which he attended in 1945.**

never disclosed to them his Jewish identity after he saw them kill a stray Jew. After many vagaries, he found himself in Piotrkow Trybunalski, the hometown of our cousins who now were in Israel. He spent the night sleeping on the grass in a park in the company of other refugees from Warsaw. Suddenly, he saw Pan Nawrocki. The Pole was leaning against a tree and gazing lethargically into the distance. He was wearing only an undershirt and long johns and a blanket wrapped about his shoulders. They recognized each other and shook hands. Then Pan Nawrocki told Bronek that he had seen the Germans kill Tatus and Dadek. That happened in early August 1944. The building at 6 Wolska Street was the headquarters of the insurgents in the Wola Borough. When the Germans stormed the building, they started to kill every man they saw, "even mice and German civilians if those were not wearing a military uniform," as Nawrocki put it, apparently because he himself was a *Volksdeutsch*, an ethnic German, which I knew because, while still living at 6 Wolska Street, I happened to see a postcard sent to him authorizing him in German to buy some rationed delicacy set aside for such as he.

He, Nawrocki, lay down in the courtyard and pretended to be dead. From a corner of his eye he saw a couple of Germans run down the stairs leading to the cellar and a moment later reappear shoving Tatus and Dadek up the stairs. Tatus took out a wad of bank notes and handed it to one of the Germans. The soldier pocketed the money and barked a command, pushing both Tatus and Dadek to face a wall. He then shot both in the nape of the neck.

The Germans left Nawrocki lying for dead but not before seizing all the women in the building, including Mamusia, for forced labor in Germany.

Bronek asked me not to relay to Mamusia Pan Nawrocki's story, and of course I agreed. We reasoned that it was better for her to hope that Tatus and Dadek would surface alive some day than to deprive her completely of that hope. I never mentioned them to her from then on, out of what I still do not see as misguided delicacy. For her part, in all those years that followed, she never once mentioned them. I believe that she inwardly knew the truth about their fate and always mourned them.

After meeting Pan Nawrocki in Piotrkow Bronek wandered through the countryside. For a while he found shelter with a Pole in Czestochowa. Then he wandered on. In a forest he encountered a detachment of the semi-fascist Polish partisans, which he joined. Had they known he was Jewish they would have killed him on the spot. He got away and reached Krakow where he was arrested during a raid and taken to the Montelupich Prison.

The Montelupich Prison is so called because it was built on real estate that used to be owned by an Italian family, the Montelupis, who held the monopoly on postal services in seventeenth-century Poland.

Bronek was placed in a cell for petty criminals. When he had to take a common shower with them, they discovered his Jewishness. At roll call the next morning one of these jailbirds denounced Bronek to the prison commandant, but a petty detail tripped him up: he did not know German so he said in Polish, "On *zydek*" (He's a Jew), pointing at my brother. The commandant did not understand Polish, so my quick-thinking brother stepped out of the row and introduced himself in his best Yiddish German as an ethnic German who had been arrested by mistake and wanted to go fight on the Eastern Front.

The commandant bid Bronek to wait in the prison yard under guard. The guard gave Bronek a broom to sweep the yard.

This episode reminds me of Agnieszka Holland's film *Europa, Europa*. In that film, a young Jew is denounced as a *Zyd* to German soldiers but his life is saved because they do not understand Polish and he himself

Eugene, Bronek, and the guerrilla brothers Borys and Zalus Mordkowicz in the Zeilsheim Displaced Persons Camp, Germany, 1946.

speaks German to buttress his claim that he is a German. Life imitates art, as that film was based on a true experience too.

As Bronek was sweeping the yard, the guard unlocked the postern in the wall to let a man in and escorted him to the prison office. My brother noticed that the postern remained unlocked. In a flash, he leaned the broom against a wall, opened the postern and leaped out.

Afterward, he kept wandering from town to town, from village to village, until finally he was liberated by the advancing Russian troops and reunited with Mamusia.

Lodz was relatively intact compared to the razed Warsaw and we stayed there for the time being. There also I met the two surviving sons of the Mordkowiczes, Zalus and Boris, when they returned from a looting trip to the part of Germany annexed by Poland under the Yalta Agreement. Over there many Germans had abandoned their homes and fled westward as the Red Army advanced, leaving behind many valuable belongings which enterprising Poles and Jews such as Zalus and Boris were appropriating and bringing back to central Poland to sell. This was called *szabrowanie,* or plain looting. When Zalus and Boris returned to Lodz together with a truck filled with valuable knickknacks and furniture, I finally had a chance to greet them after so many years.

They did not stay long, however. They left in the western direction again, this time much farther away and for good, to the American zone of Germany.

Their parents felt too old for this new adventure and stayed in Lodz. The sons crossed the new Polish-German border, passed through East Germany, entered the American zone, and ended up in the Zeilsheim displaced persons camp near Frankfurt That was a camp founded by the UNRRA (United Nations Relief and Rehabilitation Agency). It housed the so-called "displaced persons," postwar refugees who for one reason or another would not go back to their homes in east Europe. The Zeilsheim camp was mainly for Jewish survivors who felt they had no future staying in countries like Poland. To them, Poland was one vast Jewish graveyard. Besides, it was unsafe because the native Polish anti–Semites still kept killing Jews, even after the German defeat. From Zeilsheim, on the other hand, it was much easier to migrate to Palestine (as it was known then) and America and other western countries.

About a month after Zalus and Boris left for the American zone they wrote us inviting us to join them in the Zeilsheim camp. They had obtained a big apartment there and offered to share it with us. The refugees in that camp received free rations of food and free housing and could stay there until they moved on to other countries. They were free to leave the camp any time and visit neighboring Frankfurt or any other place.

After some discussion, my mother and Bronek decided to leave Lodz and journey to Zeilsheim. There was nothing for us to do in Poland. The conditions there in late 1945 were almost like during the war — bone-chilling cold and little food in a chronically poor country that was just starting to be rebuilt, languished under the oppressive blanket of communism, and was still poisoned by anti–Semitism. Besides, once we were in the American zone, our chances to leave for America would be much better. In America we had relatives, three brothers of Tatus.

We embarked on our westward trip after Bronek joined us from Krakow. We traveled by train until we reached the Polish–East German border. We had no trouble crossing that border since a sympathetic Russian-Jewish soldier drove us across it in his truck and let us off in Berlin.

But we still needed to get across to the American zone from Berlin. We took a train to the border between the Soviet and American zones. There were four of us, Mamusia, Bronek, I, and Bolek, a Polish pal of Bronek who decided to come with us. We stayed overnight in a transit camp for German refugees who intended to settle in the American zone. In those times, in the winter of 1945–46, the Berlin Wall had not yet been built and people were able to move more or less freely between the zones. The train that was supposed to take us along with the German refugees across the border to the American zone had not arrived yet, and a rumor spread that it would be delayed until the next day.

My mother, Sara, 1946, in Zeilsheim, starting a new life after the war.

The transit camp was located in a mountain valley and, since it was a beautiful day, Bolek and I decided to go for a hike in the mountains.

Bolek and I were climbing a hill when suddenly we were halted by a Soviet patrol with guns drawn. They ignored Bolek's explanations and escorted us both to a mansion that served as a local headquarters for the Soviets. An officer interrogated Bolek, who showed them some papers proving that he was a Polish citizen. They argued for a while and then shook hands.

Then came my turn. I had no identification papers on me. The officer started to question me. As he mouthed his words, I was fascinated by his metal teeth. At the time many Russians used to wear such stainless steel teeth. Of course, I could not lip-read him and pointed to my ears to show that I was deaf. Suddenly someone slammed the door behind me. I felt the shock and the blast of air and turned my face to see what happened.

It was a test to see if I was really deaf. That was enough for the officer to decide that I was shamming and was not deaf at all. He shouted to a guard to let Bolek out and my companion walked away a free man, but he also ordered my arrest as a suspicious character, all of fifteen years old, and I was led away to a room in the basement.

The room already contained a dozen or so Germans, smugglers or suspected Nazis, I could not tell which, but I felt outraged and offended to be in the same cell as they. It was so degrading. I could not stand their sight. I was sure that Bolek told Mamusia

**Me in Frankfurt, Germany, in 1947.** and Bronek what happened to me and I wondered what they were doing now about it. But I, who had been so patient so many months awaiting liberation, simply could not wait any longer for them to rescue me. I decided I had to do something myself. I sat down and wrote the following in Polish:

Comrade Officer,

Please come and free me. I am deaf and ended up here through a misunderstanding. I am a Polish Jew and have nothing to do with these Germans. My mother is missing me and I want to get back to her, please.

I knocked on the door and when the guard, who was standing outside, opened it, I gave him that scrap of paper. He closed the door. I waited. And wonder of wonders, in about fifteen minutes the door opened and an officer, not the same one, taller and friendlier, smilingly motioned for me to come out, led me outside and waved goodbye to me.

I was free! It was dawn and in the rising rays of the sun I began to walk a one-lane road toward the transit camp for refugees. In the distance, coming toward to me, was a horse-drawn buggy. As they came closer I could discern the familiar, comforting figure of Mamusia sitting in front next to the driver. She was coming to free me after Bolek, released by the Russians, returned to the refugee camp the evening before and told her what happened.

I had already been freed through my own efforts but was I ever so glad to see my mother.

# Afterword

Ever since we were reunited in postwar Poland, my mother, Bronek and I once again formed a tight and warm relationship. After crossing the border into the American zone in the winter of 1945-46, we ended up in the Zeilsheim displaced persons camp. Zeilsheim used to be a housing development for employees of the nearby IG Farben conglomerate. They had been evicted by the Allies to make room for those Jewish survivors who did not want to go back to Poland and other countries of east Europe, because to them they were now vast graveyards of their people.

The two years I had spent in that camp passed as in a blur. I attended an art school in nearby Frankfurt and Bronek took classes at Frankfurt University while Mamusia opened a grocery store in our apartment, selling herring and American canned goods to our fellow survivors. Among my strongest memories of those times is a visit to a hospital in Frankfurt. Bronek took me there for my first hearing evaluation since the war. There, I met the doctor who was to test my hearing. He wore a white lab coat and his face was perpetually screwed up in a grimace as if he had the trots and was in a hurry to reach the toilet. I offered him a cigarette. In those times cigarettes, especially American ones, were more accepted than currency. He accepted my American cigarette and, after peering into my ears and testing my hearing with a tuning fork, he gave me a copy of his diagnosis. I cannot figure out why he gave it to me unless he thought it did not matter since I was a complete moron. It said that I was *psychisch debil*, retarded. I kept that paper with his diagnosis as a souvenir for years and meant to frame it and hang it on the wall but as years passed I mislaid it somewhere. What a shame! I would have loved to hang it next to my Ph.D. diploma.

Then we were off to America where an uncle, one of my father's brothers, sponsored our journey to its shores.

Bronek, now the head of the family, orchestrated our trip. He took care of the formalities, interpreted for me at the medical examination in Bremen and then again after our ship docked in New York Harbor. Before landing we were questioned by a customs officer who, on noticing that I was deaf, asked me through Bronek what was the capital of the Soviet Union. I answered Moscow and for him this was enough proof that I was not a feebleminded and could enter the Land of Plenty.

That was in December 1947, just before New York City was engulfed by a blizzard that left in its wake a three-feet-high blanket of snow as if introducing America as a vast new continent.

Our first years in America were difficult for us. We hardly knew how to communicate in English and each one of us was desperate for any kind of work at any pay. Somehow, not only did we survive that period but due to Mamusia's insistence and loving care Bronek and I managed to graduate from college. It took Bronek nine and half years of evening studies (he did manual labor during the day) to graduate from Baruch College in New York City. And I, thanks to my wonderful mother, ultimately earned a Ph.D. degree from the George Washington University.

For the first two years I attended a high school and in my spare time pushed carts in New York's Garment Center. Finally, in 1950 I entered Gallaudet College, "The World's Only Liberal Arts College for the Deaf" as it then advertised itself. Afterward, I earned a master's and then a doctoral degree in English without ever having heard an English word. I taught English and American literature at what is now Gallaudet University. I married Claire, a woman who not only is beautiful but also has character and to whom I owe 34 years of happy married life. From her I acquired two instant children from her previous marriage, David and Evelyn. I also fathered a daughter of my own, Sabrina, another joy in my life.

After I had left for college and Bronek got married, my mother spread her wings. She acquired a broad circle of friends, widows like she, and began to be active at the local synagogue and attend bingo nights and various socials organized for the elderly. She also found a job as a companion and nurse to old and ill people, although she was no longer young herself. What free time she had she devoted to volunteer work at a home for the aged. I still have a certificate from that home, honoring her for her devotion as a volunteer. She did not stay single for long. For a woman so sociable she soon was squired by elderly bachelors one of whom, a widower, Mr. Simon, obtained her hand in marriage.

That Mr. Simon had an interesting past. He used to work as a street vendor in Algeria and after he came to America he fathered a son who became a labor union organizer and got killed in a riot.

Mr. Simon and my mother lived together for many years until he passed away. But my mother could not stay single for long. She acquired a new boyfriend, Abe, and they began to live together. Abe wanted to marry her but his family prevented him, out of fear that he would leave his money to her.

It was my mother, however, who passed away first, leaving

Claire and me in 1975, shortly after our marriage.

Abe — and not only him — desolated. The last time I had seen her was ten days previously when I came to visit her in the hospital where she had undergone cataract surgery. She smiled with such happiness to see me.

During the prescribed seven days that Bronek and I sat *shiva*, that Jewish counterpart of the Irish wake, Mamusia's apartment was continually crowded with people who came to pay their respects and brought us gifts of food. We had not known, but somehow we were not surprised, that Mamusia was so popular, that she had made so many friends and acquaintances.

One of the visitors was my mother's rabbi. He said that Mamusia was blessed because she died peacefully in her sleep on Friday at the start of the Sabbath. That was a fitting end to an exemplary life.

For some reason right now I remember two pieces of conflicting advice she gave me. In the first year of my marriage, Claire and I quarreled. I no longer remember the cause, but it was the kind of stupid spat that arises between two beings who suddenly start living together and discover each other day by day. Friction is inevitable before the point when their misunderstandings about each other become cleared up and their mutual

**Bronek and me in 1995 at one of our occasional reunions.**

prejudices are resolved into concord. At the time we had not yet reached that point and I was so angry that I decided to sleep in another room. As it happened, my mother was on a rare visit with us just then. She advised me to "talk to the wall" when I was angry. I never forgot that advice and it served me well in the years to come.

Yet years later, my mother taught me that there were times when I should not talk to the wall. Once, when Claire, Sabrina, and I journeyed to New York to visit her, she displayed an unaccustomed flash of hot temper. What caused it was a visit by Rafal, a former college chum of mine who became a stockbroker. He tried to persuade Claire and me to invest in some stocks. He both signed and spoke very clearly — so clearly that my mother heard him. This being, who had never raised her voice before,

My daughter, Sabrina, and me.

rushed into the room and, a picture of fury, pointed her finger at Rafal and then at the door, shouting "Out!" I had never seen her so angry before. Rafal smiled, bowed, and exited on kissing his hand and placing it on the mezzuza on the door. She was right about him: some time later I learned that some of Rafal's customers were suing him for embezzlement.

Writing an Afterword calls for introspection. I must confess a peccadillo. As by now the reader will have guessed, I am not such a hotshot survival artist. If I have survived those sinister wartime years it was owing more to luck than to pluck. The hurricane of war did not devastate me. It was perhaps with an excusable braggadoccio that I called myself a survival artist in the title of this memoir, simply in order to emphasize that my experiences did not break my spirit.

They did not sap my spirit but did not prepare me for the new peacetime reality. During the war I had lived friendless and isolated, if my family is not counted. Now, living in sunnier climes, I had to readjust my mentality. To meet a stranger no longer meant meeting someone potentially hostile, and new experiences now meant something pleasurable to look forward to. But this readjustment took time. I had to go through a decompression period and no place was more ideal for that than Gallaudet College in the 1950s.

To me it was also a place of culture shocks. Nothing in my previous experience had prepared me for that curious American institution of fraternity hazing. I was invited to become a frat pledge, and along with a dozen of other freshmen I became what was termed a "suppliant." We suppliants had to march everywhere, to classes and the cafeteria, in single file with wooden faces, without looking at anyone. We were not allowed to talk to any outsider, which just delighted bevies of girl students, then known as bobbysoxers, in their saddle shoes and white socks, as, screaming and laughing, they vainly tried to distract us. In the evenings we had to appear in the frat's secret den or "Shrine," nicknamed the Torture Chamber, hidden somewhere in the bowels of the men's dormitory. In that darkened room, illuminated only by candles, after our blindfolds were removed we stood in a semicircle facing the frat's pledge master, Dick, a guy who enjoyed abusing us verbally, calling us scum of the earth, shit-faces, slimebags not worthy of kissing the feet of frat brethren. For good measure, he administered to us rounds and rounds of paddling (with a paddle that we had been ordered to make and emblazon with a grinning skull just for that occasion) for every imaginable reason or no reason.

One of those evenings I was his target. He was of course familiar with my background, as in those times Gallaudet was a small college with a student body of only 250. As we stood facing him, he ordered us to stand at attention and stretch out our arms in the Hitler salute. The pledges straightened up and raised their arms. I was the only one not to do so. They all expectantly looked at me. I hesitated. Then I raised my arm too.

What I did not know then was that my gesture had other repercussions. In that darkened frat den we suppliants had not known that every night behind us stood frat brothers enjoying the spectacle of us being hazed. One of them was Bernardo, later known as the King of Deaf Theater. He was so upset by Dick's Hitler salute command and my obedient response that he cried. Later that night he complained to our pledge master about his rude and heinous order. But Dick laughed in his face. The two men came to blows and afterward never talked to each other. To this day Bernardo remains bitter about this episode. Me, I had tried to be a good sport knowing it was a jape, but this American Jew took it too much to heart.

The culminating point of my experience as a frat pledge was the Hot Dog Incident. We pledges were ordered to stage a skit night for the benefit of the other students. One Sunday evening, the auditorium was packed with practically the entire student body and some teachers as well. Punctually at seven the doors opened and the Blue Brotherhood, as the frat brethren called themselves, majestically marched double file into the Chapel Hall. Led by the Grand Rajah, they were decked out in their full regalia, hooded blue robes with skulls embroidered on them, their hands hidden in their sleeves. They sat down in unison on their seats in the first row, which was reserved for them.

That was the signal for us on the stage to begin our skits. The curtains parted and I was shown alone on the stage, sitting on the top of a ladder and broadly signing "Hot Dog!" for whatever it was worth.

But it was not until I joined the Society of Cuates that I began to fully savor the delights of life in a congenial climate.

That society was born when one day I was hailed as a *cuate* by Arturo while walking past him. I was fascinated and asked him to explain the word's meaning, because he said it with such a broad, friendly and pleasant smile, a smile that told me he was kidding me in a simpatico manner. "Cuate" is Spanish slang prevalent in New Mexico, where he came from, and it stands for "buddy" or "pal."

Thus one thing led to another, like the joke told about the man who posed for a whiskey advertisement. He had occasion to taste strong alcohol for the first time in his life and ended up an alcoholic. I ended up a cuate.

I shared with Arturo the same past: we were former street toughs and current lovers of knowledge. A third cuate, Geno, a New Mexican like Arturo, also with the same past, soon joined us.

On the campus, Arturo's reputation was lopsided. He was a first-class scholar with a first-rate mind, but to people who did not know him better, he looked like a hoodlum with the springy stance of a boxer (actually he was an intercollegiate wrestling champion) and ferocious half–Mongolian face. When the time and place were right I would introduce him to new acquaintances as the son of an Apache chief and he, grimacing fiercely and smacking his mouth repeatedly with the palm of his hand, would emit what he claimed to be an Apache war whoop.

Of course, I am oversimplifying: the society we had informally founded was a pretext for a meeting of mutually sympathetic spirits, or of cuate material as we soon began to say.

The Society of Cuates was based on democratic principles: every member was president. We had our own idol, Protocuate Vishnu, a toy gorilla on Arturo's desk to which we made obeisances. When its key was wound up, it would bare its fangs and growl "Aaaargh" and thump its hairy chest while doing a fast shuffle.

We considered *Homo sapiens* to be but a stage in the evolution of the human species toward the new man, *Homo cuatus*. We had our own cuate handshake: clasping each other's elbow. It was not really our invention: the ancient Romans had already used it, but we brazenly claimed, turning logic upside down, that they had stolen it from us, aside and apart from the pleasure we felt in that handshake's being a parody of the fraternity grip. We devised a long and intricate ritual greeting to which we resorted whenever we had an audience of gawking students, which was often. We would climb on the nearest chairs. Then, with a solemn and exalted voice and sign the first man would exclaim, "Cuate!" With equal joy and fervor, the second man would chant, "One and Indivisible!" The third man: "A Cuate is a Cuate!" The first man: "In richness and poverty!" The second man: "In sickness and in health!" The third man: "Millionaire or bum!" The first man: "Now and always!" The second man: "Ahora y siempre!" The third man: "A Cuate is a Cuate!" Then all together, with beatific smiles on our faces, standing on our chairs, we would exchange cuate handshakes.

We staged these exhibitions in public, for the edification and entertainment of our fellow students, while they looked on, tittering. Some of them wanted to join our society and we never rejected anyone but the newcomers soon would begin to drop out for in their attempts to join in the spirit of the thing they either failed to strike the right note of inspired spontaneity or could not grasp our allusions. We made good-humored sport with them and they were aware of it but did not resent us because we obviously so abounded in good will and happiness. Not so incidentally, we also founded a Cuata Ladies Auxiliary to which some congenial girls belonged.

We used to spend many evenings at a nearby diner whenever we did not date any skirts. Arturo would give a speech on, say, the sex mores and habitat of the Australian doodlebug, which he dubbed *Thalassopriapus australiensis, Linn.* Geno, with his conquistador's square-jawed deadpan face resembling a younger version of the protagonist of Tchaikovsky's Nutcracker Suite would follow this with a lecture on the applicability of Plato's Parable of the Cave:

> Cuates, just as man cannot perceive reality except as a shadow flickering on the wall of the cave, so the nature of the Woman, La Femme, conversely is perceivable as reality, not as a shadow. As tangible, graspable, embraceable and impregnable reality, as *res tegenda.* Let us therefore honor Woman, with a capital W, that noblest and most glorious phenomenon of nature whose manifold and delectable delights we are blessed to enjoy. I move that we honor womanhood by rising and observing a minute of silence.

We all voted in acclaim by raising our arms and figuratively took off our hats and held them to our hearts. We did not, however, rise from the table — just one small detail showing that the cuates knew when and where to stop.

Then Geno said, "I yield the floor to the distinguished gentleman from New York."

I took up the thread: "I thank the noble gentleman from New Mexico, and I move that for this tale we award him the Order of the Silk Garter. Cuates, now let us ask ourselves the purpose of the Cuates, of Cuatismo, a question which we never grow tired of debating and pondering and which we redefine anew each day. Our purpose is to waft an air of sunshine over the campus, to console the curvaceous lonely females and bring them the solace they so ardently desire. Our goal is to make this world a better place to carouse in, to provide out of the goodness of our hearts, a free show to the awed and amazed bleachers."

"Bleachers" was the term we applied to anyone outside the Society of Cuates, by analogy with ringside spectators watching while the torero defied and dared the snorting, hulking bull as it was pawing the sand.

I could go on and on about our cuate hijinks but let me focus only on one of our capers, the Ukulele Caper. Arturo, Geno, and I were on our way to the dining room when we noticed a broken and discarded ukulele on the sidewalk.

We commented to each other, "Hey, look, this Stradivarius, the joy-giver, the pleasure-giver, the enhancer of happiness is dead ... dead! We must let the populace know of the joy-giver's death and make sure he is duly honored."

We climbed the clock tower, lowered the flag to half mast and entered the dining room. Arturo stood on a chair. He got the students' attention and, brandishing the ukulele, proclaimed the death of Stradivarius, the world-renowned joy-giver. He declaimed, pointing at the ukulele, "Look at his lifeless, decomposing body, his collapsed lungs, the cirrhosis that ravaged his liver. (In a stage whisper he asked, "Was he an alcoholic?") Imagine, fellow students, the sufferings of Stradivarius, the joy-giver, before he died. Fellow students, the flag is lowered at half staff to honor his passing."

There was also the Toilet Paper Caper and others but decorum prevents me from devoting more space to these hijinks.

Since then years have passed but Arturo, I, and sometimes also Geno continue to meet at least once or twice each year, and sometimes more often. I and my cuata Claire fly to California or Arturo and his paramour fly to the East Coast in order to hold conferences and seminars on the theory and practice of cuatismo. We always have something new to say to each other. Voltaire's Candide ended up by cultivating his garden. We cuates are one up on him.

My bond with Bronek is as strong as ever. We keep each other posted regularly and swap news about the little comedies and tragedies coming and going in our respective families.

# Chapter Notes

## Introduction

1. Photo courtesy of Noah Lasman, a member of the Poznan Hashomer Hatzair. He survived the war by escaping from a series of small ghettos and living as a partisan in the forests and peasant barns. After the war he got a copy of that photo from Adek Redlich, another member of the Poznan Hashomer Hatzair, who survived by living in the Soviet Union.

2. Horst Biesold, *Klagende Haende* (Solms: Jarick Oberbiel, 1988).

## Chapter I

1. Martin Buber. *Die Stunde und die Erkenntnis. Reden und Aufsatze, 1933–1935* (Berlin: Schocken Verlag, 1936).

2. Frankism, an eighteenth-century messianic Jewish religious movement in Poland, supported a kind of rapprochement between the Jewish and Christian religions. Its leader, Jacob Frank, claimed to be the reincarnation of the self-declared Messiah Sabbatai Zevi. Frank was ultimately rejected by the Jewish community and his followers converted to Roman Catholicism, just as Zevi's followers had converted to Islam.

3. Waldemar Korolczak, "Charities of the Community: Jewish Relief Societies in Poznan During 1815–1914,"*Kronika Miasta Poznania. Poznanscy Zydzi* (published by the Poznan Municipal Council. Poz-

nan: Wydawnictwo Miejskie, 2006), pp. 149–177.

4. *Ibid.*

5. Wiktor Stachowiak, "Thrash Them Black and Blue," *Kronika Miasta Poznania, op. cit.*, p. 376.

6. *Ibid.*, p. 377.

## Chapter II

1. Emmanuel Ringelblum, *Notes from the Warsaw Ghetto. Notes from the Journal of Emmanuel Ringelblum*, translated and edited by Jacob Sloan (New York: ibooks, 2006), p. 126.

2. *Ibid.*

3. Gunnar S. Paulsson, *Secret City: The Hidden Jews of Warsaw, 1940–1945* (New Haven: Yale University Press, 2002).

4. Kazimierz Moczarski, *Rozmowy z katem*. Warsaw, WPN 2001. This is a record of conversations with Jurgen Stroop in his jail cell after he was extradited to Poland and before he was hanged.

5. Gusta Draengerowa-Dawidsohn, *Pamietnik Justyny* (Krakow: Zydowska Komisja Historyczna, 1946), p. 28. Memoir consisting of scraps of paper by the author, smuggled out of the prison where she was tortured to death without betraying anyone.

6. *Ibid.*, p. 14.

## Chapter III

1. Gunnar Paulsson, *Secret City: The Hidden Jews of Warsaw, 1940–1945* (New Haven: Yale University Press, 2002).

2. Simcha "Kazik" Rotem, *Memoirs of a Warsaw Ghetto Fighter: The Past Within Me.* New Haven: Yale University Press, 1994.

3. Emmanuel Ringelblum, *Notes from the Warsaw Ghetto. Notes from the Journal of Emmanuel Ringelblum.* Translated and edited by Jacob Sloan. New York: ibooks, 2006.

4. Yisrael Gutman, *The Jews of Warsaw, 1939–1943: Ghetto, Underground, Revolt* (Bloomington: Indiana University Press, 1982), p. 341.

5. Gutman, *op. cit.*

# Bibliography

Adelson, Alan, and Robert Lapides. *Lodz Ghetto: Inside a Community Under Siege.* New York: Viking, 1989.

Amery, Jean. *At the Mind's Limits: Contemplations by a Survivor on Auschwitz and Its Realities.* New York: Schocken Books, 1986.

Bauman, Janina. *Red Sky in the Morning.* New York: Free Press, 1986.

Biesold, Horst. *Klagende Haende.* Solms: Jarick Oberbiel, 1988.

*Biuletyn Zydowskiego Instytutu Historycznego w Polsce (BZIH),* 1960–1999.

Blady-Szwajger, Adina. *I Remember Nothing More: The Warsaw Children's Hospital and the Jewish Resistance.* New York: Pantheon, 1991.

Brustin-Berenstein, Tatiana. "On Hitlerian Methods of Economic Exploitation of the Warsaw Ghetto." *BZIH (Biuletyn Zydowskiego Instytutu Historycznego* 4 (1953), p. 42.

Buber, Martin. *Die Stunde und die Erkenntnis: Reden und Aufsatze,* 1933–1935.

Checinski, Michael M. "My Account of Resistance in the Lodz Ghetto." *Kwartalnik Historii Zydow* 1 (2007), pp. 94–100.

_____. *My Father's Watch: Lodz Ghetto Underground.* Jerusalem: Gefen, 1994.

Czerniakow, Adam. *Adama Czerniakowa Dziennik getta warszawskiego 6.XI. 1939–23.VII.1942.* Warsaw: PWN, 1983.

Dobroszycki, Lucjan. *The Chronicle of the Lodz Ghetto, 1941–1944.* New Haven: Yale University Press, 1984.

Draengerowa-Dawidsohn, Gusta. *Pamietnik Justyny.* Krakow: Zydowska Komisja Historyczna, 1946.

Getter, Marek. "The Blue Police in Warsaw, 1939–1944." *Studia Warszawskie* 8, pp. 215–217.

Gilbert, Martin. *The Holocaust: A Jewish Tragedy.* London: Fontana, 1987.

Goldstein, Bernard. *Five Years in the Warsaw Ghetto.* Garden City, NY: Dolphin Books, 1961.

Gutman, Yisrael. *The Jews of Warsaw, 1939–1943: Ghetto, Underground, Revolt.* Bloomington: Indiana University Press, 1982.

Harris, Frederick J. *Encounters with Darkness: French and German Writers on World War II.* New York: Oxford University Press, 1983.

Hempel, Adam. *Pogrobowcy kleski: Rzecz o policji "granatowej" w Generalnym Gubernatorstwie, 1939–1945.* Warsaw: PWN, 1990.

Hertz, Aleksander. *Zydzi w kulturze polskiej.* Warsaw: Biblioteka "Wiezi," 2003.

Jaworski, Michal. "*Plac Muranowski 7 (Fragment wspomnien).*" BZIH 90 (1974), 69–89.

*Kronika Miasta Poznania.* Published by the Poznan Municipal Council. Poznan: Wydawnictwo Miejskie, 2006.

*Kwartalnik Zydowskiego Instytutu Historycznego,* 2000–2007.

Landau, Ludwik. *Kronika lat wojny iokupacji.* 3 vols. Warsaw: PWN, 1962.

Meed, Vladka. *On Both Sides of the Wall: Memoirs from the Warsaw Ghetto*. New York: Holocaust Library, 1979.

Moczarski, Kazimierz. *Rozmowy z katem*. Warsaw: WPN, 2001.

Passenstein, Marek. "Smuggling in the Warsaw Ghetto." *BZIH* 26 (1958), pp. 42–72.

Paulsson, Gunnar S. *Secret City: The Hidden Jews of Warsaw, 1940–1945*. New Haven and London: Yale University Press, 2002.

Podolska, Aldona. *Sluzba porzadkowa w getcie warszawskim w latach 1940–1943*. Warsaw: Wydawnictwo Fundacji "Historia pro Futuro," 1996.

Prekerowa, Teresa. "Jews in the Warsaw Uprising." In *Powstanie warszawskie a perspektywy polwiecza*. Warsaw: Instytut Historyczny PAN, 1995.

Ringelblum, Emmanuel. *Notes from the Warsaw Ghetto: Notes from the Journal of Emmanuel Ringelblum*. Translated and edited by Jacob Sloan. New York: ibooks, 2006.

Rotem, Simcha "Kazik." *Memoirs of a Warsaw Ghetto Fighter: The Past Within Me*. New Haven: Yale University Press, 1994.

Sierakowiak, Dawid. *Dziennik Dawida Sierakowiaka*. Warsaw: Iskry, 1960.

Sikorski, Brunon. "Commerce in Occupied Warsaw." *Studia Warszawskie*, Vol. 7, No. 1. Warsaw: Instytut Historyczny PAN, 1971, pp. 17–85.

Skalniak, Franciszek. *Stopa zyciowa spoleczenstwa polskiego w okresie okupacji na terenie Generalnej Gubernii*. Warsaw: GK, 1979.

Trunk, Isaiah. *Lodz Ghetto: A History*. Bloomington: Indiana University Press, 2006.

Ziemian, Joseph. *The Cigarette Sellers of Three Crosses Square*. Minneapolis: Lerner Publications, 1975.

# Index

Aleichem, Scholem 17, 70
*Alice in Wonderland* 68
Amish 12, 14–15
Anielewicz, Mordecai 116–117
Anka 121
Arturo 185–188
Auschwitz 84, 91

Baluty 38, 40, 45
Bedzin 75
Belzec 73, 84
Bialik, Chaim Nahman 70
Bialystok 48, 75
Biesold, Horst 10
Bismarck, Otto von 16
Black Battalion 91
"Blue" Polish police 79, 111
Bolek 175–177
Brockwitz bei Meissen 149, 164
Buber, Martin 13

*Captain of Koepenick* (film) 41
charities, Jewish 19–20, 69
Chrobry Battalion 140
*The Cigarette Sellers of Three Crosses Square* 157
*Copperfield, David* 127
Courthouse, Grodzki 57–60
*Crying Hands* 10
Cuates, Society of 185–187
Cukierman, Antek 39, 108
Cwaniak *see* Sly
Czestochowa: history of ghetto 89–92; rescue by Dadek 93–101
Czerniakow, Adam 47, 114
Czyste hospital 52

David (first cousin) 4–5, 39
David (grandfather) 17
Dreizel, Aunt 42
Dubnow, Simon 69

Eger, Rabbi Akiva 30
*Europa, Europa* 40, 172

Felix, Minucius 86
Final Solution 90
Flaubert 121, 147
Frankists 13, 189

Gall, Yves de 148
Gallaudet College, 180, 183
Gandhi 62
Gepner, Abraham 114–115
General Government 39, 89
Geneva Convention 142–145
Gestapo 96, 100
*Glos Poznanski* 22
Golem 66
Grosberg 23, 24
Gulliver 64

Hammer 152, 160, 162
Hamsun, Knut 121
Hashomer Hatzair 3, 26–28, 70–72, 115, 169
Haskiel 39
Heep, Uriah 127
Heniek 25–28
Holland, Agnieszka 40, 172
Horthy, Admiral 2
Hutoran 73–74

Icchak *see* Cukierman, Antek
*The Idiot* 61

The Inquisition 21
Istrati, Panait 121

Jakubowski 22–23
Janka 121
*Jean Christophe* 61
*Jew Suess* 127, 135
Judenrat 56, 101

Karakul, Lt. 137–138, 150
Kasprowicz, Cpl. 149
Kazik (Simcha Rotem) 108
*kehilla* 15
Kielce 83, 85–86, 89–91, 99
Koepenick (town of) 41
*Krowki* 87

Liebeskind, Adolf 71
lifeline, concept of 121
Lutens 150–151, 156–158, 160, 163
Lodz Ghetto: establishment 39–41; living conditions 44–46; unique nature 47–48
Lynx 153–154, 160, 163–164

Maciek 159–160
Martinique 6–7
Martyr, Justin 84
Mickiewicz, Adam 13
Mietek 75–76
Miki-Bandyta 152–160
*Les Misérables* 61
Montelupich Prison 172
"mooing cow" 139
Mordkowicz family 169, 174
Mt. Pele 6
Muhlberg P.O.W. camp 144, 157

Nawrocki, Mieczyslaw 101–104, 109
Noskowicz 22
*Nowy Kurier Warszawski* 101, 111

Operation Reinhard 73, 83
Operettas, Austrian 126, 135

*Pajak* 21
*palant* 34–35
Parable of the Cave 186
Paulsson, Gunnar 105
Peretz, I.L. 70
Piotrkow Trybunalski 4, 123, 171
Plato 186
Plutarch 61
*Pod Pregierz* 21, 23

Polish-Jewish relations, history 11–15
Poznan Jews, history 15–17, 19–23
Poznan under German occupation, 1939 30–38
*psychisch debil* 179

Ravensbrueck Prayer 5
Reichsbank 5
Ringelblum, Emmanuel 46
Rolland, Romain 121
Rubinstein, Artur 14
Rumkowski, Chaim 1, 39 , 44–47
rumkies 39, 54

Saint-Pierre 6
Singer, I.B. 4
Sly 152–154
Sobibor 73, 84, 91
Sosnowiec 75
*srulki* 24
Stachowiak, Wiktor 27
Stanislavsky method 106
Stroop, Juergen 51–52, 189

tinnitus 36–37
Tlomackie, synagogue and square 50–54, 60, 64, 75
Tolstoy, Leo 145–148
Treblinka 72–74, 79, 91, 114, 144

*Umschlagplatz* 74

Vilna 48
Vulture 152, 160, 162

Warsaw: cultural life 70; deportations 72–76; establishment 42–43; social structure 44, 68; street scenes 64–68; uprising 115–117
Wells, Leon 1–2
*Werterfassung* 114
Widawa 17
Wiktor, Comrade 167–168

Zamenhof, Ludwik 13
Zegota 106
Zeilsheim Displaced Persons Camp 8, 54, 174, 175, 179
Ziemian, Joseph 159
Zionism 26–27, 70–72, 115–117
Zosia 25–26, 28, 89
Zuckerman, Antek see Cukierman, Antek